ANNOTATIONS

TO THE

HEIDELBERG CATECHISM

ANNOTATIONS

TO THE

HEIDELBERG CATECHISM

by

J. Van Bruggen

Minister of the Word of God

translated by A. H. Oosterhoff

INHERITANCE PUBLICATIONS
NEERLANDIA, ALBERTA, CANADA

Canadian Cataloguing in Publication Data

Bruggen, J. van (Jan van), 1909-1965.
Annotations to the Heidelberg Catechism

Translation of: Aantekeningen bij de Heidelbergse Catechismus.
ISBN 0-921100-33-7

1. Heidelberger Katechismus.   2. Reformed Church—Catechisms.   3. Reformed
Church—Doctrines.   I. Title.
BX9428.B7813 1991   238'.42   C91-091607-1

Originally published as *Aantekeningen bij de Heidelbergse Catechismus* by Drukkerij
Horstman, Assen, The Netherlands.
Published with permission.

Translated by A.H. Oosterhoff.

All rights reserved © 1991
by Inheritance Publications
Box 154, Neerlandia, Alberta
Canada T0G 1R0
Tel. (403) 674 3949

Printed in Canada by
Premier Printing Ltd. Winnipeg, MB

ISBN 0-921100-33-7

The main Bible translation used in this book is *The Holy Bible, Revised Standard
Version*. Copyright © 1946, 1952, 1971 by Division of Christian Education of the
National Council of the Churches of Christ in the United States of America. Also used
is the *Authorized* or *King James Version*. Some scripture passages were taken from
The Holy Bible, New International Version. Copyright © 1973, 1978, 1984
International Bible Society. Used by permission of Zondervan Bible Publishers.

The versions of the Heidelberg Catechism, other doctrinal standards, rhymed psalms
and hymns, liturgical forms, *etc.*, used in this book are those contained in *Book of
Praise: Anglo-Genevan Psalter*, rev. ed. Copyright © 1984 by the Standing Committee
for the Publication of the *Book of Praise* of the Canadian Reformed Churches.

Table of Contents

Thy words I have laid up within my heart;
I keep Thy faithful promise as my treasure,
Lest I should ever from Thy ways depart.
O LORD, how blest Thou art beyond all measure.
Thy statutes and decrees to me impart,
For in Thy law I find my greatest pleasure.

In Thy commandments I take great delight;
They are the subject of my meditation.
The path marked by Thy law I'll keep in sight
And guard myself against all deviation.
Thy holy word I'll not neglect or slight;
Thy statutes are the cause of my elation.

Anglo-Genevan Psalm 119 : 5 & 6

Foreword

A living church instructs its youth! This is age-old wisdom. The confessions were written to that end: short but effective in the Old Church and more extensive in the time of the great Reformation. The focus of the catechism of Heidelberg (1563) is also the instruction of young people. This confession looks to the future of the church!

Young people in every age have their own questions and problems. It would be imprudent to ignore these. A church which gives instruction must be up to date!

There appears to be a certain tension between the text books of earlier times and the time in which today's youth is growing up. The old text book does not seem so important to people who live centuries later.

However, in order to be able to give a sound answer to questions that arise today, we need the help of the good distinctions drawn in, and the insights of, an earlier time. That was the conviction of my father as he continued to work on and revise his *Aantekeningen bij de Heidelbergse Catechismus*. He spoke a great deal with his catechumens about their questions and showed them that sound knowledge can give you much pleasure.

The book that has now been translated into English is somewhat like a nature guide. At first blush it looks rather dry: so many names and distinctions for plants, animals and birds! But when you walk around in nature, you find a guide to be extremely useful. It opens your eyes: there is more to see than you thought at first! This book is also designed as a guide. It contains a collection of knowledge from the past that gives you insight for today.

Without one's own living relationship with the Lord and a knowledge of one's own time, this book will remain a dead letter, but when it is used in the context of such a relationship and knowledge, it can sharpen our insight and equip us readily to acquit ourselves as believers.

It is a great joy that Prof. Oosterhoff was moved to translate this book. I hope that his work will be crowned in that many will start to use it for catechesis, in the study societies and for their own studies. A living church refuses to remain ignorant!

Kampen, March 1, 1991   Jakob van Bruggen

Preface

The Rev. J. van Bruggen was a minister of the Gereformeerde Kerken in Nederland (Vrijgemaakt) for many years, until the LORD took him unto himself on June 8, 1965.

Rev. van Bruggen was the author of a number of theological publications, including *Het amen der kerk*, a commentary on the Belgic Confession, the second edition of which was published in 1965, and this book, *Aantekeningen bij de Heidelbergse Catechismus*, the fifth edition of which was also published in 1965. It bears the subtitle: *For use in the catechetical instruction in the Reformed Churches in the Netherlands* and was used for many years in those churches for this purpose since its first publication in 1951. It was also used extensively in the early years of the Canadian Reformed Churches.

As a young catechumen I had the privilege of using Rev. van Bruggen's *Aantekeningen bij de Heidelbergse Catechismus*. When my consistory asked me to teach the senior catechism class, it seemed only natural, therefore, to make use of this booklet again. My memory of its riches did not fail me. It contains a wealth of information, presented in a compact and easily readable format.

It occurred to me that it would be desirable to make this booklet available to my students and others in the English language. I am grateful to the author's widow, Mrs. J van Bruggen, and his son, Prof. Dr. J. van Bruggen, for giving me permission to prepare this translation.

I am greatly indebted to Dr. J. Faber, Prof. Emeritus, Theological College of the Canadian Reformed Churches, Hamilton, Canada, for his willingness to check the manuscript and for his helpful suggestions and comments.

A.H. Oosterhoff
London, Canada
March, 1991

INTRODUCTION

A. CATECHESIS

Catechesis is an institution of the church designed to train its young (unprofessed) members by instruction in the revealed truth and to lead them to become professing members.

Catechesis is, therefore, in the first place a task of the *Minister of the Word and the Elders*. It is not only under their supervision, but proceeds from them. It is one of the means whereby the office bearers fulfil their calling to "tend the flock of God" (1 Pet 5:2), to strengthen the weak and to lead the children to Christ (Acts 20:28; Mt 19:14). Thus, the instruction is given, pursuant to the LORD's charge, with official authority.

Catechesis is also a task of the *parents*, who have the duty to teach their children about the LORD and about his service (Ex 13:14; Deut 6:6, 7; Eph 6:4). They fulfil the calling in part by sending their children to catechism class and by ensuring that the children conscientiously do their work there. They bound themselves to this calling by their own promise at the baptism of their children when they promised to instruct them and to have them instructed in the Christian doctrine.

Further, catechesis is also *your own* task. For the LORD caused also you to belong to those with whom he established an eternal covenant of grace. And in that covenant he admonishes you to KNOW, love and obey him (Prov 8:17; Ecc 12:1). Let us therefore clearly realize at the outset that neglect of catechesis amounts to a violation of the covenant and is the first step on the road to leaving the church!

The purpose of catechesis, therefore, is that you become full-fledged members of the church. You became members when you were baptised, but you do not yet have the full rights of members, for you do not yet have access to the Lord's supper. You only receive that access when you consciously choose to accept the promise which the Lord gave you in his covenant and in which you must first be instructed. To lead you to that choice and, thus, to make you a full member of the church is the purpose of catechesis.

Catechesis seeks to attain this goal through instruction, and rightly so. For the Lord wants to lead sinners in the way they should go by instruction (Ps 25:8). The content of this instruction is the doctrine in which your parents promised to instruct you and to have you instructed. It is "the doctrine of the Old and New Testament, summarized in the confessions and taught here in this Christian Church" (Form for the Baptism of Infants, Address to the Parents, Q. 3). Our text is the Heidelberg Catechism. It *teaches* the doctrine of the Old and New Testament, summarized in the confessions. It does not stand on its

13

own, apart from the Bible, but is a guide which introduces us to the Bible. Hence, its proof texts for each answer direct us to the Bible.

NOTE: The Synod of Dort 1618/19 distinguished three forms of catechesis, namely, catechesis (1) in the home; (2) by the school; and (3) by the church. The first two fell into disuse when deformation occurred in the church. We should strive to have them reinstated!

B.   THE CATECHISM

Our Catechism was written in Heidelberg, a German city, by the professors Zacharias Ursinus and Caspar Olevianus. It was adopted by the Synod of Heidelberg in 1562 and published in 1563. This was done by order of the Elector of the Palatinate, Frederick III, who wished to reform his country, in which Lutheranism had originally taken root, into a Calvinistic one. He asked the above-mentioned professors to write the Catechism in order to lead the young people thereby to the Reformed confession.

Petrus Dathenus translated this Catechism into Dutch (1563). The Reformed Churches in the Netherlands adopted it as confession and text book for catechechetical instruction in the church at the Synod of Dort in 1574.

C.   QUESTIONS (PARTS A. & B.)

1.   What is catechesis? Who is primarily charged with it? With what kind of authority is catechetical instruction given?

2.   What task do the parents have with respect to catechesis? Why do they have this task? Why is catechesis also your task? What, therefore, does neglect of catechetical instruction amount to?

3.   Are those who are baptised already members of the church? What rights do they lack as yet? What is the purpose of catechesis? How does catechesis seek to attain this goal?

4.   What must be the content of catechetical instruction? What is our text book? What is its relationship to the Bible?

5.   Who wrote the Catechism? When was it adopted and published? On whose orders did this occur? Who translated it into Dutch? How did it become a confession of the church?

D.   COVENANT

Our Catechism, therefore, serves to bring the young people of the church to their Reformed profession of faith. The youth of the church is distinct from all other young people. Not as though they were better, but because they are *baptised.* And *in that baptism* the LORD has recognised them as "heirs of the covenant." Baptism served "to seal" also to them "His covenant." (For the quoted words, see the Form for the Baptism of Infants and read this form in its entirety carefully).

1. *Essence.*

   A covenant is a mutual agreement between two or more parties whereby they bind themselves together through promises and demands. Such a covenant also comprises the threat of vengeance for breach of the covenant. That which party A *promises* to party B, party B is entitled (and must) demand of party A, and *vice versa.*

   In his sovereign grace, it seemed good to the LORD to join himself in such a covenant to man (Adam). (Hos 6:7a states that the Israelites transgressed the covenant like Adam. The prophet, therefore, assumes that God had a covenant with Adam, just as he did with Israel. See also Rom 5:12-14; 1 Cor 15:21, 22).

   The Bible compares this covenant to a marriage (Hos 2; Ezek 16): The Bridegroom declares his love to the bride and asks for her love in return (*i.e.*, her yes); if she gives him her love in return, she receives him and eternal communion with him.

2. *Aspects.*

   The ORIGIN of this covenant rests in God's sovereign disposition (it is unilateral in its origin). Yet the LORD wanted to have a real covenant. Hence, he caused it to be BILATERAL in its CONTINUATION. Man received his office as "believer" as a real PARTY in the covenant.

3. *Parts.*

   Every covenant contains *two parts* (*Cf.* the Forms for the Baptism of Infants and of Adults), *viz.*

I. ON GOD'S PART

a. PROMISE: God promises HIMSELF ("to be God to you," Gen 17:7) and eternal communion with him.

b. DEMAND: "Walk before me, and be blameless" (Gen 17:1). The LORD, therefore, asks that man give *himself* to God by faith (that is the bride's "yes" to the Bridegroom).

II. ON OUR PART

a. PROMISE: Compliance with God's demand; the obedient love of faith.

b. DEMAND: Fulfilment of God's promise. (The "demand" on our part is our prayer: Ps 81:10, "Open your mouth wide").

God's covenant also has its CURSE/THREAT, for the event that man breaches the covenant (Gen 2:17: "in the day that you eat of it you shall die").

4. *Dispensations.*

   The covenant is, indeed, always the same, but it has not always been administered in the same way. The association between the LORD and his people has not always been regulated in the same manner. Compare in this respect the relationship between father and child. That relationship remains in existence no matter how old the child becomes. But the manner of association with the child differs depending upon whether the child is of tender years, a teenager, or an adult. The father does not deal with his child in the same way forever. So also, God has not dealt with his covenant people the same way all the time. Accordingly, we speak of different "dispensations." God established his covenant with Adam and his posterity, already before the fall. We call this the covenant of works (or the covenant of creation, or the covenant of paradise). In it, God promised Adam eternal life, not *because of* his *merit* before God, but *by* his *service* of God. But Adam broke the relationship between God and himself (through the fall, Adam's first breach of the covenant, *cf.* Hos 6:7). Thus, he forfeited the blessing of the covenant. In the place of the covenant with God, he entered into a covenant with the devil, by choosing his side and believing his word.

Although the LORD would not have done man an injustice if he, on his part, had abolished and terminated the covenant which had been broken by man, in his great mercy he set out to find the fallen Adam, when he fled, trembling, from him, and comforted him with the promise that he would give him his Son (BC, art. 17). He promised that he would break Adam's covenant with Satan (Gen 3:15: I will put ENMITY—the so-called protogospel).

The covenant, broken by Adam, is therefore *maintained* by the LORD, even though its administration is now different because of sin. This phase of the covenant is called the COVENANT OF GRACE.

We speak about the covenant of *grace* because man, having forfeited the covenant blessing because of sin, is by faith acquitted of guilt and punishment and is again entitled to the blessing of the covenant for Christ's sake, out of *grace*. Grace is favour that is forfeited. In the history of the covenant of grace we distinguish the following dispensations:

a.   Fall - Abraham

     During this period God's concern extends to all peoples.

b.   Abraham - Christ

     During this period the Lord restricts himself to Abraham's offspring. Here we can distinguish the following periods:

     i.   Abraham - Moses

          Before the law: patriarchal service.

     ii. Moses - Christ

          Under the law: ceremonial service.

c. Pentecost - Last day

Today the Lord again calls all peoples to covenant communion and the covenant service is no longer ceremonial, but in Spirit and in truth.

5. *Parties.*

The LORD *established* his covenant of grace with the fallen Adam and his descendants (it is unilateral in its establishment or *institution*). (BC, art. 17).

In Adam's descendants there are two lines: those who are true to the covenant and those who break the covenant ("sons of God" and sons "of men," Gen 6:2). The unbelieving and unrepentant covenant breakers are expelled (by the exercise of discipline) from the covenant, together with their descendants to the third and fourth generation of those who (continue to) hate the LORD. Cain was the first of them. The covenant is, therefore, not *continued* with *all* of Adam's descendants, for the unbelievers are always being expelled from it (excommunication). The covenant of grace CONTINUES with the BELIEVERS AND THEIR DESCENDANTS. (It is, thus, bilateral in its continuation. Note man's responsibility in this respect!).

The covenant is, thus, not established with every believer individually, with every baptised person, but it continues in every baptised person, while those who do not come to faith are removed from the holy line.

Some teach that those who are not elected and regenerated do not belong to the covenant. They argue that the promise of the covenant ("to be God to you," and eternal life) is meant only for those who are regenerated. (*E.g.*, the "Synodical" Reformed Churches).[1]

But the Bible teaches otherwise. Rom 9:4 teaches that the adoption as God's children, the *covenants* and the *promises* belonged to the Israelites who were lost; and Heb 3:19-4:1 tells us that one forfeits the *fulfilment* of the promise through *unbelief.*

The covenant was not established with Christ, for it is a covenant of *grace*, and no grace was shown to Christ. But Christ is MEDIATOR and SURETY in the covenant of grace because he:

a. fulfilled the demands of God's (creation) covenant (*active obedience,* *i.e.*, he did what Adam should have done, but did not do); and

b. bore the punishment of God's (creation) covenant (*passive obedience, i.e.*, he made atonement for what Adam did wrong by *suffering*

---

[1]Transl. note: The author refers to certain doctrinal decisions made by synods of the Gereformeerde Kerken in Nederland between 1942 and 1944, which were one of the main causes of the Liberation and, indirectly, of the establishment of the Canadian Reformed Churches.

the punishment).

Thus, the "covenant of works" was not abolished when the "covenant of grace" was established. In the "covenant of grace" the purpose of the "covenant of works" is achieved. The LORD has only one covenant with his people.

6. *Meaning.*

My sure comfort, both in life and death is that God, in his immeasurable and free grace, has included me in his covenant of grace, in order to bestow on me, who believes, righteousness and eternal life, because of the obedience and death of his Son.

E.   QUESTIONS (PART D)

1. Are the young people of the church better than other young people? How are the former distinguishable from the latter? What is a covenant?

2. In what relationship did the LORD place himself towards man? What does Hos 6:7a say? To what does the Bible compare the covenant?

3. On what does the origin of the covenant rest? How does it continue?

4. What did God promise in the covenant? What did he, at the same time, demand? What further aspect of the covenant is there?

5. What do we mean when we speak about "dispensations"? What do we call the covenant before the fall? How would man have received eternal life under it?

6. What did man do? And what did the LORD do then? What did we call the covenant thereafter? Why was it given that name?

7. What dispensations do we recognise in the covenant of grace?

8. With whom did the LORD establish the covenant of grace? With whom did he continue it?

9. Is it correct to say that this covenant is only for those who are regenerated? What does Holy Scripture say in Heb 3:19 and 4:1?

10. Is it correct to say that the covenant of grace was established with Christ? What relationship does Christ have toward the covenant of grace? How does he fulfil his work as Mediator?

11. What is the significance of the covenant for us?

LORD'S DAY 1

1. Q. *What is your only comfort*
   in life and death?

   A. *That I am not my own,[1]*
   but belong with body and soul,
   both in life and in death,[2]
   to my faithful Saviour Jesus Christ.[3]
   He has fully paid for all my sins
   with His precious blood,
   and has set me free
   from all the power of the devil.[5]
   He also preserves me in such a way[6]
   that without the will of my heavenly Father
   not a hair can fall from my head;[7]
   indeed, all things must work together
   for my salvation.[8]
   Therefore, by His Holy Spirit
   He also assures me
   of eternal life[9]
   and makes me heartily willing and ready
   from now on to live for Him.[10]

   [1] I Cor. 6:19, 20
   [2] Rom. 14:7-9.
   [3] I Cor. 3:23; Tit. 2:14.
   [4] I Pet. 1:18, 19; I John 1:7; 2:2.
   [5] John 8:34-36; Heb. 2:14, 15; I John 3:8.
   [6] John 6:39, 40; 10:27-30; II Thess. 3:3; I Pet. 1:5.
   [7] Matt. 10:29-31; Luke 21:16-18.
   [8] Rom. 8:28.
   [9] Rom. 8:15, 16; II Cor. 1:21, 22; 5:5; Eph. 1:13, 14.
   [10] Rom. 8:14.

2. Q. *What do you need to know*
   in order to live and die
   in the joy of this comfort?

   A. *First,*
   how great my sins and misery are;[1]
   second,
   how I am delivered
   from all my sins and misery;[2]
   third,
   how I am to be thankful to God
   for such deliverance.[3]

   [1] Rom. 3:9, 10; I John 1:10.
   [2] John 17:3; Acts 4:12; 10:43.
   [3] Matt. 5:16; Rom. 6:13; Eph. 5:8-10; I Pet. 2:9, 10.

A. NOTES

1. In the Catechism the church teaches "the doctrine of the Old and New Testaments, summarized in the confessions" (Form for the Baptism of Infants, Address to the Parents, Second Question). One might, therefore, expect that LD 1, which is an introduction to and brief summary of what follows, would ask: What is this doctrine? But the question reads: What is your only comfort? However, the word "comfort" in the Catechism has the same meaning as the word "doctrine." To call this doctrine "comfort" is Biblical. When the LORD sends Isaiah to his people to preach his word to them, he does not say (in Isa 40:1): "Teach, teach my people," but "Comfort, comfort my people." For God's doctrine (teaching, revelation) is our comfort. The Bible is a book of *comfort* (*cf.* Rom 15:4: the "comfort of the scriptures," KJV). Thus, the Catechism is not going to speak about us when it asks about our comfort, but about God's revelation, about his great works. But it also indicates at the outset what significance those have for us. They are our comfort!

2. "Comfort is a deliberation of the heart whereby we juxtapose our misery and the grace which Christ earned, so that, in considering that grace, our grief is tempered." (Ursinus, *Commentary on the Heidelberg Catechism*, LD 1, I). Comfort is, therefore, all that comforts us.

Let us take an example: A patient who has just undergone an operation suffers pain. The doctor tells him that the pain is temporary and will soon disappear. After the doctor leaves, the patient is still in pain, but he juxtaposes the doctor's reassurance and his pain, thereby meliorating his concern. In the same manner we place the misery of this life over against God's revelation of salvation. Then we are still subject to all manner of misery and adversity, but we are comforted.

3. The Catechism speaks of the ONLY comfort. There is no other. Everything which man embraces for comfort disappoints. Only that which God (the "God of *all* comfort," 2 Cor 1:3) *gives* as comfort is our comfort. That comfort is sufficient; it does not disappoint, neither in life, nor in death!

4. What, then, is our comfort? That we belong with body and soul, both in life and death, to our Lord Jesus Christ.

That we "belong" to him means that we are his responsibility. We belong entirely to him, we are his and he cares for and protects us (Rom 14:8), and we may share in his glory.

5. We became his property, because he *ransomed* us with his precious (*i.e.*, expensive) blood. 1 Pet 1:18, 19 says:

> You know that you were ransomed from the futile ways inherited from your fathers, not with perishable things such as silver or gold, but with the precious blood of Christ, like that of a lamb without blemish or spot.

1 Cor 6:20 says:

> You were bought with a price.

We are Christ's lawful possession, his inviolable property.

Nothing can alter that. Our sins cannot change it, for he made full payment for our sins. He has paid all debts. 1 Jn 1:7 says:

> . . . the blood of Jesus his Son cleanses us from all sin.

Nor can Satan change it. For Christ has redeemed us from all the dominion of the devil. The devil has no more jurisdiction over us. 1 Jn 3:8 says:

> The reason the Son of God appeared was to destroy the works of the devil.

6. Christ also preserves us as his possession. He exercises dominion over us on the basis of the right which he earned. He will not spare us all grief. Many calamities and vicissitudes are the lot of the believer. But no matter what may befall us, illness, imprisonment, or death, nothing can harm us unless our good Master permits it. He, the Saviour, will make all things serve for our salvation (Jn 10:28).

7. Christ takes his responsibility as the Lord, who owns us, very seriously. He does, indeed, exercise his right of ownership. By his Holy Spirit he assures me of eternal life as Eph 1:13, 14 says:

> In him you also, who . . . have believed in him, were sealed with the promised Holy Spirit, which is the guarantee of our inheritance. . . .

Further, he makes us heartily willing and ready from now on to live for him.

Thus, to belong to Christ is a complete comfort in life and death. He is a Master who is able to provide complete deliverance. He is entitled and has the power to remove our guilt, grief and corruption, and he shall do it. For that is why he bought us and made us his possession. Tit 2:14 says that he:

> . . . gave himself for us to redeem us from all iniquity and to purify for himself a people of his own who are zealous for good deeds.

8. Do not overlook the fact that the Catechism asks: What is *YOUR* only comfort? This is a very personal question! It is significant for each of us where we look for comfort. Is it truly your comfort, and do you rejoice in what God graciously revealed to us? Question 1 requires a decisive choice, not just once, but time and time again!

B. QUESTIONS

1. What does LD 1 provide with respect to the following Lord's Days? Is it Biblical to speak of "the doctrine of the Old and New Testaments" as "comfort"? How is that evident? When the Catechism speaks about *our* comfort, does it speak about us? What does it speak about?

2. What is comfort? Give an example to illustrate its meaning.

3. Why does the Catechism speak about the "only" comfort?

4. What, then, is your comfort? What does it mean to "belong"? What do 1 Pet 1:18 and 19, and 1 Cor 6:20, respectively, say? How did we become Christ's possession?

5. Can our sins negate the fact that we belong to Christ? Can Satan?

6. Does Christ spare us from all grief? What does he do?

7. What else does he do? What does Eph 1:14 say?

8. Why does the Catechism ask about "your" only comfort?

Q. & A. 2
WHAT WE NEED TO KNOW

A. NOTES

1. The Catechism now explains how we may enjoy this comfort, not just once, but time and time again. For the believers are not perfect in this life. It is possible for them to stumble and fall (CD V, 4) and then they have to return to the only comfort. In order to enjoy this comfort, they must have knowledge! Thus, we must know, *i.e.*, know in faith, so that we "accept as true all that God has revealed to us in His Word" (LD 7, Ans. 21).

2. The substance of what we must know, *i.e.*, the contents of Scripture, is summarized in three parts in this Answer:

first: *how great my sin and misery are* (we are miserable because we were driven out of paradise, out of communion with the LORD);

second: *how I am delivered from all my sins and misery*;

third: *how I am to be thankful to God for such deliverance.*

What is important is the HOW: *how* great my misery is, *how* I am delivered from it, and *how* I am to be thankful to God. The Bible reveals this to us. It teaches us in Eph 5:8:

. . . once you were darkness [misery], but now you are light in the Lord [deliverance]; walk as children of light [thankfulness].

These three parts also form the contents of the letter to the Romans: 1:1 - 3:20 (sin and misery); 3:21 - 11:36 (deliverance); and 12:1 - 16:27 (thankfulness). (See also Ps 130:3, 4).

3. We can distinguish between these three parts, but they always appear together. We can also distinguish the roots, trunk and crown of a tree, but none survives without the others. So also there is no true knowledge of

thankfulness without knowledge of sin and redemption, *etc*. This knowledge grows according to the measure by which the Lord gives us insight into the Scriptures and impresses its truth on our hearts.

4. The Catechism discusses the three parts in the following order:

    LD 2 - 4:   our sin and misery;

    LD 5 - 31:   our deliverance;

    LD 32 - 52:   our thankfulness.

B. CROSS REFERENCES

1. The triad "misery—deliverance—thankfulness" is repeated throughout the liturgical forms. In the Forms for the Baptism of Infants and Adults, Doctrine of Baptism, they are summarized as follows: 1. we are children of wrath [misery]; 2. God seals the covenant of grace to us [deliverance]; and 3. we are called and obliged to a new obedience [thankfulness]. Also in the Forms for the Celebration of the Lord's Supper, Self-examination, we find these three parts. They also appear in the first of the prayers: A General Confession of Sins and Prayer before the Sermon and on Days of Fasting and Prayer. See also LD 30, Q&A 81.

C. COMMENTS

1. Our Catechism discusses the three subjects which have always been considered the essentials in the instruction in faith, *viz.*, the "Apostles' Creed," the "Ten Words" and the Lord's prayer.

D. QUESTIONS

1. What does the Catechism explain in this answer? What is necessary for the enjoyment of our only comfort? Is it sufficient if we know the contents of Scripture?
2. What do we need to know? What does Eph 5:8 say? Of which book of the Bible do the three parts of our required knowledge form the contents?
3. Do these three parts arise separately and consecutively in our lives?
4. In which Lord's Days of the Catechism are each of the three parts discussed?

The First Part
OUR SIN AND MISERY

Lord's Days 2 - 4

A. NOTES

1. This part may be divided as follows:

LD 2: *the knowledge of our misery* (is from the law of God [Q&A 3], who demands love [Q&A 4], which man is incapable of [Q&A 5]);

LD 3: *the cause and extent of our misery* (its cause is not in God [Q&A 6], but in man [Q&A 7], and it extends over and through all mankind [Q&A 8]);

LD 4: *the punishment for sin* (is *just* [Q&A 9], *heavy* (now and eternal) [Q&A 10], and *certain*, because of God's justice and the gravity of the sin [Q&A 11]).

LORD'S DAY 2

3. Q. *From where do you know*
   your sins and misery?

   A. *From the law of God.[1]*

   [1] *Rom. 3: 20; 7:7-25.*

4. Q. *What does God's law require of us?*

   A. *Christ teaches us this in a summary in Matthew 22:*
      You shall love the LORD your God
      with all your heart,
      and with all your soul,
      and with all your mind.[1]
      This is the great and first commandment.
      And a second is like it,
      You shall love your neighbour as yourself.
      On these two commandments depend
      all the law and the prophets.[2]

      [1] *Deut. 6:5.*
      [2] *Lev. 19:18.*

5. Q. *Can you keep all this perfectly?*

   A. *No,[1] I am inclined by nature*
      to hate God and my neighbour.[2]

      [1] *Rom. 3:10, 23; I John 1:8, 10.*
      [2] *Gen. 6:5; 8:21; Jer. 17:9; Rom. 7:23; 8:7; Eph. 2:3; Tit. 3:3.*

THE SOURCE OF THE KNOWLEDGE OF OUR MISERY

A. NOTES

1. This Q&A is concerned with the knowledge of our sins and misery. Everyone has an awareness of and feeling about misery, about the fact that something is not right. That is why the Catechism does not ask *whether* there is misery, but "from where do you *know*" it. For sinful man lives and suffers without any understanding and awareness about how and why there is misery. One person may explain it from the fact of existence itself, another from the fact of some social regulation, a third regards it as belonging to a transitional period. But all of them lack the *knowledge*, the deep and correct insight of our sins and misery.

2. The knowledge we seek is not merely a theoretical one. It does not concern knowledge about *the*, but about *your* sins and misery. Only the broken-hearted have such a knowledge. You can find an example in Paul: "Wretched man that I am. . . ." (Rom 7:24).

3. A law is general in its application; it is a rule to live by. God instituted such a rule for each creature. He created it in such a way that it could only *live* in accordance with a particular law. Thus, a fish can only live in the water and the bird in the air. Just as the rails are designed to keep the train on track, so also the law is designed to keep each creature within the bounds set by for it. Ps 119:62 (rhymed version) says:

   . . . Great peace is theirs who honour and obey
   Thy precepts and who by Thy word are guided. . . .

4. The word "law" in Scripture denotes everything whereby God communicates his demand to us and which tells us what we must do to be saved. The word "gospel" means everything in which he unfolds his promise and tells us what he did, does and will do to save us.

5. The moral law is the law which God appointed for man's moral actions, *i.e.*, those actions which are determined by man's will. Man already knew this law when he was created, but he withdrew himself from its control and lost his knowledge of it through sin. In his maintenance of the covenant, God continued to reveal his law. He summarized it for all time in the ten words which he wrote on two tables on Sinai and which Moses gave to Israel. Thus, the law is the same before and after the fall; only its publication differs. Also in the state of glory this same law will still apply.

6. Rom 3:20 says: "through the law comes knowledge of sin." For it is the yard stick against which the lives of all people are measured. It is

acknowledged as such by those who are faithful to his covenant. They desire to do the law. Inwardly they delight to do their Father's will, but . . . they discover that they do not and cannot do his will. They learn not only that there is much evil around them, but that they themselves are by nature inclined to do just the opposite to what God wants them to do! Thus, they realize that their misery is their own corruption and that their corruption is total. They learn to confess that they are apt to fall because of their sinful nature (Ps 38:17, 18).

7. Hence, the law, as rule of thankfulness, is the source of our knowledge of our sins and misery. If it is not a person's rule of thankfulness, then it is also not the source of knowledge of his sins and misery. Only the believer knows his misery through the law and learns to know it more deeply through the law. When we, who were instructed in the Word of God, do not know our misery, it is usually not because we do not know the law, but because we deny our faith to our covenant God and do not esteem his covenant. Thereby, even our lack of knowledge of our misery renders us guilty!

B. CROSS REFERENCES

1. The law, given on Sinai, contains many rules which had significance for civil life in Israel. The Lord, as Israel's king (Israel was a theocracy), enacted them himself (Deut 17:14ff; Ex 22:26; Deut 22:8). The law also contained many provisions which regulated the OT (shadow and ceremonial) worship service. These speak of:

    a. The holy places (tabernacle, temple; now the Lord's congregation).

    b. The holy persons (high priest, priests and Levites; now Christ is our only high priest and all his believers are priests).

    c. The holy actions (purifications, offerings, prayers; now our entire lives are thank offerings).

    d. The holy times (sabbath and feast days; now our entire lives are a beginning of the eternal sabbath).

    These ceremonial provisions were fulfilled in Christ and are no longer effective. But they remain useful to us for the better understanding of the gospel. The civil provisions are, since Israel's theocracy has ceased to exist, also usually no longer relevant in their literal meaning. However, they contain many directions which are of continuing significance for us. (BC, art. 25).

2. In the CD III/IV, 5, we confess that the law "reveals the greatness of sin, and more and more convicts man of his guilt." Why is this discussed again in such detail in the Canons? See III/IV, RE 5.

C. QUESTIONS

1. Do all people have an awareness of misery? Also a knowledge of their sin and misery?
2. Are we speaking of a theoretical knowledge? Who only has the knowledge referred to in this Question?
3. What is a law? For which creatures did God appoint laws? What significance does the law have for the creature?
4. What is the "law" in Scripture? What else does Scripture contain? What is it?
5. What do we mean when we speak of man's moral actions? When did man already know the law? How did he lose this knowledge? Is the law today the same as that in paradise? Will this law also apply in the state of glory?
6. What special provisions did the Sinaitic law contain? Which matters do the provisions governing the worship service deal with? Do these still apply to us without exception? What significance do they still have?
7. How do we now learn to know our sins and misery from the law? Is it sufficient to know it by heart for this purpose? What does Rom 3:20 say?

Q. & A. 4

THE CONTENTS OF THE LAW

A. NOTES

1. In the Compendium (written in 1611 by Hermannus Faukelius, minister of the Word of God in Middelburg)[2] the question reads: "What did God command you in his law?" This makes it clearer that in the law we are concerned with God. He who violates the law, offends God, for it is "the law of God." He also violates his own duty, for the law of God demands something of *us*. It applies to *us* and concerns *us*. Note further that it *requires* something of us. The law does not just counsel, but it commands (*cf.* Ps 81:4).

2. Instead of listing each of the ten commandments one by one, the Catechism gives us the summary of the law instead. That is sufficient for the purpose envisaged by the question. For if we have broken the summary, then we have broken the whole law. By giving this summary, which illumines the deep sense of the law, the Catechism also precludes us from supposing that we have fulfilled the law through a superficial understanding of it. Compare the parable of the rich young ruler (Mt 19:16-30; Mk 10:17-31; Lk 18:18-30). A "summary" is a summing-up. Compare the concept of the "sum" in arithmetic and see Rom 13:9.

---

[2]Transl. note: The author refers to *The Compendium of the Christian Religion*, Q. 3. The Compendium is a short form of Catechism used in some Reformed Churches. Although it contains the same three parts as the HC and is based on it, the questions and answers are arranged differently. It was never adopted by the Canadian Reformed Churches.

3. *Love.* We should not *also* love God, or love him *above* all else, but we must *love* him. We love with our whole being. God does not desire merely a part of us, but our selves. More particularly, he wants us entirely, all of us, our heart, soul, mind and strength. For he is not just our Lord, he is also our Father! Kings do not demand love of their subjects, only obedience; love is what parents ask of their child and a husband of his wife. It is wonderful that God *demands love* of us! He *demands* love, because he demonstrated his love for us, having delivered us from bondage.

4. This love for God is the *first* commandment. Where this love is missing there can be no fulfilling of the law. The first table precedes the second. Further, this love of God is the *great* commandment. This is what everything depends on!

5. The second is like it. It is, indeed, the *second*, but it is like the first in origin and necessity. He who is not particular about obeying the second table of the law does not love God, despite all kinds of religiosity (1 Jn 3:17).

6. *Neighbour* means "close to." All people are my neighbours, for God created mankind out of one man. But some are closer to me than others. Those with whom I associate on a daily basis are closest to me. We must, indeed, love all men, *for the Lord's sake.* But the law is sensible and practical and demands that we begin at home.

7. *As yourself.* We must love ourselves because and in so far as we are God's creatures. That is also how we must love the neighbour.

8. *On these two commandments depend all the law and the prophets.* This means that whatever the law and the prophets command is summarized in these two commandments.

B. QUESTIONS

1. Whom do we offend when we violate the law? What else do we violate when we break the law? What is a "summary"? Why does the Catechism give a summary of the law here, instead of the full text?
2. What single word describes the demand of the law? How must we love God?
3. What does it mean that the love of God is called the "first commandment"? Why is it called the great commandment?
4. Is the second commandment less important than the first?
5. Who is your neighbour? Why must we love him? May we love ourselves?
6. What does "On these two commandments depend all the law and prophets" mean?

Q. & A. 5
HATERS OF GOD (ROM 1:30)

A. NOTES

1. *Can*: the question is not whether you did, but whether you can keep the law;

   you: note the second person singular; it concerns you;

   keep all this *perfectly*: for God, who is perfect, has no pleasure in anything that is imperfect;

   all this: for the law is one; he who stumbles in one commandment is guilty of transgressing all the commandments.

2. *No!* The Arminian says this too. But then he continues: "However, I have the *will* to do it, even though I cannot." But the Scriptural confession of the Catechism continues: "I am inclined by nature to hate God and my neighbour."

3. *By nature.* This means the state in which I was born and in which, if not renewed by God's Spirit, I live. The phrase "by nature" is added, because the bald statement that the believer hates God is false (see Ps 116:1).

4. *Inclined.* Man does not always commit all kinds of sins. But the inclination of his heart is to do them. Hence, the word "inclined" is not an excuse! The inclination is kept in check for a variety of reasons (fear of punishment, desire for honour, *etc.*).

5. *Hate.* This is the opposite of love and it is as unbounded and insatiable as love. Whereas love is the impulse to seek what is good, hate is the urge to destroy. By nature man *hates* God. His heart says, in the words of Ps 2:3:

   Let us burst their bonds asunder, and cast their cords from us.

   And Rom 8:7 says:

   For the mind that is set on the flesh is hostile to God; it does not submit to God's law, indeed it cannot.

   In this context the word "flesh" connotes man in his depravity. Sometimes it connotes man in his frailty (*cf.* Isa 40:6: All flesh is grass).

B. QUESTIONS

1. Why does the question ask whether you can keep "all this"? Further, why is perfect compliance required? Can we keep the law perfectly? Do we, of ourselves, have the will to keep it?

2. What does "by nature" mean? Does the Christian also hate God?

3. Does a person always commit all sins? Is his nature so good that he cannot commit all sins? If not, why does he not do them?

4. What does "hate" mean? What does Rom 8:7 say?

5. Which two connotations of the word "flesh" are found in Holy Scripture?

6. *Q.* *Did God, then, create man*
so wicked and perverse?

   A. *No, on the contrary,*
   God created man good[1] and in His image,[2]
   that is, in true righteousness and holiness,[3]
   so that he might rightly know God His Creator,[4]
   heartily love Him,
   and live with Him in eternal blessedness
   to praise and glorify Him.[5]

   > [1] *Gen. 1:31.*
   > [2] *Gen. 1:26, 27.*
   > [3] *Eph. 4:24.*
   > [4] *Col. 3:10.*
   > [5] *Ps. 8.*

7. *Q.* *From where, then, did man's depraved nature come?*

   A. *From the fall and disobedience of our first parents,*
   Adam and Eve, in Paradise,[1]
   for there our nature became so corrupt[2]
   that we are all conceived and born in sin.[3]

   > [1] *Gen. 3.*
   > [2] *Rom. 5:12, 18, 19.*
   > [3] *Ps. 51:5.*

8. *Q.* *But are we so corrupt*
   that we are totally unable to do any good
   and inclined to all evil?

   A. *Yes,[1] unless we are regenerated*
   by the Spirit of God.[2]

   > [1] *Gen. 6:5; 8:21; Job 14:4; Is. 53:6.*
   > [2] *John 3:3-5.*

A. NOTES

1. Job 34:10 says:

> ... far be it from God that he should do wickedness, and from the Almighty that he should do wrong.

But the sinner is always inclined to blame God for his misery and for all the evil that exists in the world. That is why the question now posed by the Catechism is necessary.

2. God created man *good*. Gen 1:31 says:

> And God saw EVERYTHING that he had made, and behold, it was VERY GOOD.

"Good" means efficacious. Man fully satisfied God's will and law. He fulfilled God's plan.

3. The word "image" used in this Answer combines the two words used in Scripture: "image" and "likeness" (see Gen 1:31). Holy Scripture, thus, uses two words for the same matter to express that matter as clearly as possible.

4. That man was God's image (not image bearer) means that he resembled God. Similarly, children sometimes resemble their father and it is then sometimes said: those children are the image of their father. When God looked down on Adam, he saw him exercising righteous dominion over all creatures (Gen 1:28; Ps 8). Therein God saw his own image, just as a king sees his image reflected in a faithful viceroy who administers the king's laws. Thus, man showed himself to be God's image in all his conduct by faithfully fulfilling the office (*i.e.*, duty) to which he was called as prophet, priest and king.

God had created man to this end in (*i.e.*, endowed with) "true righteousness and holiness." Man, therefore, stood in a true relationship to God, his law and his service (righteousness); and he dedicated himself fully to the Lord in complete purity. Man did not have any wrong impulse; he desired solely to devote himself faithfully to God (holiness). Eph 4:24 says:

> And put on the new nature, created after the likeness of God in true righteousness and holiness.

We know the original man, who was created in God's image, from the new nature of man (*i.e.*, the nature restored by Christ) of which the Apostle speaks. For when a new statue is made, in accordance with the original drawings, to replace one that has been destroyed, we know from the replacement what the original looked like.

The reason why God created man like this was so that he might rightly know God his Creator and also the creatures in their relationship to God. This knowledge was pure and certain in Adam; it was also sufficient for the moment, but capable of development.

5. The requirement of the law is love. It requires man to be the imitator of God, who is love. This was not impossible for man as created by God; in fact, it caused him no difficulty. For he was created in God's image. To be the imitator of God he had only to remain what he was.

6. God also made this a commandment for man. He must remain what he was and use the gifts which God had given him in accordance with their nature.

    For the Catechism says that God gave him his gifts, "so that he might rightly *know* God his Creator (*i.e.*, he had to use the gift of knowledge properly as *prophet*), heartily *love* Him (*i.e.*, he had to preserve his holiness as *priest*), and *live* with Him in eternal blessedness (*i.e.*, he had to exercise his righteousness as *king*)." Adam, therefore, fulfilled the three-fold *office*.

7. However, man profaned his office by sin. He did not faithfully devote his good gifts to God's service, but used them to obey the devil. Thereby God's image became corrupt.

    Man lost all his excellent gifts, received from God, through the fall. It is true that of all these original gifts "some small traces" remain (BC, art. 14). Further, the CD III/IV, 4, states that man still has:

    > . . . some light of nature, whereby he retains some notions about God, about natural things, and about the difference between what is honourable and shameful. . . .

    However, these remnants of his original gifts do not suffice for man to remain God's image (Jn 8:44). He misuses the remnants in unrighteousness (see CD III/IV, 4).

    In LD 12, Anw. 32, we confess that Christ restores us to a faithful fulfilment of the original duty of office and thereby renews us to the image of him who created us.

8. Thus, man did not arise out of the depths of the earth. God gave him a high position. He sinned, not because he was unable to do otherwise, or because he did not know what he was doing, but because of evil wilfulness. His fall into sin was a falling away from the most high God, also a falling away from the high position in which God placed him.

9. Man had not yet reached his ultimate destination at the time of creation. He did not yet enjoy eternal life. He was, indeed, good, but still changeable. God wanted man himself to desire the state of goodness. Augustine

said: Man had the ability not to sin. Had he made the correct choice, this would have become the inability to sin. Sadly, it became the inability not to sin.

B. CROSS REFERENCES

1. Article 14 of the BC speaks of our creation in God's image and of our fall, in consequence of which all ability to do good was lost.
2. Chapter III/IV, 1 of the CD, describes more broadly our creation in God's image and the consequences of our fall. The latter is further elaborated upon in III/IV, 4.

C. HERESIES

1. The Roman Catholic doctrine of the image of God, which that church likes to describe as the "golden rein."

D. QUESTIONS

1. Why is Q. 6 of the Catechism necessary?
2. How did God create man? What does it mean that he was created good?
3. What does it mean that man was created in God's image? Wherein did he show himself to be God's image? With what did God endow man?
4. What does it mean that man was created in "righteousness"? What does it mean that he was created in "holiness"?
5. What does Eph 4:24 say? How does this text point us to the first man?
6. To what end did God create man in his image?
7. How can you describe Adam's knowledge?
8. Was man able to keep God's law?
9. What was man's three-fold office?
10. What became of man as image of God as a result of sin?
11. Did man already have eternal life?
12. What did man's changeability consist of?

Q. & A. 7
BY MAN

A. NOTES

1. The only one who can inform us about the origin of our misery is God. Most nations have a vague tradition about a fall into sin. But only the Word of God gives us the revelation of history.
2. This Word, as well as this question about the origin of our depravity, direct us to Paradise. In connection with the previous question we saw that man, who was created good, also had to have the *will* to be good. The Lord wanted man on his part to accede to God's covenant by loving his covenant God and listening to his Word. In order that man would be

able to show that he desired to do this, God gave him the probationary command contained in Gen 2:17:

> But of the tree of the knowledge of good and evil you shall not eat, for in the day that you eat of it you shall die.

3. PROBATIONARY COMMAND: It is probationary because the Lord tested man by it.

   TREE OF THE KNOWLEDGE OF GOOD AND EVIL: Through the *presence* of this tree and the probationary command, man acquired knowledge of good *and* evil. The GOOD consisted of not eating of the tree; the EVIL of eating of it. Man was able to choose.

4. The Lord did not set a trap for man when he gave this probationary command. He warned him of the consequences of disobedience. Further, the Lord did not overburden man. He was *forbidden* to eat of only *one* tree. The Lord gave this commandment for (*i.e.*, in furtherance of) life! For the commandment enabled Adam to show that he desired to cling to the Lord, even though he did not understand fully why the Lord demanded of him what he did demand. Thereby man would achieve love *of his own free will* and surpasses all other creatures on earth.

5. It was at this point, where the Lord gave man the opportunity to proceed to love of his own free will, but where there was also the possibility that man might turn away from God, it was *here* that our misery began. For man did not obey the Lord. That was his fall. That is why he was cast down from his high position. There is not a single excuse for this disobedience. It was, says LD 4, Answer 9, deliberate, impudent disobedience. Scripture calls it folly.

6. Read the course of the temptation and man's disobedience again in Gen 3:1-7.

7. By his disobedience man cut the bond of life with the Lord. He went from a covenant with the Lord to a covenant with Satan. Immediately, this had very sad consequences for man's entire nature (*i.e.*, his existence). Everything in his nature was turned into the opposite. His knowledge became foolishness; his righteousness, unrighteousness; his holiness, impurity. Gen 3:8-13 describes how this immediately became apparent. Instead of being child of God, man became child of the devil! He chose the side of the devil and thereby obtained his nature (Jn 8:42-44; see also BC, art. 14; and CD III/IV, 1).

8. Man brought forth children of the same nature as he had become after the fall. This followed from the position in which God had placed him in creation (head of the covenant and of mankind). Gen 5:3 states:

. . . Adam . . . became the father of a son in his own likeness, after his image. . . .

Rom 5:19 says:

> For as by one man's disobedience many were made sinners. . . .

The word "many" in this text does not imply a mathematical concept. Rather, it means *all*. These all are called many, because their number is overwhelming.

Ps 51:5 says:

> Behold, I was brought forth in iniquity, and in sin did my mother conceive me.

B. CROSS REFERENCES

1. We call this congenital depravity "original pollution" (see BC, art. 15; and CD III/IV, 1, 2, 3).

2. In the Forms for the Baptism of Infants and of Adults (Doctrine of Baptism) we confess:

> . . . we and our children are conceived and born in sin and are therefore by nature children of wrath. . . .

See also the first question in the Form for the Baptism of Infants (Address to the Parents) and the second in the Form for the Baptism of Adults (Public Profession of Faith).

3. In the General Confession of Sins and Prayer before the Sermon and on Days of Fasting and Prayer (the first prayer in the Prayers section of the Liturgy, contained in the Book of Praise) we confess:

> We are deeply conscious of the fact that we are conceived and born in sin, and that all manner of evil desires against Thee and our neighbour fill our hearts.

C. HERESIES

1. Pelagianism.

2. Arminianism (Remonstrantism).

3. The denial of the existence of the spiritual world, or of its influence on this life.

D. QUESTIONS

1. What is the only source of our knowledge of the origin of our misery?
2. What does the probationary commandment say?
3. What was the purpose of the probationary commandment? Why was the tree called the "tree of the knowledge of good and evil"?
4. Was the probationary commandment a trap? Was it unbearable?
5. What does the word "fall" mean?
6. What did the fall consist of?

7. Is there any excuse for the fall?
8. Relate what Gen 3:1-7 says.
9. What are the consequences of the fall for human nature?
10. What do Rom 5:19 and Ps 51:5, respectively, say?
11. What is original pollution?

Q. & A. 8
NO ONE THAT DOES GOOD

A. NOTES

1. Answer 7 has already stated that the corruption caused by Adam's fall extends to ALL men. Q. 8 now describes how extensive this corruption is in everyone. It is so extensive that we are unable to do *any good*, but are *inclined* to all evil.

2. This confession virtually isolates Reformed Christians. Many believe that a "better person" remains in man. But Scripture says in Gen 6:5:

    The LORD saw that the wickedness of man was great in the earth, and that every imagination of the thoughts of his heart was only evil continually.

    So also, Rom 8:7 says:

    . . . the mind that is set on the flesh is hostile to God. . . .

    Man is completely corrupt.

3. Sometimes that is dramatically evident. There are people who are complete criminals. But there are also others. Indeed, most people are intent upon looking after their physical welfare, filling their position in society with honour, making themselves useful toward their fellow man by courteous behaviour, and exhibiting a certain respect for religion. Is all that not good? Indeed, these *natural, civil,* and *outwardly moral* and *religious* actions and attitudes of doing "good" have value for this life. The Lord uses them to ensure that society does not fall apart. But in all of these things man does not fulfil the law of the Lord. For he does not do them in love of the Lord. This is evident from the story about the building of the tower of Babel. Men did "good" to each other in that situation. They did not fight each other, but helped each other in complete harmony. What peace and prosperity! But in the process they helped each other unanimously to forget God and to resist his commandment! Thus, they hated God, while doing "good" toward each other!

4. We do not deny that man remained a human being after the fall. He still has his intellect and can take up a task with deliberation. Further, he has retained his will, can still make choices and does so. But he does not use these "small traces" of the excellent gifts which God gave him when he was created (BC, art. 14), to serve God; rather, he uses them in the

service of his evil designs (see esp. CD III/IV, 4, 5). These "small traces" do not give man any saving knowledge of God, but they do make him inexcusable before God, since he misuses even the good gifts which were left him (see Q&A 6, Note 7).

The Catechism says that we are *inclined* to all evil. Not every person commits every evil deed. This is not because man might still have some goodness in him, for each man is *inclined* to *all* evil. But God restrains much. He holds back much evil by means of the threat of the law and the punishment meted out by the government. Nonetheless, the inclination of the heart is against God and to do evil. Just like iron has the inclination to hurtle itself against a magnet when it comes near the magnet, so also the sinful heart is inclined to thrust itself at sin.

5. Man, therefore, has not retained any connection with good. No moral or spiritual rearmament can help. Sin is not an acquired habit; it is not something we have learned. Rather, it is inherited (Gen 8:21; Job 14:4). Only REGENERATION can give deliverance. That which exists must die in order to arise in a new life. ("This is what the immersion in or sprinkling with water teaches us" [Forms for the Baptism of Infants and of Adults (Doctrine of Baptism)]). The deliverance can only come about through a miracle of God. But before the Catechism speaks about the deliverance, it will first illuminate our depravity still further.

6. *Regeneration.* The Bible speaks of being born again (Jn 3:3, literally, the word "again" says: "from above"). This refers to the complete renewal of life. In LD 33, Q. 88, this renewal is called the "true repentance or conversion." The CD III/IV, 11, 12, speak of conversion, regeneration, new creation, resurrection from the dead, and making alive. The *Holy Spirit* works this renewal of life by *God's Word*. Ps 19:7 (KJV) says:

> The law of the LORD is perfect, converting the soul. . . .

Ps 119:50 states:

> This is my comfort in my affliction that thy promise gives me life.

Jas 1:18 says:

> Of his own will he brought us forth by the word of truth that we should be a kind of first fruits of his creatures.

Wherever this Word of God is accepted in faith, man is born anew, for, as BC, art. 24 says:

> We believe that this true faith, worked in man by the hearing of God's Word and by the operation of the Holy Spirit, regenerates him and makes him a new man. It makes him live a new life and frees him from the slavery of sin.

B. CROSS REFERENCES

1. CD III/IV, 3 states:

> . . . they neither will nor can return to God, reform their depraved nature, or prepare themselves for its reformation.

2. In CD III/IV, RE 4, this assertion is substantiated and maintained, with references to Scripture.

C. QUESTIONS

1. Is man still able to do good? Does he wan.. to do good?
2. What do Gen 6:5 and Rom 8:7, respectively, say?
3. Are all men complete criminals? In what respect do they do "good"? What value do these "good" actions have?
4. Does man not fulfil the law of the Lord when he does these "good" actions? Why not?
5. Were any traces of good gifts left to man in the fall? Is he not able to do good through them?
6. Do people always commit all sins? Is it because there is sufficient good in them that they do not? If not, why do they not commit all sins all the time? What is man's stance over against sin?
7. Can we still deliver ourselves from sin?
8. What must happen for our deliverance? Who, only, can do this?
9. What is regeneration? What does the Catechism call it in LD 33, Q. 88?
10. Who works regeneration? By what means?
11. What do Ps. 19:8 and Jas 1:18, respectively, say?

9. Q. *Is God, then, not unjust*
by requiring in His law
what man cannot do?

A. *No,*
for God so created man
that he was able to do it.[1]
But man, at the instigation of the devil,[2]
in deliberate disobedience[3]
robbed himself and all his descendants
of these gifts.[4]
[1] *Gen. 1:31.*
[2] *Gen. 3:13; John 8:44; I Tim. 2:13, 14.*
[3] *Gen. 3:6.*
[4] *Rom. 5:12, 18, 19.*

10. Q. *Will God allow such disobedience and apostasy*
to go unpunished?

A. *Certainly not.*
He is terribly displeased
with our original sin
as well as our actual sins.
Therefore He will punish them
by a just judgment
both now and eternally,[1]
as He has declared:[2]
Cursed be every one
who does not abide by all things
written in the book of the law,
and do them (Galatians 3:10).
[1] *Ex. 34:7; Ps. 5:4-6; 7:10; Nah. 1:2; Rom. 1:18; 5:12;*
Eph. 5:6; Heb. 9:27.
[2] *Deut. 27:26.*

11. Q. *But is God not also merciful?*

A. *God is indeed merciful,[1]*
but He is also just.[2]
His justice requires
that sin committed
against the most high majesty of God
also be punished with the most severe,
that is, with everlasting,
punishment of body and soul.[3]
[1] *Ex. 20:6; 34:6, 7; Ps. 103:8, 9.*
[2] *Ex. 20:5; 34:7; Deut. 7:9-11; Ps. 5:4-6; Heb. 10:30, 31.*
[3] *Matt. 25:45, 46.*

LORD'S DAY 4
Q. & A. 9
CULPABLE INABILITY

A. NOTES

1. In the preceding Lord's Days we confessed that man *cannot* fulfil the law
    of God, not even in part. The question now being asked is, therefore,
    cogent: Is it not an injustice on God's part to require of man what he is
    unable to do? For it is unjust to demand of a child what only an adult can
    do. But the sinner is not a child. He was supplied with the tools to
    complete the required work (*God so created man that he was able to do
    it*). But man threw his tools away (*robbed himself . . . of these gifts*). He
    did not do this in ignorance, but in deliberate disobedience. Foolishly, he
    placed the suggestion of the devil above God's commandment. That is
    why his inability is culpable.

2. No one will contradict that all this applies to Adam. But what about us?
    For we never enjoyed the gifts that Adam received. It is, therefore,
    understandable that the Compendium inserts the following question at this
    point:[3] "Does the disobedience of Adam concern us?" and the Answer
    reads: "Yes, indeed, for he is the father of us all and we have all sinned
    in him." The Catechism does the same here by speaking about *man* and
    intimating that the action of *the first* man concerned all his descendants.

3. Adam was not just any man, one of many. For people do not stand on
    their own. God made all mankind out of one person (Acts 17:26). He
    created mankind so that they stood in relationship to each other, as an
    organic whole, in the same manner as the branches are connected to the
    tree and the members of your body to your head. But we can say more.
    The cohesion of man is not just material, it is also spiritual. There is not
    only the bond of blood, but also that of the covenant, the covenant of
    works (see Introduction, D, 4)!

4. In accordance with this covenant Adam is not just our *father*, but also our
    legal *representative*. Our relationship to Adam is so close that Scripture
    says: BECAUSE ALL MEN SINNED (Rom 5:12).[4] Adam did not merely
    sin for us, or also on our behalf, but we ourselves sinned in him (that is

---

[3]Transl. note: See footnote 2, *supra*, Q. 11.

[4]Transl. note: The Dutch Statenvertaling reads "in whom all sinned." In a brief passage, which has not
been translated, the author refers to the Dutch Nieuwe Vertaling which reads the same as the English
versions. He concludes that it may be the correct translation and that, in any event, this version did not alter
the meaning as indicated by its marginal notes. The context in the English versions makes it clear that all
men sinned in Adam.

how close and real the relationship is). We ourselves have, in him, rejected our excellent gifts!

5. Hence, we are culpable in Adam. Even before we commit any actual sin, we are already guilty before God (Ps 51:7). Rom 5:19 says:

> For as by one man's disobedience many were made sinners, so by one man's obedience many will be made righteous.

This guilt of Adam's, which extends to us, is called original guilt (see also 1 Cor 15:21ff).

6. We already spoke about original pollution. Hence, we distinguish between *original guilt, i.e.,* that in Adam we are culpable before God; and *original pollution, i.e.,* that the corrupted nature of Adam extends to us.

7. Our sinful hearts resist the allegation that we are guilty in Adam. They protest our inclusion in Adam's guilt. But was God not free to create man as he wished, and was he not entitled to establish the covenant? It is not what God did that made us miserable. We are miserable because we ruined what God made good and we employ the good things God gave for corrupt purposes. It behooves us only to be silent and to pray to the Lord. He also works deliverance according to the same law of "one for all."

B. CROSS REFERENCES

1. See BC, art. 15 about original sin.

2. Also the CD I, 1 confesses the righteousness of God in the condemnation of sinners.

3. The CD III/IV, 1-3 also speak of the fall and its consequences.

4. Note also how this confession is reflected in the first question in the Form for the Baptism of Infants (Address to the Parents) and the second question in the Form for the Baptism of Adults (Public Profession of Faith).

C. QUESTIONS

1. Why is it that man cannot keep God's law?

2. Does Adam's disobedience concern us?

3. Was Adam more than just our father?

4. How did God create mankind?

5. What binds us together in addition to the bond of blood?

6. What does Scripture say in Rom 5:12 and 19, respectively?

7. What is original guilt? What is original pollution?

Q. & A. 10
GOD PUNISHES

A. NOTES

1. Punishment is retribution; it serves to restore the law that was broken. Of course, the punishment must be commensurate with the crime (Ex 21:24, 25). God's law was broken by our sin. To restore the broken law the offender must now undergo punishment. He who does evil must suffer evil!

2. Or do you suppose that God might let the sin go unpunished? But he is TERRIBLY DISPLEASED with all sin. Hab 1:13 says:

    Thou who art of purer eyes than to behold [*i.e.*, tolerate] evil. . . .

    God's anger is his hatred of and opposition to sin. God's entire holy being abhors sin. He is not indifferent to it. Scripture even says in Ps 7:11:

    God is a righteous judge, and a God who HAS INDIGNATION EVERY DAY.

    His anger is terrible! Ps 90:11 says:

    Who considers the power of thy anger, and thy wrath according to the fear of thee?

    God is not a judge who punishes because the law prescribes it but who is himself unmoved by the offence. On the contrary, God *himself* in his anger opposes the sinner. God's entire holy being opposes itself to the sinner.

3. While man's anger works unrighteousness, God's anger is righteous. He does not become angry because he is evil, but because he is holy. He does punish in holy passion, but "by (*i.e.*, in accordance with) a just judgment." Thus, from him to whom much has been given, much will be demanded. It shall be more tolerable for Tyre and Sidon than for Capernaum and Bethsaida (Mt 11:20-24).

4. God judges both original as well as actual sins. The latter are those we do ourselves, by commission or omission.

5. God's punishment is in part "natural" in the sense that it flows "naturally" from sin (sin punishes itself: adultery, intemperance). In part it is "external" in the sense that it is imposed on the offence by God. It is *temporal*, since it is experienced already in this life (in all interruptions of wealth and peace: sickness, war, discord, contrition), and *eternal* (after this life). Scripture depicts eternal punishment mostly in images, such as: outer (most extreme, worst) darkness, unquenchable fire. Just as no eye has seen what God has prepared for those who love him, so also the heart of man has not conceived what God will do to those who hate him.

2 Thess 1:9 says:

> They shall suffer the punishment of eternal destruction and exclusion from the presence of the Lord and from the glory of his might.

6. The essence of the punishment is the CURSE. It is the personal displeasure of God. It arises first in God's heart: he HATES the workers of iniquity; then in his word: he has no kind words for them but curses them; finally in his deed: he gives them over to corruption—God pushes them away from himself!

B. QUESTIONS

1. What is punishment? What is its purpose? What principle must it satisfy?
2. What is God's anger? What is God's position over against sin? What is "original" sin? What is "actual" sin?
3. How does God punish sin? Who bears the heaviest punishment?
4. With what does God punish sin?
5. What are "temporal" and "eternal" punishments?
6. What is the essence of punishment?
7. What do Hab 1:13 and Ps 90:11, respectively, say?

Q. & A. 11
GOD IS FAITHFUL

A. NOTES

1. Here the Catechism demonstrates the futility of the final attempt to escape the argument. The sinner refuses to accept that he, dead in sin and misdeeds, is subject to eternal punishment. When he knows of no other escape, he says in a frivolous and unconcerned manner, "but God is merciful"! This is true. Rom 5:8 says:

> . . . God shows his love for us in that while we were yet sinners Christ died for us.

But in his mercy God does not abandon the word he has spoken. He is just and his justice, *i.e.*, the fact that he keeps the word he has spoken, requires that sin be punished by the most severe, *i.e.*, everlasting punishment.

2. This punishment is not too heavy, for: (a) the sin was committed against the most high majesty of God; and (b) by its nature the sin was eternal, since it was not subject to repentance.

3. The sinner also deserves to be punished in body and soul. For he sins with both body and soul. He will, therefore, be punished accordingly, unless he be delivered by Christ.

4. It is evidence of God's mercy that he causes this to be preached to us so seriously and with insistence. Thereby he urges us to consider as yet what

serves for our peace and, knowing the fear of the Lord, to repent.

5. It behooves us to consider eternal punishment in humility. The subject contains many mysteries.

B. CROSS REFERENCES

1. This Answer of the Catechism is repeated almost word for word in the CD II, 1.
2. See also BC, art. 20 about the justice of God.

C. HERESIES

1. The doctrine of conditional immortality. According to this doctrine no person is immortal unless he satisfies the condition of faith. Hence, so it is supposed, only the believers will have eternal life, while the unbelievers will cease to exist when they die (Jehovah's Witnesses).
2. Others are of the view that all persons in hell will, in time, come to repentance. This is in direct conflict with Scripture.

D. QUESTIONS

1. Is God not also merciful? How has he demonstrated his mercy?
2. Does God in his mercy set aside the punishment?
3. Is eternal punishment not too heavy?
4. Is eternal punishment only a spiritual suffering?
5. Is it not cruel to speak to man of everlasting punishment in this short life?
6. What is the doctrine of conditional immortality?
7. What other heresies which deny the eternal nature of the punishment do you know?

The Second Part

OUR DELIVERANCE

Lord's Days 5 - 31

A. NOTES

1. In the work of the Lord concerning our deliverance we can distinguish the following aspects:

   a. THE ACQUISITION OF THE DELIVERANCE.

   This is the work of God done FOR us by the Saviour, Jesus Christ. He fulfilled this work in the state of humiliation. That is when he satisfied God's justice for us and in our place and acquired our deliverance for us, *i.e.*, it became HIS possession.

   b. THE APPROPRIATION OF THE DELIVERANCE.

   This is that work of the Lord whereby he brings the deliverance obtained by Christ TO us and makes it our OWN. We also call it the application or the distribution of salvation. Christ does this in his state of exaltation by the Holy Spirit. This is God's work IN us.

   Lord's Days 5 and 6 speak of the ACQUISITION of the deliverance and confess that it was only obtained for us by the Mediator, Jesus Christ.

   Lord's Days 7 - 31 speak of the APPROPRIATION of the deliverance and confess that this happens by faith.

2. The distinction between obtaining and appropriating the deliverance was distorted by the Arminians (Remonstrants). They taught that Christ died for *all* people and obtained forgiveness of sins for *all*, and that it now depends upon *us* to appropriate this work (see CD II, RE 6). However, both are the work of God! Christ has obtained the deliverance only for those to whom it is appropriated and it is appropriated only to all those for whom Christ obtained it.

B. QUESTIONS

1. Which Lord's Days speak about the deliverance?
2. What distinctions do we draw in the work of deliverance?
3. What is obtaining the deliverance? Who obtained it? When did he complete it? How did he complete it?
4. What is appropriation of the deliverance? Is it also known by other terms? Who completes this work? When does he do so?
5. What do we confess in Lord's Days 5 and 6? What do we confess in Lord's Days 7 - 31?

§I. THE ACQUISITION
OF THE DELIVERANCE
BY OUR MEDIATOR JESUS CHRIST

Lord's Days 5 - 6

12. Q. *Since, according to God's righteous judgment*
we deserve temporal and eternal punishment,
how can we escape this punishment
and be again received into favour?

A. *God demands that His justice be satisfied.[1]*
Therefore full payment must be made
either by ourselves or by another.[2]

> [1] *Ex. 20:5; 23:7; Rom. 2:1-11.*
> [2] *Is. 53:11; Rom. 8:3, 4.*

13. Q. *Can we ourselves make this payment?*

A. *Certainly not.*
On the contrary, we daily increase our debt.[1]

> [1] *Ps. 130:3; Matt. 6:12; Rom. 2:4, 5.*

14. Q. *Can any mere creature pay for us?*

A. *No.*
In the first place,
God will not punish another creature
for the sin which man has committed.[1]
Furthermore,
no mere creature can sustain
the burden of God's eternal wrath against sin
and deliver others from it.[2]

> [1] *Ezek. 18:4, 20; Heb. 2:14-18.*
> [2] *Ps. 130:3; Nah. 1:6.*

15. Q. *What kind of mediator and deliverer*
must we seek?

A. *One who is a true[1] and righteous[2] man,*
and yet more powerful than all creatures;
that is, one who is at the same time true God.[3]

> [1] *I Cor. 15:21; Heb. 2:17.*
> [2] *Is. 53:9; II Cor. 5:21; Heb. 7:26.*
> [3] *Is. 7:14; 9:6; Jer. 23:6; John 1:1; Rom. 8:3, 4.*

LORD'S DAY 5
Q. & A. 12
No Reconciliation Except Through Satisfaction

A. NOTES

1. In the confession of our deliverance, we must not neglect anything contained in the part about our sin and misery. For God does not overlook any aspect of our misery at all. That is why the second part of the Catechism begins with a full admission of the conclusion to which we came in the part on our sin and misery, *viz.*, that "according to God's righteous judgment we deserve temporal and eternal punishment." The question is then asked: How, or by what means (for it will not be automatic), can we escape the punishment and be received again into God's favour?

2. *Escape this punishment* is not the same as *be again received into favour.* For one can give a guilty person a discharge, thereby absolving him of the punishment, without accepting him into favour again (see 2 Sam 14:24).

   Escape this punishment means to escape God's covenant wrath.

   Be again received into favour does not mean that God extended grace in the sense of guilt-forgiving favour to Adam before the fall. Rather it means: share again in God's covenant blessing, in his communion.

3. The deliverance will only happen if justice has its course. Isa 1:27 states:

   > Zion shall be redeemed by justice, and those in her who repent, by righteousness.

   For God is just. He maintains his word once spoken forever. Ex 23:7 says:

   > . . . for I will not acquit the wicked.

   And Ex 34:7 says:

   > . . . who (*i.e.*, the LORD) will by no means clear the guilty. . . .

   In order to achieve reconciliation (*i.e.*, to restore the friendly relationship) with God, satisfaction must occur. *God demands that his justice be satisfied.*

   We must make PAYMENT to God's justice. The noun "payment" indicates precisely what the matter is all about. For when PAYING it is essential that you hand over exactly what is demanded. Otherwise you are not given a receipt, or remission, for you have not paid. Further, "payment" connotes a *quid pro quo* for what is required. Paying does not confer a right, but fulfils an *obligation*! This "payment" must be FULL, says the Catechism.

4. Already in Paradise man had to "pay," *i.e.*, fulfil the demand of the covenant. This payment meant that the law had to be fulfilled completely. Thus, this is the *first* thing that we must pay: we must be obedient in our actions and fulfil the law. This is *active obedience*. After the fall the obligation to suffer the punishment was added to this obligation. This is *passive obedience*.

5. WE must pay. Payment must be made by man, from whom God has expected it from the beginning.

   This payment must be made *either by ourselves or by another*. But also in the latter situation, WE must do it through the other person. Hence, we must take an active part in the payment made by Christ, *viz.*, by our faith, which places Christ's satisfaction before the Father, with the supplication that he will show us grace for Christ's sake. Man does not earn anything with this "payment." He merely accepts what God gives.

B. QUESTIONS

1. Why does the Catechism ask in Q. 12 how we can escape the punishment?
2. What does "escape this punishment" mean? What does "be again received into favour" mean?
3. What does Isa 1:27 say? What is necessary for reconciliation? What is reconciliation?
4. What does the word "payment" connote?
5. What did man already have to pay in Paradise? What was added to that after the fall?
6. What do the terms "active obedience" and "passive obedience" connote?
7. Who must pay? How must we pay? If payment is made by "another," do we have nothing to do with it? Do we, in that manner, still give something to God?

Q. & A. 13 and 14
NEITHER MAN NOR OTHER CREATURE CAN MAKE SATISFACTION

A. NOTES

1. The Catechism now asks first whether "we ourselves" can make the required payment. But that is impossible, even though the sinner believes that he can do so in various ways, such as: sacrifices, repentance, self improvement, good works, *etc.* Man has devised many ways to make God content. But no matter what he does, he increases his debt daily.

   This is not hard to understand. Man is duty-bound to make full payment, *i.e.*, to fulfil the law, every day. But no matter what he does, he cannot fulfil the law. That is why he increases his debt day by day. Even the converted, those who desire to serve God, must pray every day: "Forgive us our debts. . . ."

2. *Guilt* must be distinguished from *sin*. But it must never be separated from it, for sin is guilt! But sin is the crime, the wrongdoing, whereas guilt is

the crime which is accounted to us (*i.e.*, brought into account, put on our account).

3. Is there somewhere, perhaps, a *mere creature* that can pay for us? The question contemplates a creature that is endowed only with the powers of a creature, one that has only created powers at its disposal.

4. But no "mere creature" can pay for us, for:

   a. *God will not punish another creature for the sin which man has committed.* Payment must be made to God by a *human* being. Ezek 18:4 says:

      . . . the soul that sins shall die.

   b. *No mere creature can sustain the burden of God's wrath and deliver others from it.* The creature can suffer that wrath and will do so. But "payment" implies an action of which one can say at some point: It is finished. And a creature cannot do that. The finite cannot bear away the infinite. Nah 1:6 says:

      Who can stand [*i.e.*, stand firm] before his indignation? Who can endure the heat of his anger?

   (See also LD 6, Q&A 16 and 17, Note 2).

5. In Israel the LORD used sacrifices of animals in the service of reconciliation. But those did not reconcile. Heb 10:4 says:

   For it is impossible that the blood of bulls and goats should take away sins.

   Israel knew that too. Ps 40:3 (rhymed version) begins:

   No sacrifice didst Thou, O LORD, require. . . .

   These sacrifices taught the people of Israel the necessity of the only sacrifice of Christ and assured them it would be brought.

B. QUESTIONS

1. Can we "ourselves" make the required payment? How does man try to do this? What does he accomplish thereby?
2. What is the distinction between "sin" and "guilt"?
3. What is meant by the expression "mere creature"?
4. Why can a mere creature not pay for us?
5. What does Nah 1:6 say?
6. What was the purpose of the sacrifices in Israel?

Q. & A. 15
A MEDIATOR IS NEEDED!

A. NOTES

1. The question, "What kind of mediator and deliverer must we seek?" does not, of course, imply that we ourselves are going to determine that issue in the Catechism. Also in this Answer the Catechism merely confesses, *i.e.*, repeats, what the Word of the Lord tells us.

2. A mediator is someone who works in a conciliatory manner between two or more parties. He reconciles the offended party to the offender. Generally, in such circumstances, it is usually possible for the mediator to persuade both parties to concede something and bring about the reconciliation thereby. But, as between the offended God and offending man, there can be no question of concession, for:

   a. the sinner has nothing to concede; he has only guilt; and

   b. God neither can, nor will retreat from his righteous demand for justice in any way. He overlooks nothing.

3. Hence, in order to effect reconciliation, the Mediator between God and man must:

   a. make satisfaction for the injustice that was done (by his passive and active obedience) - this is the acquisition of the reconciliation; and

   b. ensure that the sinner does not harden himself in his sin and continues to offend God - this is the appropriation of the reconciliation.

   Thus, the Mediator has to act as *vicarious Surety*. He has to take our place. That is how he is the Deliverer!

4. We must *seek* this Mediator. This does not mean that we should try to find him somewhere. God has given him and made him known. But we must seek the Mediator who has been revealed to us. We must go to him, plead on his completed work, and follow him.

5. The requirements of the Mediator are: He must be a true and righteous (*i.e.*, not guilty, holy) man and also true God.

B. CROSS REFERENCES

1. You will find the term "Surety," used above, also in CD II, 2.

C. QUESTIONS

1. Does the Catechism itself determine what kind of Mediator we require? What does it do, then?

2. What is a mediator? Can reconciliation between God and man occur by each party conceding something? Why not?

3. What must the Mediator do to accomplish reconciliation? How must he, therefore, act?
4. What does it mean that we must seek the Mediator?
5. What are the requirements for the Mediator?

16. *Q.* *Why must He be a true and righteous man?*

   A. *He must be a true man*
      because the justice of God requires
      that the same human nature which has sinned
      should pay for sin.[1]
   He must be a righteous man
      because one who himself is a sinner
      cannot pay for others.[2]

   [1] *Rom: 5:12, 15; I Cor. 15:21; Heb. 2:14-16.*
   [2] *Heb. 7:26, 27; I Pet. 3:18.*

17. *Q.* *Why must He at the same time be true God?*

   A. *He must be true God*
   so that by the power of His divine nature[1]
   He might bear in His human nature
   the burden of God's wrath,[2]
   and might obtain for us
   and restore to us
   righteousness and life.[3]

   [1] *Is. 9:5.*
   [2] *Deut. 4:24; Nah. 1:6; Ps. 130:3.*
   [3] *Is. 53:5, 11; John 3:16; II Cor. 5:21.*

18. *Q.* *But who is that Mediator*
   who at the same time is true God
   and a true and righteous man?

   A. *Our Lord Jesus Christ,[1]*
   whom God made our wisdom,
   our righteousness and sanctification
   and redemption (I Corinthians 1:30).

   [1] *Matt. 1:21-23; Luke 2:11; I Tim. 2:5; 3:16.*

19. *Q.* *From where do you know this?*

   A. *From the holy gospel,*
   which God Himself first revealed in Paradise.[1]
   Later, He had it proclaimed
      by the patriarchs[2] and prophets,[3]
      and foreshadowed
      by the sacrifices and other ceremonies
      of the law.[4]
   Finally, He had it fulfilled
      through His only Son.[5]

   [1] *Gen. 3:15.*
   [2] *Gen. 12:3; 22:18; 49:10.*
   [3] *Is. 53; Jer. 23:5, 6; Mic. 7:18-20; Acts 10:43; Heb. 1:1.*
   [4] *Lev. 1:7; John 5:46; Heb. 10:1-10.*
   [5] *Rom. 10:4; Gal. 4:4, 5; Col. 2:17.*

A. NOTES

1. The Catechism now explains *why* the Mediator has to satisfy the requirements listed previously. He must be TRUE MAN because, as 1 Cor 15:21 says:

> For as by a man came death, by a man has come also the resurrection of the dead.

God demands justice demands it (see LD 5, Q&A 12, Note 5; and Q&A 13 and 14, Note 4).

He must also be a RIGHTEOUS MAN. Heb 7:26 states:

> For it was fitting that we should have such a high priest, holy, blameless, unstained, separated from sinners, exalted above the heavens.

A person who is a sinner himself increases his debt daily (see LD 5, Q&A 13 and 14, Note 1). Such a person is therefore not able to pay his own debt, let alone the debt of any other person.

2. Further, the Mediator must be TRUE GOD, "in order to conquer death by his power" (BC, art. 19). His divine nature had to give him the power to sustain him so that, in his human nature, he could suffer the wrath of God fully, so that he could complete his task. If you place a man at the sea side to empty the sea, he will never finish the job. Neither would a creature ever finish the job of emptying the cup of God's wrath. But God picks up that sea in one go in his eternal power in order to cast it where he wishes! The Mediator can empty the cup of God's wrath and finish it. In addition, the Mediator must *obtain*, *i.e.*, earn, our deliverance. A mere man cannot earn it. Even if he completes everything demanded of him, man has merely done what it was his duty to do. In order to earn deliverance, the Mediator must be God (Heb 5:8, 9). And he must be God in order to be able to give us what he obtained. No man can change another man's heart. Only God can do that.

B. QUESTIONS

1. Why must the Mediator be true man? Why must he be righteous man?
2. Why must he be true God? (Give three reasons!)

Q. & A. 18

OUR LORD JESUS CHRIST

A. NOTES

1. "But who is. . . ." It seems as though the Catechism asks this question with a certain amount of embarrassment: "Who is *that* Mediator . . . ?" For it has become very clear from the requirements he must satisfy that we cannot produce such a Mediator. We on our part, therefore, have no prospect whatsoever of deliverance. But the Answer may be joyful, for God has given him!

2. Our Lord Jesus Christ is that Mediator who at the same time is true God and true and righteous man.

    He is true GOD. Thus, 1 Jn 5:20 says:

    > This [*i.e.*, Jesus Christ] is the true God and eternal life.

    And Rom 9:5 (NIV) says:

    > . . . Christ, who is God over all, forever praised!

    He is also true MAN. Thus, Lk 2:7 says:

    > And she gave birth to her first-born son. . . .

    Further, 1 Tim 2:5 states:

    > For there is one God, and there is one mediator between God and men, the man Christ Jesus.

    Moreover, he is RIGHTEOUS man. He was not included in Adam when he fell away from God and is, therefore, not subject to original sin. Neither did he have actual sin. 1 Pet 2:22 says:

    > He committed no sin; no guile was found on his lips.

    (See also Jn 8:46).

3. In the Answer the Catechism quotes 1 Cor 1:30, to make it very clear that this Mediator is a free gift of the grace of our God.

    He is given to us for wisdom. We are foolish in sin. Even the wise of this world cannot find true wisdom (1 Cor 2:20). But Christ is given us for wisdom. We become wise again when we know and accept him in faith.

    He is also given to us for righteousness. We cannot produce righteousness before God; we cannot pay the demand of the law. But when we accept Christ in faith as the sacrifice for our sins we are again (as we were in Paradise) righteous before God.

    Further, he was given to us for our sanctification. We lack it. But when we accept Christ in faith, we are sanctified by the Holy Spirit.

    What we had in Paradise—righteousness and holiness—but which we lost through sin (forever!), we received again in Christ and we are made partakers of it by faith in him. Thus, he is, indeed, our *redemption*. Now we still sigh with much sorrow and imperfection. But when Christ returns he will redeem us completely.

B. QUESTIONS

1. What do the requirements of the Mediator make clear?
2. Who is our Mediator? Demonstrate from Scripture that he is: (a) true man; (b) righteous man; and (c) true God.
3. Which text does Answer 18 quote? What does this text clearly demonstrate?
4. Why was Christ given to us? What have we, therefore, received again in him? How do we become partakers thereof?

Q. & A. 19

THE HOLY GOSPEL

A. NOTES

1. In this Answer the Catechism discloses the source from which it derived what it has said to this point. What was said in LD 5 and 6 is not some ingenious discovery of our own. It was drawn together in faith out of, and confessed in accordance with the holy gospel. We confess in this Answer that the Word of God itself says this.

2. The word "gospel" means: good news, glad tidings. We should not immediately suppose that this word refers to one of the four first books of the NT. For there is but one gospel. The first four books of the NT give us a (not the only!) fourfold description of the gospel. The gospel is the always continuing proclamation of salvation of God. Thus, it is a *work*, not a book.

3. This proclamation began in Paradise, immediately after the fall, in the so-called PROTOGOSPEL (Gen 3:15). All subsequent promises are comprehended in it and arise out of it. The prefix "proto-" means "giving rise to." All the subsequent promises are further, clearer and more detailed explanations of what the Lord promised already in Paradise when he said: "I will put enmity [*i.e.*, destroy the intended friendship] between you [*i.e.*, the serpent, the devil] and the woman, and between your seed [the seed of the serpent, *i.e.*, haters of God] and her seed [*i.e.*, Christ and those who are his]; he [*i.e.*, Christ] shall bruise your head, and you shall bruise his heel [the victory will be won only in a bloody conflict; and that is how it happened on the cross on Golgotha]."

4. Thus, God himself revealed the gospel in Paradise. To reveal means to bring out into the open, to make known what was hidden.

5. Thereafter, God had this gospel proclaimed by the patriarchs and prophets. Patriarchs are men regarded as fathers, not just of a family, but

of a whole nation. Prophets are persons who speak the Word of God. Thus, the revelation of the gospel followed its course of *history*.

6. God also gave visible instruction to Israel of what he thus made known by his prophets. He did this by "the sacrifices and other ceremonies of the law." Thus, the paschal lamb, the sin offering, and all of Israel's temple service with its high priest, priests, *etc.*, pointed to Christ (see LD 2, Q&A 3, Note 6).

7. Finally, the gospel was fulfilled in Christ. Jn 1:17 says:

> For the law was given through Moses; grace and truth came through Jesus Christ.

In him, all of God's promises were proved true and faithful.

B. CROSS REFERENCES

1. God continues to spread the gospel that has been fulfilled. The CD I, 3 says:

> . . . God mercifully sends heralds of this most joyful message to whom He will and when He wills.

C. QUESTIONS

1. What is the source of our knowledge about what has been said about the Mediator thus far?

2. What does the word "gospel" mean? What does it denote?

3. Who revealed it at first? What does Gen 3:15 say?

4. What are patriarchs? What are prophets? What else did God do in the OT in addition to having the gospel preached?

5. In whom is the gospel fulfilled?

Addendum to Q. & A. 19
REVELATION

A. NOTES

1. The BC speaks more extensively about revelation, the way in which God makes himself known to us, which is also his gospel, in arts. 2-7. Article 2 says that we know God by two *means*, *i.e.*, in two ways. We can only have such knowledge of God as he himself gives us, and he gives us this knowledge in two ways.

2. The FIRST MEANS by which God makes himself known to us is "the creation, preservation, and government of the universe." In this work of God we recognize the Worker. God's works display his qualities (Ps 19:1), and the course of history shows his power and government (Ps 33:10, 11a).

3. This revelation is directed to ALL people. Hence, it is called the *general revelation.*

   The church may not neglect this source of the knowledge of God, as happens too often. The renewed creation will provide material to praise God for ever (Rev 4:11).

4. This general revelation is not sufficient for salvation. For, although it teaches us that God exists, and also in part what he is (great, almighty, wise and good), it does not tell us what God means *for us*, nor about his will. It does not teach us about his grace in Jesus Christ.

   In addition, our understanding has been obscured. We see only partly and cannot read the book of the general revelation except through the glasses of the special revelation.

5. Yet, this general revelation is not without significance. Article 2 says that it is "sufficient to convict men and to leave them without excuse." No one will be able to say in the final judgment that he did not know of God's existence. Rom 1:20-21 states:

   > So they are without excuse; for although they knew God they did not honor him as God or give thanks to him, but they became futile in their thinking and their senseless minds were darkened.

6. The SECOND MEANS whereby God makes himself more clearly and fully known to us is his divine Word.

   We sometimes call this revelation by the Word *special revelation*, because of (a) its *means*, (b) its *content*, and (c) its *destination*.

7. The MEANS of this clearer and fuller revelation are special. For we do not receive the clearer and fuller knowledge from what was already given in creation, but from what God has said many times and in many ways to the fathers (Heb 1:1). In so speaking, God did sometimes make use of the powers which already existed in creation. He spoke to the fathers by:

   a. APPEARANCES: column of smoke, the Angel of the Lord, *etc.*;

   b. PROPHESY: lot (urim and thummim), internal and external address, dream, vision;

   c. WONDERS: God's intervention in the "ordinary course of events": passage through the Red Sea, healings, *etc.*

8. The CONTENT of the special revelation is special. It is the counsel of God for the deliverance of sinners: simply put, that is Jesus Christ. No one could or was entitled to expect that God wants to save sinners, people who hate him.

   The Lord did not present us with the full content all at once. The special revelation was presented over the course of time and reached its zenith in Jesus Christ (see LD 6, Ans. 19).

He is God's clearest *appearance* (Jn 14:9; Heb 1:3a).

He completes the *prophesy* (Heb 1:1; Jn 17:6a).

He is THE *wonder* (1 Tim 3:16).

9. The DESTINATION is also special. For this revelation is not directed to all people, but to those peoples and men to whom God, in his good pleasure, sends his gospel (CD II, 5; and III/IV, 7). What a privilege that we received it also! We can only give proper thanks for that by preserving the gospel and propagating it.

10. So far as we know, the preservation and propagation of the God's spoken Word until Moses' time took place orally. This was possible originally. But when man multiplied on the earth and his life span was cut short, the danger of corruption of the gospel increased. That is why, as art. 3 of the BC states:

> . . . in His special care for us and our salvation, God commanded His servants, the prophets and apostles, to commit His revealed Word to writing. . . .

In this process of recording, not everything was written down (Jn 21:25), only that which the Lord deemed necessary for all times and all peoples, for his praise and our salvation.

B. HERESIES

1. Agnosticism (the idea that God is unknowable).
2. Proofs for the existence of God.
3. Atheism (denial of God).
4. Naturalism.
5. Deism.

C. QUESTIONS

1. In which articles does the BC speak about revelation and the Holy Scriptures? By which means do we know God? Can we, of ourselves, know God? What is the first "means" by which we know God?
2. What do Ps 19:2 and Ps 33:10-11a, respectively, say?
3. How many forms of revelation do we recognise? Is the general revelation sufficient for salvation? Why not? What do we learn from it about God?
4. What is the significance of the general revelation?
5. Why do we call God's revelation in his Word "special"?
6. By what means did God speak to man?
7. What is the content of the special revelation? To whom is it directed?
8. How was the special revelation propagated originally? Why could this not continue? What did the Lord do then? Is everything God said written down?

HOLY SCRIPTURE

A. NOTES

1. The Bible (the word derives from the Greek, *biblia*, *i.e.*, books, *viz.*, of the OT and NT) is, therefore, the record (notation) of the revelation. But the record itself is also *revelation*. For, although the Bible was written by men, the product of their work is not a human and, therefore, imperfect, but a divine book. For the Holy Spirit inspired the writers of the Bible to write what they did. The Bible clearly teaches this inspiration. Thus, 2 Pet 1:21 says:

    Because no prophecy ever came by the impulse of man, but men moved by the Holy Spirit spoke from God.

    Similarly, 2 Tim 3:16 says:

    All scripture is inspired by God. . . .

    This inspiration is further confirmed by the following:

    a. The prophets were aware that they did not speak and write their own words, but the Word of God (Ex 17:14; Jer 13:16; Hos 1:1).

    b. Christ accepted the OT as the Word of God (Mt 5:17-18; Lk 24:27; Jn 5:39).

    c. Before they became active in their office, Christ gave the Holy Spirit to his apostles. For it was he who was to remind them of all that Christ had told them, guide them in all truth, and declare to them the things that were to come (Jn 20:22; 14:26; 16:13). Consequently, the apostles demand acceptance of their word as the Word of God (1 Thess 2:13).

2. The inspiration did not destroy the individuality of the writers (that is what the mechanistic view of inspiration holds). On the contrary, they worked in accordance with their own capacities and according as they had received talents (see Lk 1:3).

    In this connection, the difference in language and style among the different writers is remarkable. That is why we adopt the *organic view* of inspiration and maintain that inspiration is that work of God's Spirit whereby he:

    a. made the writers of the Bible by means of upbringing, education, experience, *etc.*, into the kinds of persons that he required (PREPARATION);

    b. urged them irresistibly to write, sometimes by direct command, at other times by guidance of circumstances (INSTIGATION);

    c. led them in their investigations infallibly to the truth (DIRECTION); and

    d.   prompted them with those words and thoughts which most accurately reflected God's intention (EVOCATION).

3. Thus, the Bible is a book which God has given to us. We receive its books, says the BC, art. 5:

> . . . as holy and canonical, for the regulation, foundation, and confirmation of our faith.

"Canonical" derives from "canon," which means "rule of conduct."

4. Therefore, we believe without any doubt all that is contained in Scripture. We do that, not so much because the church teaches it, but, as the BC, art. 5 states:

> . . . especially because the Holy Spirit witnesses in our hearts that they [*i.e.*, the books of the Bible] are from God, and also because they contain the evidence thereof in themselves.

Only God can convince a person that his Word is truth. We cannot prove it to anyone. We can only direct a person to the Word itself. The Holy Spirit testifies in it. And we are joined to Scripture by this testimony, which he causes to resound in our hearts by faith. This testimony does not, therefore, have its own content, separate from Scripture, but the Holy Spirit uses it to make us submit ourselves to the content of Scripture.

5. The attributes of Scripture are:

    a. *Divine Authority.* See Note 3. It is the end of all dispute.

    b. *Perspicuity.* Although some parts of it are difficult to understand (2 Pet 3:16), that which is necessary for our salvation and for the service of God is made clear (Ps 119:105). The Church of Rome teaches wrongly that only the clergy can explain Scripture. Thereby it places life in bondage to the "church."

    c. *Sufficiency.* Art. 7 of the BC states: "We believe that this Holy Scripture fully contains the will of God and that all that man must believe in order to be saved is sufficiently taught therein." Contrary to what Rome teaches, no tradition of the church is necessary to complement it (Rev 22:18, 19).

    d. *Necessity.* Jn 5:39 states that no one can know the Lord Jesus Christ outside of Scripture.

It behooves us to give Holy Scripture the honour to which it is entitled in accordance with these attributes!

6. The Bible is divided into two parts:

    a. The Old Testament, consisting of 39 books, which belong to the old dispensation of the covenant. It is written in Hebrew, the language of the people of the Old Covenant.

b. The New Testament, consisting of 27 books, which belong to the new dispensation. It is written in Greek, the international language at the time.

Article 4 of the BC lists the books.

We no longer have any of these books in original manuscript. We only have copies. Sometimes there are differences, usually minor, between these copies. It is the purpose of *text criticism* to discover the correct rendering of the text. That is something different from *Scripture criticism*. The latter does not, in reverence to Scripture, seek the correct rendering of the text, but seeks to subject it to human reason. That is the work of unbelief.

7. We use the Revised Standard Version of the Bible. It was prepared by the Division of Christian Education of the National Council of the Churches of Christ in the United States of America. The first edition of the New Testament was published in 1946; the Old Testament was published in 1952, and the second edition of the New Testament was published in 1971. The Revised Standard Version is an authorized revision of the American Standard Version which was published in 1901 and which in turn was a revision of the Authorized or King James Version. The latter was prepared in 1611 by special command of His Majesty, King James I. Another modern version is the New International Version, published by the International Bible Society in 1985. It is desirable to use a sound modern translation, since our knowledge of Hebrew and Greek is better today than it was when earlier translations were prepared, and also because the English language has changed over time and in the process the meaning of some words and expressions has changed.[5]

B. COMMENTS

1. We distinguish the canonical from the apocryphal (*i.e.*, concealed) books. The latter were present in the synagogue, but remained hidden (hence, their name), and were not read in public (see BC, art. 6).

2. The Bible also contains the words of sinners and even of the devil. We must, therefore, determine whether a particular passage from Scripture tells us of an historical event, or whether it states a commandment that must be followed. Further, we must constantly ascertain what a particular passage meant originally and what its meaning is for today (*cf.*, *e.g.*, the fourth commandment).

---

[5]Transl. note: It will be understood that the contents of this Note were changed to reflect the situation in the English-speaking world.

C. HERESIES

1. The view that Holy Scripture is merely a human record of revelation.
2. The Anabaptist idea of the internal light.
3. Barthianism, which states that the Word only becomes the Word of God when it intervenes subjectively in our lives.
4. Undervaluing the OT.
5. The belief that the OT and the NT are opposed to each other.

D. QUESTIONS

1. What is the Bible? Is it a human book? Why not? What do 2 Pet 1:21 and 2 Tim 3:16, respectively, say? Give three proofs of the inspiration of Scripture.
2. How can you show that inspiration did not destroy the individuality of the writers? List the four aspects which we distinguish in speaking of the inspiration of Holy Scripture, and describe each of them.
3. What does it mean that we call books of the Bible canonical? Why do we receive the books of the Bible as canonical? In what does the work of the Holy Spirit testify?
4. List the attributes of Scripture and state what each of them means.
5. How many parts does Holy Scripture have? In what language was each written? What is text criticism? What is Scripture criticism?
6. Which Bible translation do we use? Which others do you know about? How did each of them originate? Why do we use a sound modern translation?

§II. THE APPROPRIATION OF THE DELIVERANCE IN THE WAY OF FAITH

Lord's Days 7 - 31

This Section discusses successively:

1. The necessity of faith (LD 7, Q&A 20).
2. The essence of faith (LD 7, Q&A 21).
3. The content of faith (LD 7, Q&A 22 - LD 22, Q&A 58).
4. The benefit of faith (LD 23, Q&A 59 - LD 24, Q&A 64).
5. The realization of faith (LD 25, Q&A 25a).
6. The strengthening of faith (LD 25, Q&A 25b - LD 30, Q&A 82).
7. Keeping the faith pure and the preservation in faith (LD 31, Q&A 83 - 85).

20. *Q. Are all men, then, saved by Christ*
    just as they perished through Adam?

    A. *No. Only those are saved who by a true faith*
       are grafted into Christ and accept all His benefits.[1]
       [1] *Matt. 7:14; John 1:12; 3:16, 18, 36; Rom. 11:16-21.*

21. *Q. What is true faith?*

    A. *True faith is a sure knowledge whereby I accept as true all*
       that God has revealed to us in His Word.[1]
       At the same time it is a firm confidence[2] that not only to
       others, but also to me,[3] God has granted forgiveness of
       sins, everlasting righteousness, and salvation,[4] out of mere
       grace, only for the sake of Christ's merits.[5]
       This faith the Holy Spirit works in my heart by the gospel.[6]
       [1] *John 17:3, 17; Heb. 11:1-3; James 2:19.*
       [2] *Rom. 4:18-21; 5:1; 10:10; Heb. 4:16.*
       [3] *Gal. 2:20.*
       [4] *Rom. 1:17; Heb. 10:10.*
       [5] *Rom. 3:20-26; Gal. 2:16; Eph. 2:8-10.*
       [6] *Acts 16:14; Rom. 1:16; 10:17; I Cor. 1:21.*

22. *Q. What, then, must a Christian believe?*

    A. *All that is promised us in the gospel,[1] which the articles of*
       our catholic and undoubted Christian faith teach us in a
       summary.
       [1] *Matt. 28:19; John 20:30, 31.*

23. *Q. What are these articles?*

    A. *I.   1. I believe in God the Father almighty,*
                 Creator of heaven and earth.
       II.   2. I believe in Jesus Christ,
                 His only begotten Son, our Lord;
             3. He was conceived by the Holy Spirit,
                 born of the virgin Mary;
             4. suffered under Pontius Pilate,
                 was crucified, dead, and buried;
                 He descended into hell;
             5. On the third day He arose from the dead;
             6. He ascended into heaven,
                 and sits at the right hand
                 of God the Father almighty;
             7. from there He will come to judge
                 the living and the dead.
       III. 8. I believe in the Holy Spirit;
             9. I believe a holy catholic Christian church,
                 the communion of saints;
             10. the forgiveness of sins;
             11. the resurrection of the body;
             12. and the life everlasting.

A. NOTES

1. Compare the expression "saved by Christ" with LD 5, Q&A 12, Note 2. What the question asks is whether all men again share in the communion with God through Christ.

2. All men are damned through, or in, Adam. They are not merely damnable, but damned. And not all are delivered out of their damnation by Christ. Holy Scripture teaches this clearly. Thus, Mt 22:14 says:

   For many are called, but few are chosen.

   It is true that 2 Pet 3:9 states that the Lord does not wish that any should perish, but that all should reach repentance, but this does not mean that all will be saved. Rather, it means that the Lord postpones the judgment in his forbearance, so that all his elect should come to faith and repentance. Similarly, while 1 Tim 2:4 says that God desires all men to be saved, this means that he desires that all kinds of people, rich and poor, distinguished and simple, be saved. These and other texts do not contradict the fact that the gate that leads to life is narrow and that those who find it are few (Mt 7:14).

3. The CD II, 6, states:

   That, however, many who have been called by the gospel neither repent not believe in Christ but perish in unbelief does not happen because of any defect or insufficiency in the sacrifice of Christ offered on the cross, but through their own fault.

   For the death of the Son of God is, as CD II, 3 states:

   . . . of infinite value and worth, abundantly sufficient to expiate the sins of the whole world.

   (*Cf.* 1 Jn 2:2).

   But this sacrifice, which is sufficient for the whole world, only bears fruit and was also brought only for those who *believe* in Christ. Thus, Jn 3:36 says:

   He who believes in the Son has eternal life; he who does not obey the Son shall not see life, but the wrath of God rests upon him.

   Similarly, in Jn 17:9, the Saviour says:

   I am praying for them; I am not praying for the world but for those whom thou hast given me, for they are thine.

   Christ has, therefore, brought his sacrifice, which was sufficient for all, only for those who are his (CD II, 8).

4. Thus, only those who believe in Christ are saved by him—those *who by*

a true faith are grafted into Christ. For by *faith* we become one plant with him (being grafted into him): we become one body with him. Faith is the means whereby we embrace Christ (*accept all his benefits*), and whereby the life-giving nourishment of the vine (Christ) passes to the branches (members of the covenant). (Jn 15:1-8; Rom 11:16-24). In that we become one body with Christ by faith, all that is his becomes ours, and we become partakers of the treasures which he earned.

5. The Catechism speaks of being grafted, thus using the passive voice, for this is something that God does. We do not do it. We do not make ourselves a part of Christ. The Holy Spirit does that. But he does it through faith! Thus, our responsibility is not excluded. For the Lord *calls* us to faith. (For further detail, see CD III/IV, 9-10).

6. Faith is, therefore, necessary for us to be delivered by Christ. The requirement of faith did not just appear after the fall. Also Adam in Paradise found life only by faith. But faith did acquire a different content after the fall. It is now directed to Christ and accepts his benefits.

B. CROSS REFERENCES

1. The CD I, 4 states:

> The wrath of God remains upon those who do not believe this gospel. But those who receive it and embrace Jesus the Saviour with a true and living faith are delivered by Him from the wrath of God and from destruction, and are given eternal life.

(*Cf.* Jn 3:16; Mk 16:16).

2. The BC, art. 22 also states:

> . . . the Holy Spirit kindles in our hearts a true faith. This faith embraces Jesus Christ with all His merits, makes Him our own and does not seek anything besides Him.

C. HERESIES

1. Universalism.

2. Arminianism.

3. The idea that faith does nothing but make us realize that we have been ingrafted into Christ immediately (without means).

4. False passivity.

D. QUESTIONS

1. What do Lord's Days 7 - 31 successively speak about? Are all men saved? Prove that Holy Scripture rejects this question. What does it mean when Holy Scripture says that God desires all men to be saved? Why are not all who are called also saved?

2. Is Christ's work not sufficient for all? Who alone benefits from this work? For whom was it accomplished?

3. What happens through faith? What does faith do?
4. Who grafts us into Christ? What means does he use?
5. Was the demand to believe made only after the fall? What did change after the fall?

Q. & A. 21
KNOWLEDGE AND CONFIDENCE

A. NOTES

1. This question asks: What is *true* faith? For there is also an imitative, artificial faith. But it is not faith, any more than artificial sweetener is sugar, although it may look like sugar. Imitative faith is a reaction to the Word, but not an acceptance of the Word, as true faith is. Scripture calls this faith dead. Jas 2:20 says:

    . . . faith apart from works is barren.

    We recognize the following faith-like reactions to the Word:

    a. *Historical "faith."* It does not contradict Scripture, believes that the facts related in Scripture happened, but is then indifferent to the Word and does not work repentance.

    b. *Temporal "faith."* This runs away with the content of the Bible, thinks it interesting and loves to talk about it, but it has no depth; it is not real. That is why it ends when difficulties or oppression arise. It only exists for a time.

    c. *Miracle "faith."* This believes, on the basis of Scripture, that miracles can happen and likes miraculous events, but does not repent in obedience.

    (For all of these, see Mt 13:1-23, the parable of the sower).

2. The Catechism gives two marks of living, true faith:

    a. KNOWLEDGE: sure (*i.e.*, certain) knowledge whereby we accept God's Word as true.

    b. CONFIDENCE: whereby I apply God's promise to myself.

    The KNOWLEDGE referred to is not simply an intellectual knowledge, but a knowledge in love. It is a knowledge whereby we accept as true all that God has revealed to us in his Word, whereby we approve it, concur in it, and assent to it. We say "Amen" upon it. When the Catechism also speaks about CONFIDENCE, it does not refer to something distinct from this knowledge. This confidence is not something that can accompany the knowledge (and it is good when it does), but does not have to (and that is allright too); rather, knowledge and confidence are one in this context. True faith is *not only* knowledge, *but also* confidence. It is both. It is such a knowledge that it includes confidence. We see this beautifully in the life of Abraham, of whom Rom 4:18 testifies:

> In hope he believed against hope, that he should become the father of many nations; as he had been told, "So shall your descendants be."

3. This knowledge and confidence extends to the entire Word of God. Faith accepts ALL that God has revealed in his Word. It does not judge and criticize the Word, but accepts it and obeys it. (See LD 23, Q&A 59).

   And the firm confidence is that God granted forgiveness of sins for the sake of Christ's merits not only to others, but also to me. Faith calls out "mine," "that's for me," in response to God's promises, meaning: that suits me and I want to have it, I draw it to me. Thus, faith appropriates, draws towards itself what the Lord promised to his covenant people ("others"). We acknowledge and understand that the promises which God gave to his people, and in them to us, apply not only to others, but also to us!

4. True faith, therefore, does not mean: "having confidence in something." Everyone has that, simply because everyone was created to be dependent and needs something in which to trust. Rather, it is placing confidence in the revealed promise of God. Faith does not exist when Scripture is rejected, nor when a person does not know the Word at all. Further, disdain for the Word is not a work of faith. On the contrary, faith says: I chase after it and expect my salvation from it.

5. Faith in Christ is nothing else than to *accept as true all that God has revealed to us in His Word.* For Christ comes to us in that Word, both in the OT and in the NT. By accepting the Word as true, we surrender ourselves to him. There can, therefore, be no faith in Christ if Scripture is rejected.

6. The person who works this faith is the Holy Spirit. He kindles it in our hearts by the gospel. (We will discuss this in greater detail in LD 25, Q&A 65). Through this faith we receive forgiveness of sins, everlasting righteousness and salvation. (We will deal further with this in LD 23).

B.   CROSS REFERENCES

1. See Q&A 20, Cross References 1 and 2.

2. CD V, 10 states that the assurance of the forgiveness of sins

   > . . . is not produced by a certain private revelation besides or outside the Word, but by faith in the promises of God. . . .

   Read the rest of this article also.

C.   HERESIES

1. The idea that faith is produced by ourselves.

2. The idea that Christian faith and communion with Christ can coexist with rejection or criticism of Scripture.

3. The idea that faith is only the inclination to accept what the church regards as true.

4. The idea that there is a "kernel of faith" which is placed in us apart from the gospel.

D. QUESTIONS

1. Why does the Catechism ask about "true" faith? Is there also an imitative faith? Is it a true faith? What does Scripture call it? How many types of this imitative faith do you know? In which parable do we read about them?

2. Which marks of true faith does the Catechism list? What kind of knowledge is meant? Is the confidence separate from the knowledge?

3. What must we know? What must we have a firm confidence about?

4. Is "believing in something" also true faith? Does faith exist separate from Scripture?

5. Who works faith in us? By what means? What do we receive by faith?

Q. & A. 22 and 23
THE CATHOLIC FAITH

A. NOTES

1. Question 23 asks what a Christian *must* believe, not what he believes. For faith is incomplete for each Christian; it is full of error and fault. That is why we must constantly compare our faith with what is necessary for faith, *viz.*, God's Word. And we must not burden each other with, or bind to, anything other than what is necessary for faith.

2. One could say: A Christian must believe all that God has revealed to us in his Word (see Answer 21), but the current Answer states: "All that is promised us in the gospel." For the Word of the Lord is full of promises. In his Word the Lord does not just say: I am X, and this is what I do, but I am he who does all this for you who believe in me.

When the Answer speaks of promise, we should note carefully that this is God's promise. People will sometimes say: Oh, well, what's a promise? But when God promises, it is certain; he grants what he promises. But only if we *believe* the promise! The Lord did, indeed, promise Canaan to all the Israelites who set out from Egypt (*i.e.*, he, on his part, granted it), but the majority never entered Canaan and did not receive it, because of their *unbelief* (Heb 3:19).

3. All that is promised us in the gospel is summarized in "the articles of our catholic and undoubted Christian faith."

A "*summary*" is a brief summation. (*Cf.* the "sum" in arithmetic).

An "*article*" is a part, or a member. The confession is one body which consists of more than one member. He who treats one member ill, injures the *body*! (*Cf.* the word "*all*" in LD 23, Q. 59).

The faith described in the articles is *"catholic,"* i.e., universal. It is the faith of the church of all ages. And it is *"undoubted,"* i.e., it has never been called into question by the church. We may not do this either. To call into question, to doubt, is sin; it makes God a liar. Further, it is called *"Christian,"* for is revealed by Christ, has him as content, and affords communion with the Triune God through him.

4. We call these articles the Apostles' Creed. Not because it was drafted by the apostles, for it developed out of the confession of faith in the Father, the Son and the Holy Spirit, originally asked at baptism. It was not until the year 500 that it had attained its present form. But it presents us with the faith taught us by the apostles. Hence its name.

5. The Canadian Reformed Churches[6] give a more detailed account of the faith contained in these articles in:

   a. The Belgic Confession, containing 37 articles, and drafted by Guido de Brès in 1561. In it the church makes known to those outside the church what it believes.

   b. The Heidelberg Catechism, drafted by Ursinus and Olevianus in 1563, at the behest of the Elector of the Palatinate. In it the church instructs its children what it believes.

   c. The Canons of Dort, or the Five Articles against the Remonstrants, drafted by the Synod of Dort of 1618/19. In it the church maintains its faith against error.

   Together, these three are called: the Three Forms of Unity. For the confession demonstrates and fosters the unity of believers.

6. The church is entitled to formulate the content of Scripture in this summary fashion. For the Word was entrusted to the church. It is also the duty of the church to do so. For it was placed in this world as a pillar and bulwark of the truth (1 Tim 3:15).

7. The authority of these confessions is not superior or equal, but subservient to the Bible. The confessions do have authority, but it is *derivative* authority. The Bible has original authority. Should discrepancies between the confession and the Bible be demonstrated, the confession must be changed accordingly. Only the church can make such changes, for the confession belongs to it.

8. The confessions serve to:

   a. give public testimony of the truth of faith and the doctrine of the church (BC);

   b. preserve the truth for the coming generations (HC);

---

[6]Transl. note: The name was changed having regard to the primary audience of this translation.

c. maintain the truth over against error (CD); and

d. demonstrate and preserve the unity of the believers (Three Forms of Unity).

B. COMMENTS

1. We further willingly receive (BC, art. 9) the creeds of Nicea (about the Godhead of the Son) and of Athanasius (about the Trinity).

2. Also of importance for the knowledge of the doctrine of the church are its liturgical forms. You will find these in the back of our Book of Praise. They contain a wealth of knowledge which no one may keep buried away in a napkin (Lk 19:20).

3. The word "form" derives from the Latin "forma," and means "fixed." For the liturgical forms give a fixed expression to the confessional and liturgical actions of the church.

C. HERESIES

1. The notion that the confession promotes division.

2. The belief that the confession enslaves the conscience.

3. The idea that the confession conflicts with the belief in the sufficiency of Scripture.

4. The false contrast between "church of the confession" and "confessing church."

D. QUESTIONS

1. Why does the question ask about what is necessary to believe?

2. What must a Christian believe? What is the nature of God's Word? What does it ask of us in that respect?

3. What is a summary? Why do we speak about articles? Why is faith called "catholic," "undoubted," and "Christian," respectively?

4. How did the Apostles' Creed originate? Why is called "*Apostles'* Creed"?

5. Which other confessions do the Canadian Reformed Churches have? Relate what you know about them.

6. Is the church entitled to formulate the content of Scripture? Does it have a duty to do so?

7. What is the authority of the confessions?

8. What purpose do they serve?

9. Recite the Apostles' Creed?

LORD'S DAY 8

24. *Q.* *How are these articles divided?*

    A. *Into three parts:*
    the first is about God the Father and our creation;
    the second about God the Son and our redemption;
    the third about God the Holy Spirit
    and our sanctification.

25. *Q.* *Since there is only one God,[1]*
    why do you speak of three persons,
    Father, Son, and Holy Spirit?

    A. *Because God has so revealed Himself in His Word[2]*
    that these three distinct persons
    are the one, true, eternal God.

    [1] *Deut. 6:4; Is. 44:6; 45:5; I Cor. 8:4, 6.*
    [2] *Gen. 1:2, 3; Is. 61:1; 63:8-10; Matt. 3:16, 17; 28:18, 19;*
    Luke 4:18; John 14:26; 15:26; II Cor. 13:14; Gal. 4:6;
    Tit. 3:5, 6.

A. NOTES

1. The content of our faith is God's promise in the gospel and this promise is summarized in the Apostles' Creed (see LD 7, Ans. 22). God does not just promise something, even a lot, but he promises *himself* to us. Gen 17:7 says:

   > And I will . . . be God to you and to your descendants after you.

   Thus, the content of our faith is GOD HIMSELF. Our faith and trust are directed to HIM, and take hold of HIM. Our faith is not just an intellectual conviction that there is a God. But by our faith we rest in God; we entrust ourselves to him. All of the articles, therefore, speak about God and what he means and does for us, and what we expect from him. They speak of God the Father and *our* creation, of God the Son and *our* redemption, and of God the Holy Spirit and *our* sanctification. We express in this confession that God the Father created us and has since preserved us; that God the Son is our Redeemer by his blood; and that God the Holy Spirit sanctifies us and leads us into eternal bliss, the life everlasting.

2. That is how God graciously bound himself to us, with that promise. For we were baptized in the name of the Father, and the Son, and the Holy Spirit. The Forms for the Baptism of Infants and of Adults (Doctrine of Baptism) explain beautifully that this means that God the Father promises us that he will be our Father and provide us with all good, that God the Son promises us the washing in his blood, and that God the Holy Spirit promises us that he will dwell and work in us to impart to us all that we have in Christ. It is this promise that we grasp in faith. We put our trust in it. And, thus, we confess in the summary of our faith that God the Father is *our* Father, who as almighty Creator of heaven and earth cares for us; that God the Son is *our* Redeemer, who bought us with his blood; and that God the Holy Spirit sanctifies us and will complete our redemption.

B. QUESTIONS

1. What is the content of our faith? What did God promise us? What do we do by faith? Of whom do the articles speak?

2. What did God promise us in our baptism? What do we, therefore, profess to believe?

Q. & A. 25
HOW GLORIOUS IS THY NAME!

A. NOTES

1. In this Answer we acknowledge that we confess the Triune God (as set out in the preceding Answers), because he "has so revealed himself in his Word." For we know God from his Word and, in the light of that Word, also out of his creation and preservation of all things (BC, art. 2). God has graciously given his Name in his Word. That Name is not just any name; in it we deal with God himself. His Name is God, as he made himself known to us, as he turned to us. We know God in his Name. Scripture uses the expression "the name of the LORD" to denote God himself (see, *e.g.*, Prov 18:10). The Lord has graciously specified the one Name in the many other Names for the one Name of God, which makes known his essence, in Holy Scripture. These Names are like the many colours which together form the light. Yet, in every Name we do not deal with a part of God, but with God himself. We can see this in our own language too. For example, we use the several names: seed, fruit, grain, food, *etc.*, to refer always to the *whole* kernel of grain.

2. We distinguish the Names of God as follows:

    a. PROPER NAMES, *e.g.*, God, LORD.

    b. ATTRIBUTES (1 Pet 2:9), or perfections, *e.g.*, the Holy One.

    c. PERSONAL NAMES, *e.g.*, Father, Son and Holy Spirit.

3. The PROPER NAMES, those which are God's own and which no other has are:

    a. GOD (Hebr.: *Elohim*; in abbreviations: *El*, as in Bethel. It is a plural form to denote a fullness of power). This name teaches us to know God as Creator of and Ruler over all.

    b. LORD (JHWH, Yahweh; not Jehovah). God makes himself known to his people with this name as "I AM WHO I AM," the Faithful and Unchangeable One (Ex 3:14; 6:1ff).

    c. Lord, *i.e.*, Master, Ruler, Owner.

    d. LORD of Hosts (Yahweh Zebaoth). These hosts are: Israel (2 Sam 6:2), the stars (Ps 3:6), and the angels (Isa 37:16).

4. The ATTRIBUTES. These describe what God is, make known his Essence. Article 1 of the BC states that God is:

    a. ONE. There is only one God (Deut 6:4; 1 Cor 8:4-6). Polytheism, the doctrine that there are many gods, is as foolish as Atheism, the doctrine that there is no God.

b. SIMPLE (as distinct from complex). In God everything is a single perfection. He is not composed of parts, let alone parts in conflict with each other (1 Jn 1:5).

c. SPIRITUAL. God is a Spirit (Jn 4:24). He is above all matter.

d. BEING. God exists; he Is, the Only One who proceeds from himself.

e. ETERNAL. God is without beginning, progress, or end. Time does not apply to him. We miss today what we had yesterday, or will only have tomorrow. God does not (Ps 90:1, 2).

f. INCOMPREHENSIBLE. God exceeds our understanding. But we can know him from his revelation (Job 36:26).

g. INVISIBLE. No one can see him, although he is everywhere (Jn 1:18).

h. IMMUTABLE. There is no variation with God (Jas 1:17), not even when he repents of something (Gen 6:6). In that case something has changed with man, not with God.

i. INFINITE. God is omnipresent. He is everywhere (Ps 139:7), although not everywhere in the same way. Thus, his presence in heaven is different from his presence here and from his presence in hell.

j. ALMIGHTY. God can do everything he wants to do (Lk 1:17).

k. PERFECTLY WISE. He always chooses the best ways and means to attain the highest goal (Rom 11:33-36).

l. JUST. He rewards those who do good and wreaks vengeance on evildoers. He keeps his Word and does not treat the guilty as though they are innocent, nor the reverse (Ex 34:7).

m. GOOD. He desires the wellbeing of his creatures, especially of his elect, and shows: (i) love toward people; (ii) grace toward the guilty; (iii) mercy toward those in want; and (iv) long-suffering toward those who deserve punishment. Note also the concluding paean of art. 1 of the BC: He is the overflowing fountain of all good.

We may also mention:

n. HOLINESS. God is far removed from all sin and hates sin, for he is highly exalted above all creatures (1 Jn 1:5; Isa 6:3).

o. OMNISCIENCE. He knows and fathoms everything from eternity.

Now take a moment to think about each of these attributes and answer these questions: (i) what does it comfort me that God is like this; and (ii) what does it motivate me to do?

5. The PERSONAL NAMES. There is one God. But the essence of this God is so great that he exists in (not: out of!) Three Persons. We call this mystery the "Trinity." You will not find this word in Holy Scripture, but you will find the subject matter it denotes. In fact, it is only to be found in Scripture. For we do not know this mystery from nature, but only from the Word (Ans. 25).

6. That there is a plural in the singular of God is immediately apparent from Gen 1:26: "Let Us make man." See also Ps 110:1: "The LORD says to my Lord." As one continues, it becomes apparent that this plural is a Trinity (Isa 63:9, 10).

   In the NT this Trinity becomes apparent immediately when the birth of Christ is announced. Lk 1:35 says:

   > The Holy Spirit will come upon you, and the power of the Most High will overshadow you; therefore the child to be born will be called holy, the Son of God.

   Further, at Jesus' baptism in the Jordan, it is the Son who is baptized, while the Holy Spirit descends and the Father speaks from heaven. The three Persons are also named very clearly in the benediction in 2 Cor 13:13 and in the Great Commission (the command to baptize) in Mt 28:19.

   Yet, art 9 of the BC states:

   > All this we know both from the testimonies of Holy Scripture and from the respective works of the three Persons, and especially those that we perceive in ourselves.

   The confession does not, in the last clause, posit a second source of knowledge in addition to Holy Scripture, but makes it clear that Scripture teaches us to distinguish the three Persons not only from various texts, but also by its list of their actions. And we do notice those actions in our lives. The confession of the Trinity is not a dull theory. Every Christian knows God as the Triune One: as his Creator, before whom he is guilty; at the same time as his Redeemer, in whom all his hope is founded; and as his Sanctifier, who himself performs in him both the willingness and the works.

7. Therefore, as art. 8 of the BC states, we believe:

   > . . . in one only God, who is one in essence, in which are three persons, really, truly, and eternally distinct according to their incommunicable properties; namely, the Father, the Son, and the Holy Spirit.

   The DISTINCTIONS between the three Persons become evident in:

   a. *Their attributes.* The first Person fills the position of Father. He exists in and of himself. The second Person fills the position of Son. The Father gives him power to have life in himself (Jn 5:26). He is generated by the Father (*i.e.*, brought forth out of his being). The third person fills the position of the Spirit. He proceeds as a spirit, a breath, from the Father and the Son and returns to them. Through him God lives in all things.

   b. *Their names.* These are never used indiscriminately of the other Persons.

c. *Their works.* The Father: Creation; the Son: Redemption; the Holy Spirit: Sanctification.

All three Persons do act in all three works, but so that One of them takes the principal role. Thus, it is, indeed, the Son who redeems, but the Father sent him to redeem, and the Holy Spirit attributes the Son's work to those given to the Son by the Father.

d. *Their order of existence.* First, Second, and Third Persons. We cannot, however, assign a consecutive order, or a system of priority. All three are *equally* and from *eternity* God. And each of the three Persons partakes of the entire divine Being.

THE UNITY OF THE PERSONS. (See BC, art 10-11). It is apparent from Scripture that the Son and the Spirit are God, equally with the Father. For Scripture attributes to the Son and the Spirit, as well as to the Father:

a. *Divine names.* The Son is also known as LORD, Mighty God, Everlasting Father (Isa 9:6). And the Holy Spirit is also called God (Acts 5:3, 4).

b. *Divine attributes.* The Son is eternal and omniscient (Mic 5:1; Jn 21:17). The Holy Spirit is omnipresent (Ps 139:7).

c. *Divine works.* The Son and the Spirit were both active in creation (Jn 1:3; Ps 33:6).

d. *Divine honour.* We are baptized also in the names of the Son and the Spirit (Mt 28:19).

8. This confession of the Trinity will always exceed our understanding, but it is not contrary to reason. We do not say, as the Muslims mock: 3 = 1. For we do not say that the one Being is three Beings, but that the one Being substantiates itself in three PERSONS.

9. By this confession we understand that:

a. God, who is so rich in himself, does not need creation. He did not need it to overcome loneliness and to have company. For the Father is eternally in the company of the Son and both of them are eternally in the company of the Spirit. God is complete in himself and does not need any creature.

b. Everything that is needed for our redemption is in God. He himself, who, as Father, is our Judge, pays for our guilt as Son and sanctifies us as Holy Spirit.

B. CROSS REFERENCES

1. The BC is excellent in its detailed confession of the Trinity. Article 8 states what it means that God is "one single essence, in whom are three persons." Article 9 demonstrates in detail that this confession is scriptural.

Article 10 continues with scriptural proofs of the divinity of the Son and art. 11 does the same for the Holy Spirit.

2. In the Liturgical Forms the belief in the Trinity is expressed in a number of places. Thus, in the Forms for the Baptism of Infants and of Adults (Doctrine of Baptism), the promises of God are described in terms of the three persons of the Trinity. See also the prayers before the sacraments and the prayers of thanksgiving after the sacraments in the Forms for Baptism and for the Celebration of the Lord's Supper. In them and everywhere else the church speaks in a trinitarian manner.

C. COMMENTS

1. People have tried to categorize the attributes of God in one way or another. Thus, for example, there is the not entirely useless, but also not entirely correct classification of (a) communicable attributes (*i.e.*, those of which the creature also has some aspects), and (b) incommunicable attributes (*i.e.*, those in which the creature does not share).

2. Some have supposed that they could discern traces of the Trinity in creation. They mention, for example: the three dimensions of space, the three persons in language, the three temporal relationships, and the three articulations of living organisms. But we know the Trinity only from the Word.

3. The terms used by the church are not equivalent to the truth. Bavinck wrote: We should gladly trade them for other words if we could find better ones.

D. HERESIES

1. Polytheism.
2. Atheism.
3. Materialism.
4. Agnosticism.
5. Judaism.
6. Arianism.
7. Sabellianism.
8. Mohammedanism.
9. Modernism.
10. The doctrine of the Greek Orthodox Church that the Holy Spirit proceeds only from the Father.

E. QUESTIONS

1. From what do we know God? What did God reveal to us in his Word? What is his Name? How did God give his Name in his Word? What must one always keep in mind for each of the Names?

2. How do we distinguish God's Names?

3. List the Proper Names and state what each of them mean.

4. List seven Attributes and make sure that you can state what each of them mean.

5. Does the word "Trinity" appear in the Bible? What does appear there? Do we know the Trinity from the creation and preservation of all things? From what do we know it?

6. Give a couple of scriptural proofs for the Trinity. Does the expression in art. 9 of the BC, "the . . . works . . . we perceive in ourselves" indicate that there is a second source of knowledge of the Trinity? If not, what does the art. mean?

7. How are the three Persons distinguished? Why is the Father called Father? Why is the Son called Son? Why is the Holy Spirit called Holy Spirit? What is the special task of each of them? Did the Father ever exist apart from the Son?

8. Prove from Scripture that the Son and the Holy Spirit are God.

9. Can we understand the concept of the Trinity? Is it contrary to reason?

10. What do we understand by the confession of the Trinity?

LORD'S DAY 9

26. *Q.* *What do you believe when you say:*
    I believe in God the Father almighty,
    Creator of heaven and earth?

  A. *That the eternal Father of our Lord Jesus Christ,*
    who out of nothing created heaven and earth
    and all that is in them,[1]
    and who still upholds and governs them
    by His eternal counsel and providence,[2]
    is, for the sake of Christ His Son,
    my God and my Father.[3]
  In Him I trust so completely
    as to have no doubt
    that He will provide me
    with all things necessary for body and soul,[4]
    and will also turn to my good
    whatever adversity He sends me
    in this life of sorrow.[5]
  He is able to do so as almighty God,[6]
    and willing also as a faithful Father.[7]

[1] *Gen. 1 and 2; Ex. 20:11; Job 38 and 39; Ps. 33:6;*
   Is. 44:24; Acts 4:24; 14:15.
[2] *Ps. 104:27-30; Matt. 6:30; 10:29; Eph. 1:11.*
[3] *John 1:12, 13; Rom. 8:15, 16; Gal. 4:4-7; Eph. 1:5.*
[4] *Ps. 55:22; Matt. 6:25, 26; Luke 12:22-31.*
[5] *Rom. 8:28.*
[6] *Gen. 18:14; Rom. 8:31-39.*
[7] *Matt. 6:32, 33; 7:9-11.*

GOD THE FATHER AND OUR CREATION

LORD'S DAY 9

Q. & A. 26

THOU HAST CREATED ALL THINGS

A. NOTES

1. Gen 1:1 says: IN THE BEGINNING (*i.e.*, when time was directed to begin) GOD (the Creator is the Triune God, although in this work the Father, who created all things through the Son [BC, art. 12; Ps 33:6; Jn 1:1-3] is prominent) CREATED (creation is that act of God's almighty will whereby he, through his Word, that is, through his Son, called all things into being out of nothing) THE HEAVENS AND THE EARTH (*i.e.*, the dwelling of himself and his holy angels, *and* this world, and he made the two so that they should become one, as, indeed, they shall be in eternal glory).

2. We do not read anything further about the creation of heaven. But God created the thousands upon thousands of angels before he created heaven and probably before he created the earth. For we read that they praised God when he formed the earth (Job 38:6-7).

   The angels do not have a body as we do. Nor do they have family relationships. They also stand in another relationship to Christ, who is their Lord, but not their Redeemer. Further, they were not created in God's image. Thus they are placed lower than man. People are God's children; the angels are his servants. Scripture distinguishes archangels, seraphs, cherubs, thrones, powers, and principalities, and also names some of the angels, *e.g.*, Gabriel and Michael.

   The ORDINARY task of the angels is to praise God (Isa 6:1-4) and to protect his people (Heb 1:14; Mt 18:10). Their EXTRAORDINARY task is to serve in the revelation of God (Lk 1, *passim*; Lk 2:9; Acts 1:10).

   A number of the angels ("angel" means "messenger," "envoy"), whom God had created good, rebelled against him in deliberate sin and fell irremediably. They became wicked angels, evil spirits. Scripture calls their leader the devil (*i.e.*, liar, slanderer), satan (*i.e.*, adversary), old serpent, murderer from the beginning, god of this age, *etc.* He works in the unbelievers and against the believers, but he is subject to God's rule and must, in God's strength, be withstood by us. It is a rich comfort that, in Christ, legions of angels fight on our side against the threat of these evil spirits.

3. Of the earth, after God had created it, it was said that it was "without form and void," an as yet unformed mass, which God prepared in six days (the first and the subsequent creation). These six days can be divided into two related groups:

1st day: light	4th day: sun, moon and stars
2nd day: firmament	5th day: fish and birds
3rd day: sea, land, trees and plants	6th day: quadrupeds and creeping animals and man.

On the seventh day God rested. It was a rest of recreation in his "finished" and "very good" work.

4. Scripture does not tell us about creation so that we might know the origins of things, but so that we might know God and understand that everything is subjected to him. What a comfort this is! For the church confesses of *this* almighty God that he is my God and my Father for the sake of Christ his Son. Once God was the Father of man in the covenant and they were his children. However, through sin we turned away from him. But now all who believe in Christ receive again the privilege of being children (Jn 1:12).

B. CROSS REFERENCES

1. The BC speaks, in art. 12, about the creation of all things, and in particular about the creation of the angels, a topic which the Catechism does not address directly. Note also what art. 2 says about creation.

C. COMMENTS

1. The six days of Gen 1 were not eras. Scripture refers to each of them as "day." (Note also Ex 20:11).

2. Gen 1 mentions only tangible things. However, this means also that God created the different aspects of things, *e.g.*, time, number, motion, and colour, and he set his laws for them as well.

3. Holy Scripture does not give any basis for the doctrine of guardian angels, as promulgated by the Roman Catholic church.

D. HERESIES

1. The idea that God needed the world as object of his love.

2. The idea that God became richer through his creation.

3. Materialism.

4. Evolutionism.

5. The doctrine of pantheistic emanation.

6. Spurning of material things.

7. Deification of material things.

E. QUESTIONS

1. Who is the Creator? What does "creating" mean? What did God create?
2. Which "heaven" does Gen 1 refer to? Who live in it?
3. Are there many angels? When were they probably created?
4. In what relationship do the angels stand toward each other, toward Christ, and toward us?
5. How does Scripture distinguish the angels? Give the names of two angels.
6. What is the ordinary and what the extraordinary work of the angels?
7. What happened to a number of the angels? What is their leader called?
8. What do the devils do with respect to the unbelievers? What do they do with respect to the believers? What should we do with respect to the devils?
9. In how many days did God create the earth? What did he do on the seventh day?
10. Why does Scripture relate creation to us? What comfort is it to you that God is the Creator?

27. *Q. What do you understand by the providence of God?*

   A.   *God's providence is*
     His almighty and ever present power,[1]
     whereby, as with His hand, He still upholds
     heaven and earth and all creatures,[2]
     and so governs them that
        leaf and blade,
        rain and drought,
        fruitful and barren years,
        food and drink,
        health and sickness,
        riches and poverty,[3]
        indeed, all things,
     come not by chance[4]
     but by His fatherly hand.[5]

     [1] *Jer. 23:23, 24; Acts 17:24-28.*
     [2] *Heb. 1:3.*
     [3] *Jer. 5:24; Acts 14:15-17; John 9:3; Prov. 22:2.*
     [4] *Prov. 16:33.*
     [5] *Matt. 10:29.*

28. *Q. What does it benefit us to know*
     that God has created all things
     and still upholds them by His providence?

   A.   *We can be patient in adversity,[1]*
        thankful in prosperity,[2]
        and with a view to the future
        we can have a firm confidence
        in our faithful God and Father
        that no creature shall separate us
        from His love;[3]
     for all creatures are so completely in His hand
        that without His will
        they cannot so much as move.[4]

     [1] *Job. 1:21, 22; Ps. 39:10; James 1:3.*
     [2] *Deut. 8:10; I Thess. 5:18.*
     [3] *Ps. 55:22; Rom. 5:3-5; 8:38, 39.*
     [4] *Job 1:12; 2:6; Prov. 21:1; Acts 17:24-28.*

A. NOTES

1. The previous LD already spoke of God's providence. It referred to God's providence *and* his counsel. We should now say something about this counsel of God. For God works both in creation and in his providence in accordance with his counsel. In this respect God operates like a wise builder. Such a builder does not begin to build until he has carefully assessed and determined everything that belongs to the building process. So also God, before he made or began anything, determined everything in his eternal counsel. Holy Scripture calls this God's foreknowledge (prescience), purpose, definite plan, decree, good pleasure. GOD'S COUNSEL IS THE TOTALITY OF HIS ETERNAL DECREE ABOUT EVERY-THING THAT WILL HAPPEN IN TIME.

2. This counsel is:

   eternal: God's works are known to him from of old (Acts 15:18);

   sovereign: God does what seems good to him (Ps 115:3);

   wise: God in his counsel chooses the best means to the highest end (Rom 11:33);

   efficacious: "My counsel shall stand, and I will accomplish all my purpose" (Isa 46:10);

   all-encompassing: He "accomplishes all things according to the counsel of his will" (Eph 1:11).

3. Knowing that God has determined all things from eternity does not entitle us to sit back to see what will happen. For God's counsel does not abrogate our responsibility. The Lord, in his counsel, maintains man as a rational, moral being. Acts 2:23 mentions in one breath the definite plan and foreknowledge of God and the actions of man. Further, the Lord did not merely determine the end of all things in his counsel, but also the means whereby the end will be reached, and we are called upon to use those means. God's counsel also took sin into account. Sin was not a disappointment, a set-back for him. But neither is God the author of sin. Sin is the act of man and guilt for sin falls on man. Thus, sin cannot prevent God from reaching his goal, but must serve to reach that goal (Gen 50:20; Acts 2:23).

4. God began his creation and continues to work with it in accordance with this counsel. For the fact that he rested on the seventh day did not mean that God ceased to work (God always works [Jn 5:17]), but that he left

off creating. He did not add new creatures to creation, but began to lead creation to his goal. God, therefore, continued to work.

And if you should ask what it is that he does, then the answer is, first: HE UPHOLDS all things. He preserves (conserves) all thing from corruption. God *causes* (not: permits) all things to exist: some, such as man, he causes to exist mediately (by means); some, such as angels, immediately (without means); others, such as the sun, moon, *etc.*, by themselves; yet others, such as animals, man, *etc.*, according to their kind (Heb 1:3).

Further, we say: HE GOVERNS all things (Ps 93:1). He rules all things and guides them to his goal. Nothing is excluded from this government, not even sin, even though God is not the author of sin and is not guilty of the sins that are committed. Art. 13 of the BC states:

> For his power and goodness are so great and beyond understanding that He ordains and executes His work in the most excellent and just manner, even when devils and wicked men act unjustly.

We can, therefore, say of every one of man's actions that God does it *and* that man does it. But God and man do not act in the same manner and for the same purpose in that action. For example, when in former days a "surgeon" used a leech to draw the poisoned blood from a person's limb, it might be said that the leech healed the person, or that the surgeon did it. But the leech did it only to satisfy itself, whereas the surgeon did it to help the patient. That is how the Lord caused Joseph to be sold into Egypt and his brothers did the selling. The brothers sinned in doing so, since they did it entirely to indulge their hatred; but God wrought a great work in so doing, in order to keep his people alive (Gen 50:20).

God normally governs in accordance with established rules. This makes it possible for us to take precautions. We are obliged to do so, for God's governance of all things does not abrogate our responsibility.

5. Do you wonder how God does all this? BY WORKING TOGETHER WITH ALL THINGS. His power flows as *first cause* in all powers, which work in the world as *second cause*. But in so doing, God does not demand of any creature that it act contrary to its nature or will.

Ivy, a monkey and man, all three can climb a tree. And when they climb, it is God's power which allows them to do so. But that power operates in a different way in each of them, so that each creature acts in accordance with its own nature and pursuant to its own will. That is how God also works together with all our thoughts, words and actions. Prov 16:1 states:

> The plans of the mind belong to man, but the answer of the tongue is from the LORD.

This applies also to our sinful thoughts and deeds, but the responsibility for the sins rests upon us. God does, indeed, give the power by which we sin, but WE use it to sin (see Isa 10:5-7).

6. We refer to all of this work of God concerning his creation as his PROVIDENCE. It is *His almighty and ever present power, whereby, as with His hand, He still upholds heaven and earth and all creatures.*

7. Providence provides rich comfort for those who know God in Christ as their Father. They know that because of God's providence nothing can happen to them by chance. There is no such thing as chance, even though we sometimes use that word (Lk 10:31). We must make the confession about the providence of God true in our lives, so that, acknowledging God's hand in everything, we are patient in adversity, thankful in prosperity and, as regards the future, have confidence that nothing can separate us from God's love.

8. To be thankful does not mean having a pleasant feeling and displaying a satisfied disposition. Rather, it means that we use God's gifts in accordance with the rule of thankfulness (the law!) and serve the Lord with those gifts.

   To be patient does not mean that we must bear suffering impassively, without emotion. Instead, it means that we must bear the cross willingly and for the Lord's sake.

9. Note that the Catechism speaks of common things: rain and drought, leaf and blade, *etc.* He who does not see the hand of the Lord in everyday things, but only in extraordinary ones, does not live out of the faith which is confessed in this LD.

B. CROSS REFERENCES

1. The confession of the providence of God in art. 13 of the BC is beautiful. In this art. we confess, in connection with the inscrutability of God's rule, that we are content to be "pupils of Christ."

2. The comfort of God's rule is confessed also in the Forms for the Baptism of Infants and of Adults (Doctrine of Baptism). There we confess that God provides us with all good and averts all evil or turns it to our profit.

C. COMMENTS

1. During the time of the special revelation, God often did miracles, unheard-of deeds. We may no longer expect them today. But God still does spiritual miracles every day: he regenerates men and revives the church.

D. HERESIES

1. Pantheism.

2. Deism.

3. The belief that the taking of special precautions conflicts with the confession of the providence of God.

4. The belief that only natural events are subject to the providence of God, and not man's moral actions.

5. The idea that one can only say that sin is permitted by God.

6. Naturalism (which denies the existence of miracles).

7. Supranaturalism (which purports to explain miracles).

8. Expecting signs and miracles in normal times.

E. QUESTIONS

1. What is God's counsel? What names does Scripture use for it?

2. Which attributes of God's counsel do you know? What does Isa 46:10 say?

3. Does God's counsel abrogate our responsibility? What does Acts 2:23 say?

4. Did God's counsel also take sin into account? Does that not make God the author of sin?

5. What does God do with creation after he created it? What does it mean when we confess that God still upholds everything? What does it mean that God still governs everything? Does God also rule over sin? How does he uphold his creatures? What does Heb 1:3 say? Does God's rule abrogate our responsibility?

6. What does the fact that God works together with all things mean?

7. What, then, is God's providence?

8. To whom does this confession provide comfort? What is that comfort?

9. What does it mean to be thankful? What does it mean to be patient?

10. Wherein must we acknowledge God's hand?

GOD THE SON AND OUR REDEMPTION
Lord's Days 11 - 19

A. NOTES

1. Lord's Days 11 - 19 deal with the six clauses of the Apostles' Creed which are dedicated to God the Son and our redemption. They discuss, successively:

a.	*His names:*	Jesus, Christ, God's Son, and our Lord (LD 11-13).
b.	*His states:*	1. The state of humiliation (LD 14-16).
		2. The state of exaltation (LD 17-19).
c.	*His offices:*	The offices of Prophet, Priest and King (LD 12).
d.	*His natures:*	The divine and human natures (LD 13a, 14).

LORD'S DAY 11

29. Q. *Why is the Son of God called Jesus,*
    that is, Saviour?

    A. *Because He saves us from all our sins,[1]*
    and because salvation is not to be sought or found
    in anyone else.[2]

    > [1] Matt. 1:21; Heb. 7:25.
    > [2] Is. 43:11; John 15:4, 5; Acts 4:11, 12; I Tim. 2:5.

30. Q. *Do those believe in the only Saviour Jesus*
    who seek their salvation and well-being
    from saints, in themselves, or anywhere else?

    A. *No.*
    Though they boast of Him in words,
    they in fact deny the only Saviour Jesus.[1]
    For one of two things must be true:
    either Jesus is not a complete Saviour,
    or those who by true faith accept this Saviour
    must find in Him all that is necessary
    for their salvation.[2]

    > [1] I Cor. 1:12, 13; Gal. 5:4.
    > [2] Col. 1:19, 20; 2:10; I John 1:7.

A. NOTES

1. The names of the Mediator are so important because we know Him by
these names. The name "Jesus" was given him at God's command. Thus,
Mt 1:21 says:

> ... you shall call his name Jesus, for he will save his people from their sins.

(Cf. Lk 1:31).

2. "Jesus" is the Greek form of the Hebrew name, Joshua, which means,
"the LORD saves." It was a very common name in Israel (see Acts 13:6;
Col 4:11). We are familiar with the following from the OT: Joshua the
son of Nun, the "successor" to Moses, who led Israel into Canaan after
their forty years of wandering; and Joshua, the high priest, the son of
Jehozadak, who, together with Zerubbabel, led Israel back to Canaan after
the exile. Thus, the LORD granted deliverance to Israel through both of
them. However, they were able to effect only an earthly and temporal
deliverance.

3. Jesus, the son of God, truly saves. He does not merely deliver people
from the desert, or from exile, but from *sin! To save* or deliver means:

a. *to redeem from the power of sin* ("escape the punishment" [see LD
5, Q. 12]). Jesus brought this about by paying for our sins with his
blood (passive and active obedience).

b. *to deliver to the service of God* ("again be received into favour" [see
LD 5, Q. 12]). Jesus brings this about by regenerating us through his
Word and Spirit.

Thus, he removes both the guilt and the pollution of sin. He saves us
completely from sin.

His priesthood is permanent; it cannot pass to another person (Heb 7:24).
Nor is it necessary for another to come after him. Heb 7:25 says:

> ... he is able for all time to save those who draw near to God through him,
> since he always lives to make intercession for them.

4. Just as he is the *complete* Saviour, so also is he the *only* Saviour.
Salvation is to be sought or found in none other. Acts 4:12 says:

> And there is salvation in no one else, for there is no other name under heaven
> given among men by which we must be saved.

Our service to God (our conversion) rests solely in our bond with Christ.
In Jn 15:5, Christ says:

I am the vine, you are the branches. He who abides in me, and I in him, he it is that bears much fruit, for apart from me you can do nothing.

Q. & A. 30
JESUS ALONE!

A. NOTES

1. Originally this Answer was directed against the Roman sect. Roman Catholics are taught that salvation is to be sought:

   a. from saints (Maria; apostles; church fathers, *etc.*);

   b. in themselves (one's good works are said to be meritorious before God); or

   c. anywhere else (relics, indulgences, pilgrimages, *etc.*).

   It is true that Roman Catholics do not *say* that Jesus is not the only Saviour. But they make their belief known by what they *do and refrain from doing*. For although they dare not say that Jesus is not a complete Saviour, in fact they seek their salvation not only with Jesus, but also elsewhere.

2. Although this Answer was framed against Rome, it obviously applies also to all who, although not Roman Catholic, are guilty of the same fundamental error. Also in Christ's church there are people who seek their salvation from *others* (a minister, a deceased theological savant), in *themselves* (in their faith, their prayer, their conversion, *etc.*), or *anywhere else* (*e.g.*, those who seek their well-being in the power of organizations and who allow reason to rule them during the week, rather than Jesus).

   It must be said of all of these: They deny Jesus in their actions!

B. CROSS REFERENCES

1. The BC also constantly states that Jesus saves completely. Thus, art. 21 states:

   > We find comfort in His wounds and have no need to seek or invent any other means of reconciliation with God. . . .

   Art. 22 follows the same method as is used in Answer 30 to demonstrate the complete satisfaction of Christ.

   Art. 23 confesses that Christ's work is:

   > . . . sufficient to cover all our iniquities and to give us confidence in drawing near to God. . . .

   Art. 26 describes the sufficiency of Christ in a persuasive manner and sings a paean to it.

C. COMMENTS

1. Since only Jesus redeems us, the name "Jesuit" is an insult to him.

D. HERESIES

1. Judaism;

2. The idea that we must first be converted before we may abandon ourselves to Christ.

3. Pelagianism.

4. Arminianism (Remonstrantism).

5. Every attempt to seek one's salvation or well-being in the state or society instead of in faith in Jesus.

E. QUESTIONS (INTRODUCTION; Q&A 29 & 30)

1. What do LD 11-19 deal with? Which topics do they discuss? Which names, states, offices and natures of the Mediator do you know?

2. Why are the Mediator's names so important? Who gave him the name, Jesus?

3. What was the OT equivalent of this name? How many persons who bore the name, Joshua, do you know? What did they do? What kind of deliverance did they effect?

4. From what does Jesus save? What does this encompass? How does he do it?

5. What do Mt 1:21 and Acts 4:12, respectively, say? Is our conversion something that we add to Jesus' work?

6. Against whom was Answer 30 originally directed? With whom do they seek their salvation? How do they deny Jesus?

7. To whom does Answer 30 also apply? How do persons who are not Roman Catholic sometimes seek their salvation or well-being from others, in themselves, or anywhere else?

31. Q. *Why is He called Christ,*
    that is, Anointed?

    A. *Because He has been ordained by God the Father,*
    and anointed with the Holy Spirit,[1] to be
        our chief Prophet and Teacher,[2]
        who has fully revealed to us
        the secret counsel and will of God
        concerning our redemption;[3]
    our only High Priest,[4]
        who by the one sacrifice of His body
        has redeemed us,[5]
        and who continually intercedes for us
        before the Father;[6]
    and our eternal King,[7]
        who governs us by His Word and Spirit,
        and who defends and preserves us
        in the redemption obtained for us.[8]

[1] *Ps. 45:7 (Heb. 1:9); Is. 61:1 (Luke 4:18); Luke 3:21, 22.*
[2] *Deut. 18:15 (Acts 3:22).*
[3] *John 1:18; 15:15.*
[4] *Ps. 110:4 (Heb. 7:17).*
[5] *Heb. 9:12; 10:11-14.*
[6] *Rom. 8:34; Heb. 9:24; I John 2:1.*
[7] *Zach. 9:9 (Matt. 21:5); Luke 1:33.*
[8] *Matt. 28:18-20; John 10:28; Rev. 12:10, 11.*

32. Q. *Why are you called a Christian?*

    A. *Because I am a member of Christ by faith[1]*
    and thus share in His anointing,[2]
    so that I may
        as prophet confess His Name,[3]
        as priest present myself
            a living sacrifice of thankfulness to Him,[4]
        and as king fight with a free and good
            conscience against sin and the devil
            in this life,[5]
            and hereafter reign with Him eternally
            over all creatures.[6]

[1] *I Cor. 12:12-27.*
[2] *Joel 2:28 (Acts 2:17); I John 2:27.*
[3] *Matt. 10:32; Rom 10:9, 10; Heb. 13:15.*
[4] *Rom. 12:1; I Pet. 2:5, 9.*
[5] *Gal. 5:16, 17; Eph. 6:11; I Tim. 1:18, 19.*
[6] *Matt. 25:34; II Tim. 2:12.*

A. NOTES

1. The Greek word, Christ (in Hebr., Messiah [Jn 1:42]), means *anointed*. Anointing was very important in the OT as a symbol or sign of the *appointment* and *qualification* of office bearers. As distinguished from an occupation (such as carpenter, or clerk) which one chooses oneself, an office (such as king, or priest) is a task imposed by God. Just as today a king is crowned at his coronation as a sign that his kingly office is committed to him, so also in the OT kings were anointed (Saul by Samuel, 1 Sam 10:1; *cf.* 16:13), as were prophets (Elisha, 1 Kings 19:16), and priests (Lev 8:12; 21:10-15). Such an anointing, therefore, signified their APPOINTMENT (ordination) in the first place. Second, it also signified their PREPARATION (qualification): In the East the anointing oil, made with aromatic herbs, was used to re-equip a person, who had become fatigued by the oppressive climate, for his task. Thus, God the Lord guaranteed to a person who was appointed to a specific task, which was sealed by his anointing, that he himself would prepare him for his task. The anointing oil was a symbol of the Holy Spirit.

2. God had created man in accordance with his image, so that he was invested with the three-fold office of prophet, priest and king. But man became a servant of Satan through sin. That meant that man's call to office remained, but his qualification was lost. In order that man might faithfully fulfil his office, Jesus, THE CHRIST, became THE office bearer.

3. He was ORDAINED (*i.e.*, appointed) to this office by the Father. He says of himself that he was sent by the Father (Jn 17:3, 8, 18, *etc.*) And Scripture says in 1 Jn 4:14:

> ... the Father has sent his Son as the Savior of the world.

This ordination or appointment is from eternity. For when Prov 8:23 says: "Ages ago I was set up, at the first, before the beginning of the earth," it refers to his appointment in God's counsel (*cf.* 1 Pet 1:20: "destined before the foundation of the world").

Christ's QUALIFICATION or PREPARATION for the three-fold office that he had to fulfil as Mediator was an historical occurrence. As part of this preparation he received human nature and was equipped with everything necessary for the fulfilment of his office. Thus, he was not anointed with oil, but with *the Holy Spirit himself*. He was conceived by the Holy Spirit (Lk 1:35) and at his baptism the Holy Spirit descended upon him in the form of a dove (Lk 3:22).

4. He was anointed as prophet, priest and king. We can say this, because:

   a. he was *announced* as such in the OT: as prophet in Deut 18:18; as priest in Ps 110:4; and as king in 2 Sam 7:12-13;

   b. he was called thus in the NT: prophet in Acts 3:22; priest in Heb 5:10; and king in Jn 12:15; and

   c. he had to fulfil the three-fold original office of man in order to be a true Saviour, *i.e.*, in order to restore man to his three-fold office (in other words, because he is Mediator of the covenant).

5. The function of a prophet is to proclaim (state) God's Word (whether by reference to the past, present, or future). The function of a priest is to dedicate himself to God in love. The function of a king is to govern in obedience to God.

6. In this three-fold office, Christ not only had to do what Adam had refused to do, but he also had to suffer the punishment for Adam's three-fold failure to fulfil the office (active and passive obedience). He performed his three-fold office as Mediator BEFORE (during the OT), DURING (when he walked the earth), and AFTER (in his exaltation) his time on earth. He suffered the punishment for our neglect during his time in the flesh. In what follows we shall constantly refer to these three time periods.

7. He is PROPHET AND TEACHER in order to reveal God counsel and will concerning our redemption (God's plan of redemption) completely to us. He *is able* to do that because he knows the Father completely (Mt 11:27), since the Father revealed himself to him. Christ performed this prophetic office *before* his *humiliation* (*i.e.* during the OT) by the patriarchs and prophets. He performed it *in* his *humiliation*, when, by his words and works, he made the Father known (gave an exegesis, Jn 1:18) to us; and when he also suffered the punishment for the abandonment by us of our prophetic office, since he was not believed, but mocked as prophet. And he performs it in his *exaltation* in which the Spirit, given by him to his church, guides the church into all the truth (Jn 16:13).

   He is HIGH PRIEST. *Before* his *humiliation* he performed his priestly office by prefiguring himself in the priests of Israel. *In* his *humiliation* he performed the office by sanctifying the Father in love; bearing the punishment for our violation of the priestly office by giving himself as an atoning sacrifice; and by praying for and blessing those who are his. In his *exaltation* he performs the office by appearing before the Father as our intercessor and advocate (1 Jn 2:1; Rom 8:34; Jn 17:24); and by blessing us.

   He is KING. As such, *in the OT* he protected and ruled his people by the patriarchs, judges and kings of Israel. *In his humiliation* he governed all creatures obediently and bore our punishment, in that he was rejected and held up to ridicule as king. *In his exaltation* he protects and rules his people by his Spirit and Word and governs all creatures.

8. We tend to speak separately of each of the three offices. But Christ always fulfilled all three together in all his words and deeds. Thus, for example, his miracles are *prophetic* (revealing God's salvation), *priestly* (blessing with his redemption) and *kingly* (ruling over creation). In Adam the three offices were also conjoined. He did not have three offices, but one three-fold office. Only during the time that Israel existed as a nation was this unity broken. It was rare for anyone to hold more than one office.

9. It behooves us to honour Christ in this three-fold office, by letting him teach us as our highest *Prophet*, by trusting in his one *priestly* sacrifice, and by submitting ourselves willingly to his *royal* dominion.

B. CROSS REFERENCES

1. Art. 21 of the BC states:

> We believe that Jesus Christ was confirmed by an oath to be a High Priest for ever, after the order of Melchizedek.

(See Heb 7).

C. QUESTIONS

1. Which name in the OT compares to the name, "Christ"? What does it mean? Which two matters did anointing signify in the OT? What is an office?

2. Who were anointed in the OT dispensation? Give an example of each. Of whom was the anointing oil a symbol? Why was it so apt as a symbol of that person?

3. Who was first appointed to an office? What was his office? Are we still bound to this office? Are we still qualified for it?

4. When was Christ ordained? When was he qualified? What did this qualification entail? Was he anointed with oil? If not, what was he anointed with?

5. Why can we say that Christ was prophet, priest and king? What is the task of a prophet, a priest, and a king?

6. What did Christ have to do in the three-fold office in addition to what Adam did? When did he do this?

7. What does Christ do as prophet, as priest, and as king? State how he performed each office before, during and after his humiliation.

8. Did Christ perform each office separately? If not, how did he perform them? Demonstrate this by reference to miracles.

9. How must we honour Christ in his three-fold office?

Q. & A. 32

YOU HAVE BEEN ANOINTED BY THE HOLY ONE

A. NOTES

1. The believers were first called "Christians" (followers of Christ) in Antioch (Acts 11:26). This name was probably intended as a term of abuse originally, but it became an honorific, because people realized, correctly, that this name expressed the fact that they were partakers of Christ's anointing, *i.e.*, that they were partakers of the Holy Spirit.

2. We are members of Christ by faith (*cf.* LD 7, Ans. 20), *i.e.*, members of his body. That is how we are partakers of his anointing and bear the "office of all believers." Scripture calls all believers "saints." This means that they hold an office, *viz.*, to dedicate themselves to God. They can, indeed, be unfaithful to their office (*i.e.*, be Christians in name only), but that does not mean that they no longer hold the office. Scripture clearly states, in 1 Jn 2:27:

    . . . the anointing which you received from him abides in you.

    The anointing is the heritage of the people of the covenant.

3. This anointing, which is accompanied not only by the *appointment* to, but also by the *qualification* for the office, has in view the three-fold office:

    a. As *prophet* the member of the covenant must confess Christ's name (*i.e.*, his revelation, his entire work), and must accept it in faith and make it known in word and walk of life.

    b. As *priest* he must offer himself as a living sacrifice to Christ (*i.e.*, as *thank* (peace) offering; Christ himself is the sole *guilt* offering!):

        i. *positively*: by presenting his body "as a living sacrifice, holy and acceptable to God," as his "spiritual worship," *i.e.*, his deliberate worship and dedication (Rom 12:1); and

        ii. *negatively*: by not becoming conformed to the world (*i.e.*, to maintain the same lifestyle as that maintained by the world), but by changing (undergoing a metamorphosis, adopting another lifestyle) through a renewal of his mind (in accordance with an inner renewal of life) (Rom 12:2).

    c. As *king* he must, with a free (*i.e.* delivered of the curse and fear of the law) and .good (*i.e.*, sincere in his desire to serve God) conscience:

        i. fight against sin and the devil (and all other enemies) in this life; and

        ii. reign with Christ eternally over all creatures after this life.

4. Our communion with Christ becomes a living communion in which the office bearer can faithfully perform his office. Thus, we are prophets only by believing in Christ as prophet; we are priests only by accepting his sacrifice; we are kings only by submitting ourselves to him. This office is given to each member of the covenant.

5. Because of sin, the performance of the office of all believers is often deficient. That is why Christ also gave the special offices of the covenant to his congregation. He gave apostles as well as prophets, evangelists as well as pastors and teachers, to equip the saints for the work of ministry (Eph 4:11). Paul distinguishes two types of special office:

   a. Offices which only existed during the first period of the Christian church, when the Bible was not yet complete. These were:

      i. apostles: the 12 appointed by Christ as such, as witnesses during the entire time of his sojourn on earth; they had a foundational office: the task of the apostles was to be the foundation of the church (Eph 2:20);

      ii. prophets: (*e.g.*, Agabus [Acts 11:28; 21:10; *cf.* 1 Cor 14]) had the task of teaching the believers who had already been gathered and to build them up; and

      iii. evangelists: (*e.g.*, Philip [Acts 21:8]) assisted the apostles in their missionary work.

   b. Offices which Christ gave to the church for the duration of this dispensation. These are:

      i. pastors and teachers: these are the same as the elders "who labour in preaching in teaching" (1 Tim 5:17); they are our "teaching elders," or ministers; their task is to administer the word (and the sacraments) of the covenant;

      ii. elders: these are the elders who rule (1 Tim 5:17) and who have supervision over the congregation in which they have been appointed as overseers by the Holy Spirit; their task is to care for the congregation (Acts 20:28; *cf.* 1 Pet 5:2-3), and administer the discipline (threat) of the covenant; and

      iii. deacons: these care for those in need (Acts 6:1-6); their task, therefore, is to administer the communion of the covenant.

Christ gave these special offices "*to equip the saints for the work of ministry*," *i.e.*, in order to activate and stimulate the "saints," or members of the covenant, or holders of the office of all believers, who fail to perform their office properly because of sin, so that they might perform it as faithfully as the angels in heaven (see Eph 4:12).

Not all believers can hold the special offices. Paul says in 1 Cor 14:34: "the women should keep silence in the churches."

B. CROSS REFERENCES

1. We pray for the faithful performance of the three-fold office in the Prayer of Thanksgiving in the Forms for the Baptism of Infants and of Adults.

2. Art. 28 of the BC speaks about the office of all believers.

C. COMMENTS

1. Some people believe that the office of evangelist is also a continuing office intended specifically for the propagation of the gospel. They do not regard it as belonging to the office of ministers of the Word who are ordained (or installed) as missionaries.

D. HERESIES

1. All forms of hierarchy, especially the Roman distinction between the clergy and the laity.

2. The Anabaptist avoidance of the world.

3. Barthianism.

E. QUESTIONS

1. Where were the believers first called "Christians"? What does this name denote?
2. In what way do we, therefore, partake in the anointing of Christ?
3. Was this anointing promised to us?
4. Which three offices does a Christian hold? What is his task in each office?
5. How only can he perform the offices?
6. What assistance does God give to the general office?
7. Which are the special offices? What is the task of each?
8. To what end were the special offices given?
9. Can everyone hold a special office?

33. *Q. Why is He called God's only begotten Son,
since we also are children of God?*

A. *Because Christ alone
is the eternal, natural Son of God.[1]
We, however, are children of God by adoption,
through grace, for Christ's sake.[2]*

> [1] *John 1:1-3, 14, 18; 3:16; Rom. 8:32; Heb. 1; I John 4:9.*
> [2] *John 1:12; Rom. 8:14-17; Gal. 4:6; Eph. 1:5, 6.*

34. *Q. Why do you call Him our Lord?*

A. *Because He has ransomed us,
body and soul,[1]
from all our sins,
not with silver or gold
but with His precious blood,[2]
and has freed us
from all the power of the devil
to make us His own possession.[3]*

> [1] *I Cor. 6:20; I Tim. 2:5, 6.*
> [2] *I Peter 1:18, 19.*
> [3] *Col. 1:13, 14; Heb. 2:14, 15.*

A. NOTES

1. *God's only-begotten Son.* This name denotes the relationship between the Mediator and God the Father (the word "Lord" describes his relationship to us), and thereby contrasts it with *our* relationship to the Father. We confess, therefore, the difference between the Mediator's position of Son and the believers' position as children.

2. *Only-begotten.* This signifies two things: (a) that there is only one Son; and (b) that he was born of God. The latter means that just as the Father has life in himself, so also he gave the Son power to have life in himself (Jn 5:26). Further, the Word (*i.e.,* the Son) was "with God," *i.e.,* enjoys personal communion with the Father, from eternity (Jn 1:1). Moreover, as only-begotten Son, he is the object of the Father's highest, fullest and undivided love.

3. *Eternal.* Jn 1:1 speaks of what already "was," *i.e.,* existed, "in the beginning." He "was" already God's Son before the beginning of creation. He is thus uncreated.

4. *Natural.* He is "of one substance with" the Father. Jn 1:1 says:

    . . . the Word was God.

Note that Christ is not "similar" to, but equal with the Father. He is God, just like the Father and the Holy Spirit.

5. *Alone.* Christ alone is the divine Son of the Father. He is the reflection of the Father's glory and the copy of his being. Heb 1:3 says:

    He reflects the glory of God and bears the very stamp of his nature, upholding the universe by his word of power

6. *We are also God's children.* The angels are sometimes also called "children of God" (Job 38:7, "sons"), as are the judges of the earth (Ps 82:6). But in his covenant, God adopted man to be his children in a very unique sense. Scripture does, nonetheless, draw distinctions. First, all who embrace God's covenant in faith are entitled to bear the name "children of God" (Gal 3:26). But, second, Scripture also uses this name to refer to all who were born under the covenant, even though they broke the covenant by rejecting the blessing of the covenant, *i.e.,* Christ (Rom 9:4). Calvin says that God made his covenant with all of Abraham's children and that, therefore, all are children of God, although we must distinguish between children according to the flesh and children according to the spirit. The NT uses two expressions to refer to the children (or "sons") of God. The one, translated as "adoption as children" refers to a legal

status; the other refers to a living communion through spiritual renewal by the Holy Spirit.

7. The believers and their descendants are not *by nature* children of God, but are his children by adoption, through grace, for Christ's sake. By nature they are also children of wrath, who are not able to enter the kingdom of heaven unless they are born anew, that is, unless, by means of a miracle of God, their lives are radically renewed.

8. The fruit of this adoption, accepted in faith, is that we are also heirs: heirs of God and fellow heirs with Christ. This means that, with God in Christ, they will receive all things (Rom 8:17ff).

B. CROSS REFERENCES

1. Art. 10 of the BC states:

> We believe that Jesus Christ according to His divine nature is the only-begotten Son of God, begotten from eternity, not made, nor created — for then He would be a creature — but of the same essence with the Father, equally eternal, *who reflects the glory of God and bears the very stamp of His nature*, and is equal to Him in all things.

2. See also the Athanasian and Nicene creeds.

C. HERESIES

1. Arianism.

2. Modernists.

D. QUESTIONS

1. What is the difference between the third and fourth names of the Mediator?
2. What does "only-begotten" mean?
3. Why is Christ called the ETERNAL Son of God? Why is he called the NATURAL Son of God? Why is he alone called these things?
4. Who are called children (or, sons) of God in the Bible?
5. How do we distinguish between the two kinds of children of God?
6. Are we God's children "by nature"? How, then, are we his children?
7. What is the fruit of the adoption as children?

Q. & A. 34
OUR LORD

A. NOTES (*CF.* LD 1, Q&A 1)

1. Lord: This name designates the relationship between the Mediator and those who are his. He became our Lord, because he acquired ownership in us and made us his possession. He did that by purchasing us with his blood and so delivering us from the bonds of the devil and death. He did

not pay this costly price to the evil one, but to God. We had come under the power of the evil one, since God had given us over to him because of our sins. Satan was like the keeper of our prison. Further, by his temptation he led us to the point where God gave us up to him. The ransom must, therefore, be paid, not to the unrighteous jailer, but to the righteous judge.

2. To be Christ's possession means to belong to him, to be his responsibility. It includes our duty to serve him with all the love of our heart.

3. We confess the certainty of our redemption in the names, "Son of God" and "our Lord." For, since the Mediator is the "Son of God," sent by God himself, it is beyond any doubt that God will not reject him; and, since he is "our Lord," we are unable to reject him: he rules over us!

B. QUESTIONS

1. How did Christ become our Lord?
2. To whom did he pay the ransom? Why?
3. What does it mean that we are Christ's possession? What does that include?
4. What do we confess in the names "Son of God" and "our Lord"?

THE STATES OF THE MEDIATOR
Lord's Days 14 - 19

A. NOTES

1. The word, "state," denotes a person's legal status. It is guilty or not guilty and is determined by the sentence of the Judge. It is not determined by what a person is. A person may be a thief, but be found not guilty for lack of evidence. Then he IS, indeed, a thief, but his STATE is not guilty (innocent). The reverse is also possible.

2. When we speak of the STATE of the Mediator, therefore, we refer to his LEGAL STATUS towards God. Although without sin, he stood (laden down with his people's guilt because of his Suretyship) *guilty* before God. And he was humiliated, came under the wrath of God. This lasted until he fulfilled all suffering for our sins. Not until then did God declare him righteous by raising him from the dead (Rom 4:25). At that point the *state of exaltation* begins.

3. We distinguish four steps (stages) in the *state of humiliation*. For the humiliation deepened with every step. These steps are:

   a. His mean (lowly) birth.

   b. His suffering.

   c. His death.

   e. His burial.

   His entire state of humiliation is summarized in and characterized by the expression in the creed: "descended into hell."

4. Lord's Days 14-16 deal with the state of humiliation. Lord's Days 17-19 deal with the state of exaltation. Three Lord's Days are, therefore, devoted to each state.

THE STATE OF HUMILIATION
Lord's Days 14 - 16

LORD'S DAY 14

35. Q. *What do you confess when you say:*
He was conceived by the Holy Spirit,
born of the virgin Mary?

A. *The eternal Son of God,*
who is and remains true and eternal God,[1]
took upon Himself true human nature
from the flesh and blood of the virgin Mary,[2]
through the working of the Holy Spirit.[3]
Thus He is also the true seed of David,[4]
and like His brothers in every respect,[5]
yet without sin.[6]

[1] *John 1:1; 10:30-36; Rom. 1:3; 9:5; Col. 1:15-17; I John 5:20.*
[2] *Matt. 1:18-23; John 1:14; Gal. 4:4; Heb. 2:14.*
[3] *Luke 1:35.*
[4] *II Sam. 7:12-16; Ps. 132:11; Matt. 1:1; Luke 1:32; Rom. 1:3.*
[5] *Phil. 2:7; Heb. 2:17.*
[6] *Heb. 4:15; 7:26, 27.*

36. Q. *What benefit do you receive*
from the holy conception and birth of Christ?

A. *He is our Mediator,[1]*
and with His innocence and perfect holiness
covers, in the sight of God,
my sin, in which I was conceived and born.[2]

[1] *I Tim. 2:5, 6; Heb. 9:13-15.*
[2] *Rom. 8:3, 4; II Cor. 5:21; Gal. 4:4, 5; I Pet. 1:18, 19.*

LORD'S DAY 14
Q. & A. 35 - 36
BORN OF WOMAN

A. NOTES

1. The human birth of our Lord Jesus Christ places us before the ultimate miracle. He who lacked a mother in heaven, lacked a father on earth. For the angel gave this message to Maria (Lk 1:35):

> The Holy Spirit will come upon you, and the power of the Most High will overshadow you; therefore the child to be born will be called holy, the Son of God.

Further, Jesus' birth was not like ours, his lot. Rather, it was his deed! Phil 2:7 says that he:

> . . . emptied himself, taking the form of a servant, being born in the likeness of men.

The Saviour also said constantly: I have come. What love! He wanted to enter into our filthy existence and assume our lot of curse and shame. How zealous he was for God's justice, saying in Ps. 40:7-8:

> Lo, I come . . . to do thy will, O my God.

2. Born as man, he was like man in every respect. The Catechism emphasizes that he assumed the true human nature from the flesh and blood of the virgin Mary. Article 18 of the BC also strongly emphasizes this when it states:

> He truly assumed a real human nature *with all its infirmities.*

And Rom 8:3 says that he was sent "in the likeness of sinful flesh." The gospel portrays the Lord as true man. Even his contemporaries said: "Is not this the carpenter, the son of Mary and brother of James and Joses and Judas and Simon, and are not his sisters here with us?" (Mk 6:3). To be rejected, therefore, is the Anabaptist belief that Jesus brought his human nature with him from heaven and merely passed through Mary in his human form, as light passes through a window. Already the apostle John fought against the Docetists, who maintained that Jesus only had the appearance of a body. (See 1 Jn 4:2-3).

3. While maintaining the foregoing, we must quickly add that he was "without sin." Heb 4:15 says:

> For we have not a high priest who is unable to sympathize with our weaknesses, but one who in every respect has been tempted as we are, yet without sin.

He did not have original sin. For, being in the bosom of the Father, he did not fall along with mankind when they fell in Adam. Nor did he have actual sins.

4. His divinity was not changed into human nature at his birth. He remained what he was (God) and he became what he, until then, was not (man). The divine person of the Son, who is God from eternity, also took upon himself human existence at his birth. From then on, the two natures existed in the one person.

   Thus, everything that the Mediator did in his human nature was the work of the Son of God. This imparted a divine and everlasting value to his work. 1 Jn 1:7b states:

   > . . . the blood of Jesus his Son cleanses us from all sin.

   (See CD II, 4).

5. He is also the true seed of David, by being born of Mary and by being acknowledged as son by Joseph. Lk 1:32b says:

   > . . . and the Lord God will give to him the throne of his father David.

   Thus, it is he to whom and by whom all the promises made in the OT to David and his descendants will be fulfilled. (Read Ps 72 in this context).

6. We already discussed the necessity of his birth in connection with LD 5, Q&A 12-15 and LD 6, Q&A 16-17.

7. In Q. 36 the Catechism again asks about the benefit. Note the personal tone of the A.: ". . . my sin, in which I was conceived and born." But, while my conception was already wrong because of Adam's sin, which is also mine, Jesus restored EVERYTHING that I did wrong, even my conception. And he covers my unrighteousness with his righteousness.

B. CROSS REFERENCES

1. Art. 18 of the BC speaks extensively about the incarnation of Jesus Christ.

2. Art. 19 of the BC gives a broad discussion of the union of and the distinction between the two natures of Christ in the one person of the Son.

C. COMMENTS

1. The Mediator unites the two natures (divine and human) in the one (divine) person of the Son. Both natures retain their distinct properties. The divine nature remained uncreated, eternal, omnipresent. The human nature remained created, temporal, finite. While Christ's human nature obtained immortality by his resurrection, it remained a true human nature.

   Concerning the union of these two natures (at Christ's birth), we confess that they are so closely united that they were not even separated by his death. The divine nature always remained united with the human nature, even when he lay in the grave.

   In this union the natures (according to the Council of Chalcedon, AD 451) remained:

   a. without confusion: each nature remains independent;

b.	without change:	each nature retains its own properties;
c.	without separation:	they are always and for eternity united in one person; and
d.	without division:	the *whole* human nature and the *whole* divine nature remain joined together.

Points a. and b. were directed against Eutyches (abbot of a monastery at Constantinople), who taught that after his incarnation Christ had only one nature (the two natures, when united in the incarnation, were "melted down" into a new "divine-human nature"), so that his human nature was not like ours (water mixed with wine). This idea was incorporated in the Lutheran and the ethical theologies.

Point c. was directed against Nestorius (patriarch of Constantinople), who separated the two natures of Christ to such an extent that the unity of the person was in danger of being lost (water mixed with oil).

Point d. was directed against Apollinaris, according to whom the Son merely assumed our body.

Thus, the Council of Chalcedon only rejected the heresies and declared how the union of the natures did not take place. How the union did take place exceeds our understanding.

The Roman doctrine of Mary's immaculate conception is in conflict with, *inter alia*, Lk 1:47, in which Mary informs us that she needs a Saviour.

Christ did not become man in order to bridge the "contrast" between God and man, between time and eternity, so that he would also have come in our nature apart from the fall. There was no contrast between God and man originally. There was distance, but not a distance which was not bridged by the covenant. Christ became man to save *sinners*.

D. QUESTIONS (INTRODUCTION; Q&A 35-36)

1. What does the concept of a person's "state" denote? What determines a person's state?
2. What are the states of the Mediator? How did he stand towards God in the state of humiliation and in the state of exaltation, respectively?
3. Which stages do we distinguish in the state of humiliation?
4. Who was Jesus' Father? Was Jesus' birth his deed?
5. What do Lk 1:35, Phil 2:7 and Heb 4:15, respectively, say?
6. What did the Docetists and the Anabaptists, respectively, teach about Jesus' human nature?
7. Did Jesus have communion with sin through his birth?
8. Was his divinity changed into human nature? How do we say that the two natures are united?
9. What does it mean that he is the true seed of David?
10. Why was it necessary that Jesus became man?
11. What benefit do we receive from the holy conception and birth of Christ?

37. Q. *What do you confess when you say*
　　　 that He suffered?

　　 A. *During all the time He lived on earth,*
　　　　 but especially at the end,
　　　　 Christ bore in body and soul
　　　　 the wrath of God against the sin
　　　　 of the whole human race.[1]
　　　 Thus, by His suffering,
　　　　 as the only atoning sacrifice,[2]
　　　　 He has redeemed our body and soul
　　　　 from everlasting damnation,[3]
　　　　 and obtained for us
　　　　 the grace of God, righteousness, and eternal
　　　　 life.[4]

　　　 [1] *Is. 53; I Tim. 2:6; I Pet. 2:24; 3:18.*
　　　 [2] *Rom. 3:25; I Cor. 5:7; Eph. 5:2; Heb. 10:14; I John 2:2; 4:10.*
　　　 [3] *Rom. 8:1-4; Gal. 3:13; Col. 1:13; Heb. 9:12; I Pet 1:18, 19.*
　　　 [4] *John 3:16; Rom. 3:24-26; II Cor. 5:21; Heb. 9:15.*

38. Q. *Why did He suffer under Pontius Pilate as judge?*

　　 A. *Though innocent, Christ was condemned*
　　　　 by an earthly judge,[1]
　　　　 and so He freed us
　　　　 from the severe judgment of God
　　　　 that was to fall on us.[2]

　　　 [1] *Luke 23:13-24; John 19:4, 12-16.*
　　　 [2] *Is. 53:4, 5; II Cor. 5:21; Gal. 3:13.*

39. Q. *Does it have a special meaning*
　　　　 that Christ was crucified
　　　　 and did not die in a different way?

　　 A. *Yes.*
　　　　 Thereby I am assured
　　　　 that He took upon Himself
　　　　 the curse which lay on me,
　　　　 for a crucified one
　　　　 was cursed by God.[1]

　　　 [1] *Deut. 21:23; Gal. 3:13.*

A. NOTES

1. Christ suffered in BODY and SOUL. 1 Pet 2:24 says:

   He himself bore our sins in his body on the tree. . . .

   Isa 53:11 speaks of the "travail of his soul." Although the punishment of Christ's body was heavy, there are those who have undergone worse torture. However, no one has suffered as much as Jesus. For a person's suffering is not measured by what is done to him, but by the manner in which he undergoes it. (A child who loves his father suffers more under his father's anger than one who does not trouble himself about his father. Is not also one person more sensitive than another?) Hence, with respect to Jesus' suffering, we must pay more attention to the travail of his soul than the stripes which were inflicted upon him.

2. His suffering lasted the entire time of his life on earth. Already immediately after his birth his suffering came upon him, including the infanticide committed by Herod, and it followed him in mockery and contempt, misunderstanding and insinuation, and open rejection. It broke him in pieces, "especially at the end" of his life, in Gethsemane, before the Sanhedrin, Pilate and Herod, and on Golgotha.

   The suffering in his suffering was that he understood in faith that he bore the wrath of God in all that came upon him (CD II, 4).

   That he bore the wrath of God "against the sin of whole human race" does not mean that he redeemed the entire human race. But those whom he redeemed lay, together with the human race, under the curse which extended to that entire race. That is why he could not deliver without undergoing the wrath of God against the whole human race. Thus, his suffering is, indeed, sufficient for the redemption of the sins of all men, but is intended only for, and benefits only, the believers.

3. Christ's suffering was not a tragic fate, a lot which everyone deplores. That is why the Apostles' Creed says that he suffered under Pontius Pilate. This does not simply date his suffering (and should, therefore, not be considered together with the words which follow in the Apostles' Creed), but points to the *character* of Jesus' suffering. The *Judge* declared him guilty. Thereby he sanctioned what happened to him up to that point (rejection of his word; arrest). And thereby the rest of his suffering (death) did not acquire the character of a misdeed, regretted by everyone, but of the execution of an officially sanctioned human judgment. One must remember in this context what Ps 82:1 says:

117

> God has taken his place in the divine council; in the midst of the gods he holds judgment.

That is how the "chastisement which made us whole" was upon him (Isa 53:5).

4. Isa 53:5 continues: "and with his stripes we are healed." For his suffering was a sin offering. He suffered in our place. 1 Pet 3:18 says:

> For Christ also died for sins once for all, the righteous for the unrighteous, that he might bring us to God. . . .

So also, Mt 20:28 says:

> Even as the Son of man came not to be served but to serve, and to give his life as a ransom for many.

The text refers to the sum of money paid to redeem prisoners. Thus, also Gal 3:13 says:

> Christ redeemed us from the curse of the law, having become a curse for us. . . .

B. CROSS REFERENCES

1. Art. 21 of the BC speaks extensively about the suffering of the Lord "to purge away our sins," and of his complete satisfaction to still God's anger. See also art. 20.

2. The CD II, 1-4, speak more fully about the "death of the Son of God," which was abundantly sufficient for the expiation of the sins of the entire world.

3. See also the Form for the Celebration of the Lord's Supper (Remembrance of Christ): "We are to remember Him in the following manner. . . ."

C. QUESTIONS

1. Wherein did Jesus suffer? What aspect of his suffering deserves our greatest attention?
2. When did he suffer? What did he suffer?
3. Did Christ redeem all men by his suffering? Was his sacrifice not sufficient for that purpose?
4. What is the character of Christ's suffering?
5. What is the fruit of Christ's suffering for those who are his?
6. What do 1 Pet 3:18, Mt 20:28 and Gal 3:13, respectively, say?

40. *Q.* *Why was it necessary for Christ*
    to humble Himself even unto death?

    A. *Because of the justice and truth of God[1]*
    satisfaction for our sins
    could be made in no other way
    than by the death of the Son of God.[2]
    [1] *Gen. 2:17.*
    [2] *Rom. 8:3; Phil. 2:8; Heb. 2:9, 14, 15.*

41. *Q.* *Why was he buried?*

    A. *His burial testified*
    that He had really died.[1]
    [1] *Is. 53:9; John 19:38-42; Acts 13:29; I Cor. 15:3,4.*

42. *Q.* *Since Christ has died for us,*
    why do we still have to die?

    A. *Our death is not a payment for our sins,*
    but it puts an end to sin
    and is an entrance into eternal life.[1]
    [1] *John 5:24; Phil. 1:21-23; I Thess. 5:9, 10.*

43. *Q.* *What further benefit do we receive*
    from Christ's sacrifice and death on the cross?

    A. *Through Christ's death*
    our old nature is crucified,
    put to death,
    and buried with Him,[1]
    so that the evil desires of the flesh
    may no longer reign in us,[2]
    but that we may offer ourselves to Him
    as a sacrifice of thankfulness.[3]
    [1] *Rom. 6:5-11; Col. 2:11, 12.*
    [2] *Rom. 6:12-14.*
    [3] *Rom. 12:1; Eph. 5:1, 2.*

44. *Q.* *Why is there added:*
    He descended into hell?

    A. *In my greatest sorrows and temptations*
    I may be assured and comforted
    that my Lord Jesus Christ,
    by His unspeakable anguish, pain, terror, and agony,
    which He endured throughout all His sufferings[1]
    but especially on the cross, has delivered me
    from the anguish and torment of hell.[2]
    [1] *Ps. 18:5, 6; 116:3; Matt. 26:36-46; 27:45, 46; Heb. 5:7-10.*
    [2] *Is. 53.*

A. NOTES

1. In Israel, capital punishment took place by stoning. The Israelites did not exclude the possibility that the person who was stoned might have repented while dying and have been received in grace. But with abominable offenders they nevertheless, after the stoning, hung the soulless body on a tree outside the city. Thereby they indicated: "Lord we did what we could to this offender, but we could not completely mete out the punishment which he deserved. We lack the power to do so. We can only kill the body, but Thou canst also kill the soul. That is why we deliver him up to Thee." That is why Gal 3:13 says:

> Cursed be every one who hangs on a tree.

And this is what happened to Christ. He became a curse for us when, in his suffering outside the gate, he hung on the cross.

2. Christ suffered death fully. He suffered the temporal death. He suffered the spiritual death, for God withdrew his grace from him (but this did not make him powerless for good). And he suffered the eternal death (Mt 27:46). This was necessary because of the righteousness and truth of God. The Notes to LD 5, Q&A 12 explain why God's justice required it. But God's truth also demanded it. For God had stated that the sinner would die! And is God's Word not the truth? The Notes to LD 5, Q&A 13 further explain that only the death OF THE SON OF GOD could PAY for sin.

3. It is important that the Catechism ask Q. 42. The law of Christ as our surety does not seem to make sense. For, if Christ died for us, why do we still have to die? But the law of Suretyship is correct here too. For our death is quite different from Christ's death. In 1 Thess 4:14 it is said of Jesus that he *died*, but of those who are his that they *have fallen asleep*. Our death is, therefore, a passage (not an entrance; it rests in faith!) into eternal life. This is a benefit whereby we are completely delivered from sin.

It is a wise ordinance of the Lord that we must die. Otherwise we should have to fight against sin until the last day, or else it would be apparent of ALL on this side of the grave who will go to heaven and who are excluded from heaven!

4. The death of Christ does not just bear fruit for us when we die. Already in this life we have peace with God by faith, because of his death. And he puts to death our old nature, *i.e.*, our old way of existence, full of sin,

121

by the power whereby, until his death, he rejected sin. This does not mean that the evil desires are removed completely from those who are his, but they no longer reign in them (Ans. 43; CD V, 3).

B. COMMENTS

1. Death by crucifixion was humiliating and painful. The Romans used it, but only for non-Romans. A Latin writer stated: "A Roman not only does not die on the cross; it never even crosses his mind."

C. QUESTIONS

1. Why, exactly, did Jesus die on the cross?
2. What does it mean that God's justice demanded that Christ die?
3. What does it mean that God's truth required his death?
4. Why is our death insufficient and the death of the Son of God alone sufficient to pay for sin?
5. What is the fruit of Christ's death in connection with our death, our status before God, and our life?

Q. & A. 41
BURIED

A. NOTES

1. Christ's burial must be accepted for what it was, as this Answer does. Hence, one must also have regard to Jn 19:31-38. If Jesus had just been in a state of suspended animation, there would have been no reconciliation for our sins.

2. But the burial is more than just evidence of his death. It is also an aspect of his humiliation, one to which the sinner, who is told: "you are dust, and to dust you shall return" (Gen 3:19), is directed. Our Surety had to suffer also this galling humiliation.

3. Christ was consciously in the grave. Also there his divine nature was not separated from his human nature (BC, art. 19).

B. QUESTIONS

1. Why was Jesus buried?
2. What else did his burial encompass?

Q. & A. 44
DESCENDED INTO HELL

A. NOTES

1. When it mentions the descent into hell, the Apostles' Creed does not treat this as a fifth step in the humiliation which supposedly came about after Christ's death. Rather, it characterizes all of Christ's suffering when it says that he descended into hell.

2. Jesus did not go to hell after his death. The words on the cross to the murderer and that whereby he commended his spirit to the Father clearly prove it.

3. The Roman Catholics say that Jesus went to hell after his death to redeem the souls of the OT saints from limbo. The Lutherans believe that he went to hell to preach his triumph to the devils. Further, by an erroneous appeal to 1 Pet 3:19-20, it has been asserted that Christ went to hell after his death to preach the gospel to the damned.

4. Christ was never in hell. But he did undergo the suffering which the inhabitants of hell undergo and which make that place "hell." Throughout his time on earth he experienced the wrath of God, for it was directed against him, and on the cross he said himself that God had forsaken him. Christ had to undergo this hellish agony before his death, in order that he could experience it in his *body*. Thus, he suffered inexpressible sorrows. While it is possible for us to understand another person's suffering in part (to understand it fully one has to have undergone the suffering oneself), Christ's suffering is a mystery. We know it only through the revelation of the Word, but even when we accept this revelation in faith, there remain unfathomed depths in that suffering for us.

5. Christ was forsaken by God in all his suffering, so that we might nevermore be forsaken by him and might be assured in our severest temptations that he has delivered us from all hellish agony and pain.

B. COMMENTS

1. Older Bible translations, such as the KJV, often use the word, "hell," in the sense of "Sheol," or "realm of the dead." Thus, *e.g.*, Ps 16:10 (KJV) says: "For thou wilt not leave my soul in hell."

C. QUESTIONS

1. What does the clause "He descended into hell" in the Apostles' Creed signify?
2. Where did Jesus go when he died?
3. Who maintain that he was in hell after his death?
4. When and how did he, then, descend into hell? Why did this have to occur before his death?
5. Can we understand the suffering of Christ? How do we know it?
6. How does his descent into hell benefit us?

THE STATE OF EXALTATION

Lord's Days 17 - 19

A. NOTES

1. In the state of exaltation the Mediator stands justified before God and receives payment for his work from God for himself and his church (Phil 2:9). In Phil 2:8 Paul says that Christ showed complete obedience to the Father, and then v. 9 continues: "THEREFORE God has highly exalted him."

2. In this state we again distinguish four stages (steps): Resurrection, Ascension, Seated at God's right hand, and Return on the clouds.

3. In this state Christ dispenses the salvation, which he earned through his suffering, to those who are his. (See also LD 5-6).

B. QUESTIONS

1. How does the Mediator stand before God in the state of exaltation? What does he receive in this state?

2. What stages do we distinguish in this state? What does the Mediator do in this state?

45. *Q.   How does Christ's resurrection benefit us?*

    A.   First,
           by His resurrection
           He has overcome death,
           so that He could make us share
           in the righteousness
           which He had obtained for us
           by His death.[1]
      Second,
           by His power
           we too are raised up
           to a new life.[2]
      Third,
           Christ's resurrection
           is to us a sure pledge
           of our glorious resurrection.[3]

[1] *Rom. 4:25; I Cor. 15:16-20; I Pet. 1:3-5.*
[2] *Rom. 6:5-11; Eph. 2:4-6; Col. 3:1-4.*
[3] *Rom. 8:11; I Cor. 15:12-23; Phil. 3:20, 21.*

A. NOTES

1. The Catechism immediately asks about the *benefit* of the resurrection and does not speak first about its *fact*. Indeed, it cannot say anything about the *fact*, for the Lord did not permit anyone to witness it.

   In the days when the Catechism was composed, the fact of the resurrection was not denied among Christians. It is different today. Liberal theologians have taught that Jesus did not truly rise from the dead, but that he merely rose in the disciples' imagination. However, this assertion is in direct conflict with the reports of the evangelists. Those who believe the assertion must reject the reports of the evangelists as fantasy or lies.

   It is impossible to maintain that the fact of the resurrection is not so important, but that the idea of the resurrection is what matters. How could a dead Jesus possibly benefit us? His teachings and example are not sufficient for us. We need Christ himself. Paul writes to the church at Corinth (1 Cor 15:17):

   > If Christ has not been raised, your faith is futile.

   It is not our calling to prove the resurrection. God requires us to proclaim it and we must urge the hearers to accept it in faith. It is our task to expose the unsoundness and untenability of the arguments against the resurrection.

2. Acts 1:3 says that Christ presented himself to his apostles alive after his passion by many proofs, appearing to them during forty days. The Scriptures mention the following appearances:

   a. Mary Magdalene (Jn 20:11-18);
   b. The other women (Mt 28:8-10);
   c. Simon Peter (Lk 24:34; 1 Cor 15:5);
   d. The disciples from Emmaus (Lk. 24:13-34);
   e. The disciples without Thomas (Jn 20:19-23);
   f. The disciples with Thomas (Jn 20-29);
   g. At the sea of Tiberias (Jn 21:1-24);
   h. More than 500 brothers (1 Cor 15:6);
   i. James (1 Cor 15:7a);
   j. At the ascension (Acts 1:4-12).

   Further, also: Stephen, Saul, John on Patmos.

3. The Lord arose with the same body with which he had been laid in the grave. But it was changed in quality. It was initially glorified.

4. Scripture speaks not only of Christ rising from the dead, but also of his being raised. The resurrection of Christ was the work of the Triune God. The Father raised him and thereby announced that the Surety had fully satisfied the debt (Rom 4:24). The Son rose himself and thereby powerfully demonstrated that he is the Son of God (Rom 1:4). And the Holy Spirit was also active in the resurrection (Rom 8:11).

5. Christ conquered death through his resurrection. He did not thereby merely escape death for a shorter or longer period (Lazarus), but, having been subject to the power of death, he acquired power over death. His resurrection was, therefore, not a return to this life, but an entry into life eternal.

6. Through his death (*i.e.*, all his suffering) Christ earned our justification. He is able to obtain our justification through his intercession, in which He pleads for our acquittal on the basis of his completed work. He makes us accept our acquittal in faith (*Justification*).

7. Through his power we are raised to a new life. Our old nature was a life of enmity toward God, a life in which we were dead and deaf to God's Word. But the risen Christ raises us to a new life in which we seek the Lord and respond to his Word (*Sanctification*).

8. Finally, Christ's resurrection is a sure pledge for us of our *glorious* resurrection (*Glorification*).

   The resurrection is, therefore, the evidence of our justification, the power of our sanctification and the pledge of our glorification.

B. CROSS REFERENCES

1. BC, art. 19, states that Christ conquered death by his power.
2. BC, art. 20, confesses that God raised Christ "for our justification."

C. QUESTIONS

1. Why does the Catechism not speak about the fact of the resurrection? Is the fact of the resurrection accepted by all who call themselves Christians?
2. What do liberal theologians assert about the resurrection? How do you counter that assertion?
3. Is it important that Christ has in fact risen from the dead?
4. How can we be sure about the fact of the resurrection? Which appearances do you know of?
5. With what kind and what quality of body did Christ rise?
6. How else do the Scriptures speak about the resurrection? Whose work was the resurrection?
7. What did the Father make manifest by raising Christ?

8. Did Christ return to this life as a result of the resurrection?
9. What benefit do we receive from Christ's resurrection? (Name three benefits).

46. Q. *What do you confess when you say,*
       He ascended into heaven?

    A. *That Christ, before the eyes of His disciples,*
       was taken up from the earth into heaven,[1]
       and that He is there for our benefit[2]
       until He comes again
       to judge the living and the dead.[3]
       [1] *Mark 16:19; Luke 24:50, 51; Acts 1:9-11.*
       [2] *Rom. 8:34; Heb. 4:14; 7:23-25; 9:24.*
       [3] *Matt. 24:30; Acts 1:11.*

47. Q. *Is Christ, then, not with us until the end of*
       the world, as He has promised us?[1]

    A. *Christ is true man and true God.*
       With respect to His human nature
       He is no longer on earth,[2]
       but with respect to His divinity, majesty, grace,
       and Spirit He is never absent from us.[3]
       [1] *Matt. 28:20.*
       [2] *Matt. 26:11; John 16:28; 17:11; Acts 3:19-21; Heb. 8:4.*
       [3] *Matt. 28:18-20; John 14:16-19; 16:13.*

48. Q. *But are the two natures in Christ not separated from*
       each other if His human nature is not present
       wherever His divinity is?

    A. *Not at all,*
           for His divinity has no limits
           and is present everywhere.[1]
       So it must follow that His divinity is indeed beyond
           the human nature which He has taken on
           and nevertheless is within this human nature
           and remains personally united with it.[2]
       [1] *Jer. 23:23, 24; Acts 7:48, 49.*
       [2] *John 1:14; 3:13; Col. 2:9.*

49. Q. *How does Christ's ascension into heaven benefit us?*

    A. *First,*
           He is our Advocate in heaven
           before His Father.[1]
       Second,
           we have our flesh in heaven as a sure pledge
           that He, our Head, will also take us,
           His members, up to Himself.[2]
       Third,
           He sends us His Spirit as a counter-pledge,[3]
           by whose power we seek the things that are
           above, where Christ is, seated at the right hand
           of God, and not the things that are on earth.[4]
       [1] *Rom. 8:34; I John 2:1.*
       [2] *John 14:2; 17:24; Eph. 2:4-6.*
       [3] *John 14:16; Acts 2:33; II Cor. 1:21, 22; 5:5.*
       [4] *Col. 3:1-4.*

A. NOTES

1. Just as the Scriptures speak of Christ RISING from the dead and of his BEING RAISED, so it speaks of his ASCENSION and of his BEING TAKEN UP into heaven (Eph 4:8-10; Acts 1:11). Christ's ascension was not an assault on a barred fortress, but a reception into the Father's house, which was opened to him because of his completed work.

2. The ascension of Christ was truly an ascension into heaven. He went from the earth into heaven while his disciples were looking on. We have to describe the ascension so precisely, and the Catechism gives a detailed explanation of it, because the Lutherans deny the reality of the ascension. They believe that although the divine and human natures of the Mediator were not commingled, the characteristics of each were transferred to the other. Just as iron when held in the fire does not become fire but adopts the characteristics of fire in that it becomes hot, so the human nature of Christ, although it did not become divine, is said to have adopted the characteristics of the divine nature. According to the Lutherans, the ascension, therefore, meant that Christ's human nature then became *omnipresent*. They emphasize Jesus' own statement, "I am with you always, to the close of the age" (Mt 28:20), to support their argument. But the Catechism clearly teaches in Answer 47 that the doctrine of the omnipresence of Christ's human nature does not follow ineluctably from that statement. Further, the Lutherans' attempt to demonstrate the incorrectness of Answer 47, by asserting that it teaches a separation of the two natures of Christ, is fully refuted by Answer 48. (At this point, read Answer 47 and 48 carefully).

   This Lutheran doctrine is to be rejected, because it:

   a. leads to a misconception of the Lord's supper in the Lutheran doctrine of consubstantiation, *i.e.*, that Christ is BODILY present in, with and under the symbols of the Lord's supper (see LD 28-30, Note 7); and

   b. derives from the old heresy that that which is mortal is inferior and must first be deified in order that it may be appreciated. But the ascension teaches the exact opposite. (See what follows).

3. In his ascension Christ did not leave the earth and abandon it as something inferior. He did not thereby turn away from the perishable world for ever. On the contrary, he only left for a time. He will return. This was announced right away at the ascension (Acts 1:12), and the Catechism places that in the foreground. The ascension was not an

abandonment of the earth, but the reunion of heaven and earth in principle. It will be followed by the actual, complete reunion on the last day, when the dwelling of God shall be with men (see LD 9, Q&A 26, Note 1). For there is no breach between heaven and earth because heaven is spiritual and the earth perishable, but because there is sin on earth. That is what Christ rejected and for which he atoned. That is why heaven opened for him and why it will open for his entire church because of his redemptive work. Further, he ascended into heaven "for our benefit," that is, to bring about the complete reunion of his church (and therein of the earth) with heaven.

4. That is what the Catechism confesses in its teaching in Answer 49 of the BENEFIT to us of Christ's ascension. It describes this benefit for us in three points:

   a. He is now our Advocate BEFORE HIS FATHER. He has been allowed to approach God's throne in heaven as our ADVOCATE (defence counsel).

      As our Advocate, he demands our acquittal on the basis of *his completed work*. John 17:24a says:

      > Father, I desire that they also, whom thou hast given me, may be with me where I am. . . .

      He is entitled to demand! And Satan, the accuser of the saints, has to be silent before Christ's intercession. What a marvellous benefit of the ascension this is!

   b. In the second and third parts of Answer 49 the Catechism speaks of a pledge and a counter-pledge. To understand this concept, think of a couple who are being married and who give each other rings as pledge and counter-pledge. The man gives the woman the ring as pledge (visible evidence) of his fidelity and receives from her the ring as pledge of her faithfulness. In the same way Christ took a pledge from us, a souvenir (our flesh), and gives us a counter-pledge (his Spirit). He will, being of OUR flesh, always remember us and work on our behalf, and he wants us, through his Spirit, always to think of him and to live for him. The Catechism portrays a wonderfully tender and close relationship in its metaphor of pledge and counter-pledge!

      Christ, therefore, took along our flesh in the ascension. He did not leave it behind, as one leaves one's work boots at the door before entering the house, as if our flesh was not suited to heaven. That is why his ascension IN OUR FLESH is our guarantee that we shall also go there. That is certain, for he is our HEAD. If a swimmer keeps his head above the waves, his body will presently rise above them. Now the waves of sin still wash over us constantly, but our Head is above the waves!

c.   He sends us his Spirit as a counter-pledge. We must not forget Christ. The Spirit teaches us to seek the things that are above. That does not mean that we should escape from the world and withdraw ourselves from life in quiet contemplation. The things that are above are love, holiness, obedience, peace, *etc*. To seek those things here, means being holy and obedient in love and being peacemakers HERE and IN and WITH this life. In that way we do not abandon the world for the sake of heaven and do not forget heaven for the sake of the world, but heaven and earth are united. Col 3:1, 2 says:

> If then you have been raised with Christ, seek the things that are above, where Christ is, seated at the right hand of God. Set your minds on things that are above, not on things that are on earth.

And Jn 16:7 says:

> Nevertheless I tell you the truth: it is to your advantage that I go away, for if I do not go away, the Counselor will not come to you; but if I go, I will send him to you.

(See also Phil 3:20).

B.   CROSS REFERENCES

1.   The BC, art. 26 speaks extensively and with great comfort about Christ's intercession.

C.   QUESTIONS

1.   What other expression does the Bible use in place of ascension, and what does that mean?
2.   What do the Lutherans say about the ascension? On what do they base their opinion?
3.   What passage of Scripture do the Lutherans rely on in support of their opinion?
4.   Does this text lead ineluctably to the Lutheran doctrine? Why not?
5.   Why is it so important to reject the Lutheran doctrine on this point?
6.   Did Christ reject the earth as inferior in the ascension?
7.   Why is there a breach between heaven and earth?
8.   What was obtained in principle in Christ's ascension?
9.   In how many points does the Catechism describe the benefit of the ascension? Name the points.
10. What does Christ do as our Advocate? What is the basis of his defence?
11. What does the Catechism mean when it speaks of pledge and counter-pledge?
12. What pledge did Christ take from us? What does it guarantee?
13. What pledge does he send us? What does it do?
14. What do Col 3:1, 2, and Jn 16:7 and 17:24a, respectively, say?

50. Q. *Why is it added,*
     And sits at the right hand of God?

    A. *Christ ascended into heaven*
       to manifest Himself there
       as Head of His Church,[1]
       through whom the Father governs all things.[2]

       [1] *Eph. 1:20-23; Col. 1:18.*
       [2] *Matt. 28:18; John 5:22, 23.*

51. Q. *How does the glory of Christ, our Head,*
     benefit us?

    A. *First,*
          by His Holy Spirit
          He pours out heavenly gifts
          upon us, His members.[1]
       Second,
          by His power
          He defends and preserves us
          against all enemies.[2]

       [1] *Acts 2:33; Eph. 4:7-12.*
       [2] *Ps. 2:9; 110:1, 2; John 10:27-30; Rev. 19:11-16.*

52. Q. *What comfort is it to you*
     that Christ will come to judge
     the living and the dead?

    A. *In all my sorrow and persecution*
       I lift up my head
       and eagerly await
       as judge from heaven
       the very same person
       who before has submitted Himself
       to the judgment of God
       for my sake,
       and has removed all the curse from me.[1]
       He will cast all His and my enemies
          into everlasting condemnation,
       but He will take me and all His chosen ones
          to Himself
          into heavenly joy and glory.[2]

       [1] *Luke 21:28; Rom. 8:22-25; Phil. 3:20,21; Tit. 2:13, 14.*
       [2] *Matt. 25:31-46, I Thess. 4:16, 17; II Thess. 1:6-10.*

A. NOTES

1. Christ's being seated at the right hand of God is closely related to the ascension, but also distinguishable from it. It points to the PURPOSE of the ascension and tells us its destination. (Of Elijah we read that he went up into heaven, but not that he was seated at God's right hand). Ps 110:1 says:

> The LORD says to my Lord: "Sit at my right hand."

In Acts 7:56 we read of Stephen:

> . . . and he said, "Behold, I see the heavens opened, and the Son of man standing at the right hand of God."

(See also Mt 26:64; 28:18).

2. Among us, to be seated at someone's right hand means to receive the place of honour. That was also the case in the Scriptures. (See 1 Kings 2:19 and Mt 20:21). However, we should not understand the expression, "sits at the right hand of God," in the creed literally. God is a Spirit and, therefore, we can only speak of his hand in a metaphorical sense. We have to understand this expression in accordance with its *intent*. Thus, it means that ALL AUTHORITY and the HIGHEST HONOUR were conferred on Christ.

When Christ says in Mt 28:18, "All authority in heaven and on earth has been given to me," he does not refer to his almighty power, but to all authorities that exist among the angels and the kings and peoples in heaven and on earth.

3. This authority and honour were GIVEN to him, who was first humiliated for our sins, in order that he MANIFEST himself as Head of his Church. He WAS always the Head of the church, but now it becomes apparent. Now he manifests himself to be Head of the church. And the Catechism says that the Father governs all things through HIM. God governs all things (by his providence, see LD 10). But now we learn that God does this THROUGH Christ. All Christ's providential rule is, therefore, for the salvation and glory of his church.

4. In our discussion of the ascension in the previous LD we saw what Christ now does for us in heaven. In this LD we learn that his honour and power in heaven are so great that thereby he rules us and governs all things. He does not only send us his Spirit to draw us to heaven (LD 18), but through the Spirit he also pours out heavenly gifts upon his members here on earth. Thereby he causes them to live according to a *heavenly*

lifestyle here. Heavenly gifts are those which, poured out from heaven, prepare us for heaven: regeneration, sanctification. And from heaven he defends us here on earth by his power against all enemies who seek to withstand him, and he preserves us. (2 Tim 4:17, 18).

B. COMMENTS

1. No person (pope) or assembly (synod) is entitled to presume to place himself or itself over the church. We have one Master: Christ. People and assemblies may only *serve* in the church, and lead the members to acknowledge Christ as the Only Head of the church. The church must, therefore, not be governed by decree, but by instruction, through the declaration of the Word of Christ the King.

2. There was no chair or pew in the temple. A priest was not allowed to sit down at any time. He was never finished with his service, because the blood of goats and bulls did not remove sin. But the only High Priest, Jesus, did finish his service. He was entitled to sit!

C. QUESTIONS

1. What is the distinction between the ascension and Christ's sitting at God's right hand?
2. Prove from the Holy Scriptures that Christ is seated at God's right hand.
3. What does it mean that he sits at God's right hand? What authority did he receive?
4. Why did he receive this authority and honour?
5. How does his being seated at God's right hand benefit us?
6. Who governs the church, therefore, and how must the office bearers govern?

Q. & A. 52
COME, LORD JESUS

A. NOTES

1. Christ's return on the clouds will be visible to everyone (Acts 1:11; Rev 1:7). It will also come suddenly and unexpectedly, as a thief in the night (Mt 24:37, 38). No one knows when it will occur. Mk 13:32 says:

> But of that day or that hour no one knows, not even the angels in heaven, nor the Son, but only the Father.

The Scriptures do describe for us many signs which point to the approach of his return: Wickedness will be multiplied (Mt 24:12); the revelation of the man of lawlessness, the anti-Christ (2 Thess 2:9-12); wars and rumours of wars (Mk 13:7, 8); earthquakes in divers places (Lk 21:25-27); severe persecution of the church (Mt 24:14); preaching of the gospel to all nations (Mt 24:14). These signs are a constant warning to mankind: Behold, he comes!

2. He will come in great glory. Mt 25:31 says:

When the Son of man comes in his glory, and all the angels with him, then he will sit on his glorious throne.

Then heaven and earth will pass away and new heavens and a new earth will appear (2 Pet 3:7-12). But first, the dead will be raised. All the nations will be gathered before him and he shall separate them from each other, as a shepherd separates the sheep from the goats (Mt 25:32). And each person will receive what he has done in the body, whether good or evil (2 Cor 5:10b). The question will then be whether our deeds were done out of *faith*, which unites with Christ.

3. The Catechism only asks about the COMFORT that the article about Christ's return to judge the living and the dead affords us. For Christ's return is the great comfort of the church. Here it is oppressed and the cause which it espouses is reviled and held in contempt. But, says the BC, art. 37 of the faithful and elect:

> ... their cause—at present condemned as heretical and evil by many judges and civil authorities—will be recognized as the cause of the Son of God.

Then (says Answer 52),

> He will cast all His and my enemies
>> into everlasting condemnation,
> but He will take me and all His chosen ones
>> to Himself
>> into heavenly joy and glory.

That is why, says art. 37 of the BC:

> ... the thought of this judgment is horrible and dreadful to the wicked and evildoers, but it is a great joy and comfort to the righteous and elect. For then their full redemption will be completed and they will receive the fruits of their labours and of the trouble they have suffered.

Therefore, the Bride and the Spirit pray, "Come Lord Jesus!" Do we have this longing? He who makes Christ's cause on earth his own has it! But, where the Maranatha prayer is no longer heard, faith is in decline.

B. CROSS REFERENCES

1. Read especially the BC, art. 37, every word of which speaks of the expectant longing of the martyred church.

2. The expectation of the Lord's return is also echoed in the Prayer before Baptism of the Forms for the Baptism of Infants and Adults:

> ... and at the last day may appear without terror before the judgment seat of Christ Thy Son.

C. QUESTIONS

1. How will Christ return? When will he return? Name the signs which precede his return. What do these signs mean?
2. What will Christ do upon his return? According to what will he judge?
3. Why is Christ's return such a comfort for the church?
4. Does the church long for Christ's return?

D. HERESIES

1. MILLENNIALISM. This word derives from the Latin, *mille*, meaning "thousand," and *annus*, meaning "year."[7] It denotes the heresy concerning the thousand year reign of Christ, sometimes known as the "millennium" (see Rev 20:2, 4, 6). Millennialism is quite old and widespread. It is found among the Apostolics, the Russellites (Jehovah's Witnesses), the Mormons, and all kinds of Adventists, but each group has its own concept of the millennium.

    The millennialists teach that Christ will return twice. During his first return he will conquer the anti-christian power; bind Satan; raise the faithful who have died; gather the congregation around him, especially the Jews who have been converted and have been returned to Palestine; rule over the world out of the midst of this congregation; and cause a period of spiritual growth and material prosperity to begin for his people. Some expect that Christ will then reside in Jerusalem, others (the Mormons) that he will govern from Utah, while still others point to heaven as Christ's residence during this time. At the end of the period Christ will return to heaven and Satan will be released. Shortly thereafter, Christ will return the second time. Then ALL people will be raised and the final judgment will take place. Millennialists differ about the details of this heresy (*e.g.* about the duration of the millennium, its commencement, and the place of the Jews in it).

    Millennialists appeal to Scripture, especially the prophets, in support of this heresy. It is not possible for us to consider each of the passages relied on to defend the heresy. It is not necessary either, for the essence of the "evidence" from the Scriptures adduced by millennialists lies in Rev 20. If IT gives us an image of the millennium taught by millennialists, some of the texts they adduce from the prophets could possibly be interpreted in the manner they suggest. But if Rev 20 teaches something different from what the millennialists suppose, their explanations of the several prophesies are baseless.

---

[7]Transl. note: In The Netherlands the preferred name for this heresy is "chiliasm." Hence, in the original, the author explained its derivation from the Greek, *chilios*, meaning "thousand."

Rev 20 does not say that Satan shall be totally powerless on earth for one thousand years, but that he was bound so that he should deceive the NATIONS no more. He has been unable to do that since Christ's exaltation at the right hand of the Father. Since that time we live in the millennium. (1000, *i.e.*, 10 x 10 x 10, is a symbolic number and denotes a long and complete period of time).

Rev 20 also does not say that the elect will reign with Christ ON EARTH after a first resurrection. In Rev 20:4 John does not say that he saw the souls of those who had been beheaded for their testimony to Jesus being RAISED. Rather, he saw them ALIVE (*i.e.*, in heaven) and there they (the souls!) shared in Christ's heavenly reign.

Millennialism is a very dangerous and harmful heresy:

a.   It gives a totally erroneous picture of the relationship between the Old and the New Testament. The New Testament is not the fulfilment of the Old according to millennialism. The Old Testament will only be fulfilled later, during the millennium. For now we are merely marking time. In this manner the proper understanding of the Scriptures is hindered.

b.   It sounds the death-knell for Christian life. According to millennialism Christ has not yet begun to reign. But in truth he is King today and is entitled to be served everywhere. However the millennialists scorn all Christian action. They are content to speak and preach passively.

According to Russell, the father of the Jehovah's Witnesses, Christ did return in 1874 and since 1914-18 we live in the millennium. The invisible presence of Christ on earth is supposedly proved by the many inventions and discoveries which have happened since the beginning of the millennium!

LORD'S DAY 20

53. *Q.* *What do you believe*
    concerning the Holy Spirit?

   A. *First,*
        He is, together with the Father and the Son,
        true and eternal God.[1]
        Second,
        He is also given to me,[2]
        to make me by true faith
        share in Christ and all His benefits,[3]
        to comfort me,[4]
        and to remain with me forever.[5]

[1] *Gen. 1:1, 2; Matt. 28:19; Acts 5:3, 4; I Cor. 3:16.*
[2] *I Cor. 6:19; II Cor. 1:21, 22; Gal. 4:6; Eph. 1:13.*
[3] *Gal. 3:14; I Pet. 1:2.*
[4] *John 15:26; Acts 9:31.*
[5] *John 14:16, 17; I Pet. 4:14.*

GOD THE HOLY SPIRIT AND
OUR SANCTIFICATION
Lord's Days 20 - 24

LORD'S DAY 20

Q. & A. 53

THE COMFORTER

A. NOTES

1. LD 20 brings us to the third part of the Apostles' Creed. It speaks of the Holy Spirit, the third Person of the Triune God (LD 8). Together with the Father and the Son, he is true and eternal God. That is why the creed says, "I believe IN the Holy Spirit." That the Holy Spirit is himself God is evident from the fact that Scripture accords him divine *names* (Acts 5:3, 4), *attributes* (Ps 139:7, 8), *works* (Gen 1:2b), and *honour* (Mt 28:19). (See further the annotations to LD 8).

    He is not merely a power of God, or an influence which proceeds from God, but an independent Person. 1 Cor 2:10 says:

    > For the Spirit searches everything, even the depths of God.

    Further, we can grieve the Holy Spirit (Eph 4:30).

2. This third Person is called SPIRIT, not because he is more spiritual than the Father or the Son, but because of the manner of his existence. For he proceeds like a breath from God and returns to him, just like a person's breath proceeds from him and returns to him. He is called HOLY, not because he is holier than the Father or the Son, but because his special work is the sanctification of all things.

3. The Catechism only speaks of the work of the Holy Spirit in the church, *i.e.*, of his work which is designed to redeem and preserve the Lord's people. But his sphere of operation is much wider than the church. It is he who gives life, and all knowledge and learning is his. Ps 104:30 says:

    > When thou sendest forth thy Spirit, they are created; and thou renewest the face of the ground.

    (See also Ex 31:3).

4. The believer confesses about the Holy Spirit, "*He is also given to me.*" This means, in the first place, that we do not have the Holy Spirit of ourselves. Alas, the spirit of wickedness dwells in our old nature. Further, we cannot earn the Holy Spirit; he must be GIVEN to us.

    How can the confessor say with such certainty that the Spirit *has been* given him? Only through faith in God's promise. For when we were baptised in the Name of the Holy Spirit, the Holy Spirit testified and assured us by that holy sacrament that he would dwell and work in us, and would impart to us what we have in Christ.

5. The Holy Spirit was given to us in order to make us by true faith share in Christ and all his benefits. It is necessary for us to enter into a living communion with Christ, our complete Saviour. That is what the Spirit does, by working faith in us, the faith whereby we are grafted into Christ (LD 7). The Holy Spirit does this through the preaching of the Word (LD 25, Ans. 65), through which he causes us to know ourselves and teaches us to flee to Christ.

6. He COMFORTS us. The word, "comforter," is the same as intercessor, defence counsel, barrister, advocate. Christ is our advocate at the right hand of the Father. There he pleads our cause, pointing to his completed work. The Holy Spirit is our comforter in us. He pleads here with us and, through the Word, points us to Christ's completed sacrifice and to the Father's promise. Thereby, he helps us in our weakness and prays for us (Rom 8:26, 27).

7. He will be with us FOR EVER (Jn 14:16). He can withdraw himself and his gifts from us. He does this when we sin and grieve him (Eph 4:30). The promise that he will be with us for ever was given to us for our comfort and to prevent us from becoming despondent (Ps 51:13).

   The Scriptures also speak about the blasphemy against the Holy Spirit, or the sin against the Holy Spirit. This sin can only be committed by those who were familiar with the gospel. It consists of this that one who knows better resists the gospel and rejects what he knows to be the work of God by calling it the exact opposite. This sin will not be forgiven. It is not followed by repentance. Hence, it may safely be stated as a rule that he who fears that he has committed this sin, has not committed it (Heb 6:4-8; Mt 12:31, 32).

B. CROSS REFERENCES

1. The BC, art. 11 also confesses that the Holy Spirit is true and eternal God.

2. The confessions speak of the work of the Holy Spirit in many places. I draw the following to your attention: CD III/IV, 3, 6, 11, and 16; V, 5 and 6.

3. Also the Forms for Baptism (Doctrine of Baptism) describe the work of the Holy Spirit in their definition of the promise which is sealed in baptism. The Forms refer to: indwelling, cleansing and renewal.

4. The prayer before the Lord's supper in the Forms for the Celebration of the Lord's Supper ask that God work in us through the Holy Spirit.

C. QUESTIONS

1. What does LD 20 say first about the Holy Spirit? How is it evident that the Holy Spirit is himself God? Is he simply a power of God? What is he then? What does Eph 4:30 say?

2. Why is he called Spirit? Why HOLY SPIRIT?

3. Where else, in addition to the church, does the Holy Spirit work? What does he do there?

4. Why must the Spirit be GIVEN to us? For WHAT PURPOSE is he given to us? How can the believer say with certainty that the Spirit has been given him?

5. What does the Holy Spirit do in us? Who is our Advocate in heaven? How does the Holy Spirit comfort us?

6. Can the Holy Spirit depart from God's people? But what does he do? What do you know about the sin against the Holy Spirit?

54. Q. *What do you believe*
concerning the holy catholic Christian church?

A. *I believe that the Son of God,[1]*
out of the whole human race,[2]
from the beginning of the world to its end,[3]
gathers, defends, and preserves for Himself,[4]
by His Spirit and Word,[5]
in the unity of the true faith,[6]
a church chosen to everlasting life.[7]
And I believe that I am[8]
and forever shall remain
a living member of it.[9]

[1] *John 10:11; Acts 20:28; Eph. 4:11-13; Col. 1:18.*
[2] *Gen. 26:4; Rev. 5:9.*
[3] *Is. 59:21; I Cor. 11:26.*
[4] *Ps. 129:1-5; Matt. 16:18; John 10:28-30.*
[5] *Rom. 1:16; 10:14-17; Eph. 5:26.*
[6] *Acts 2:42-47; Eph. 4:1-6.*
[7] *Rom. 8:29; Eph. 1:3-14.*
[8] *I John 3:14, 19-21.*
[9] *Ps. 23:6; John 10:27, 28; I Cor. 1:4-9; I Pet. 1:3-5.*

55. Q. *What do you understand by*
the communion of saints?

A. *First,*
that believers, all and everyone,
as members of Christ
have communion with Him
and share in all His treasures and gifts.[1]
Second,
that everyone is duty-bound
to use his gifts
readily and cheerfully
for the benefit and well-being
of the other members.[2]

[1] *Rom. 8:32; I Cor. 6:17; 12:4-7, 12, 13; I John 1:3.*
[2] *Rom. 12:4-8; I Cor. 12:20-27; 13:1-7; Phil. 2:4-8.*

56. Q. *What do you believe*
concerning the forgiveness of sins?

A. *I believe that God,*
because of Christ's satisfaction,
will no more remember
my sins,[1]
nor my sinful nature,
against which I have to struggle
all my life,[2]
but He will graciously grant me
the righteousness of Christ,
that I may never come into condemnation.[3]

[1] *Ps. 103:3, 4, 10, 12; Mic. 7:18, 19; II Cor. 5:18-21;*
I John 1:7; 2:2.
[2] *Rom. 7:21-25.*
[3] *John 3:17, 18; 5:24; Rom. 8:1, 2.*

A. NOTES

1. The word "church" connotes something that belongs to the Lord. The word probably evokes the idea of "house," so that it is permissible to speak of "The House of God" (see 1 Tim 3:15; 1 Pet 4:17). For that is what the church is, the house of God, the temple which he chose for himself and which he builds. Holy Scripture uses the word "congregation," which is a translation of the Greek word *ekklèsia*. (*Cf.* Fr., *église*). It denotes the gathering of the people called together by the government in olden times, to impart information. The church also has that characteristic. It is a congregation which is called together; it is called by one person (God), while others come to it (the members).

2. You should note that the creed states, "I *believe* the church." It does *not* say, "I believe IN . . . ," but only, "I believe. . . ." Hence, there is a distinction between this article and the preceding ones. In those it said, "I believe IN. . . ." That means, from the Scriptures I *know* and *entrust* myself to God the Father, the Son and the Holy Spirit. We do not entrust ourselves to the church, nor do we rely on her. But we do *believe* the church, that is, we know it only from the *Word*.

3. The Word of the Lord always speaks in terms of promise and demand, in accordance with the two parts of the covenant. It speaks that way about the church, too.

   The church is *promised* to us and *demanded* of us. The Bible tells us what God will do in respect of the church *and* what he demands of us in respect of the church.

   God's promise concerning the church is that he chooses it, redeems it by his Son, and sanctifies it through his Spirit. (Isa 43:1-3; Mt 16:18; Jn 10:28-30). His demand is that we maintain the unity of the church and serve its preservation and increase in all our words and actions. (Eph 4:1-5; Rom 12:10). The Catechism speaks mainly about God's promise concerning the church. That promise is also confessed in art 27 of the BC. Articles 28-9 of the BC discuss God's demand in detail. Article 28 states that everyone is obliged to join the true church, while art. 29 discusses the distinction between the true and false church.

4. The BC uses two words for the church. Article 28 says, "this holy ASSEMBLY and CONGREGATION is the assembly of the redeemed and there is no salvation outside of it." Thus, it calls the church a CONGREGATION (L.: *congregatio*), or gathering, for Christ gathers the believers; he brings them together (collects them) as one flock (*cf.*, *e.g.*, a stamp COLLECTION). But this CONGREGATION is also an ASSEMBLY (L.: *coetus*), *i.e.*, a meeting. Those, whom Christ gathers, also assemble; they *come together*; they seek each other. The Word of the Lord motivates them to do so.

5. It is beautiful and deserves our attention that the Catechism begins its description of the church by pointing to the Son of God, our Lord Jesus Christ. For it is he

145

who gathers, defends and governs the church. God has anointed him as king over Zion (Ps 2:6). Thus, no true communion with the church is possible without communion with Christ. Article 27 of the BC says that the church is "a holy congregation and assembly of the true Christian believers." True, the church contains hypocrites (those who pretend, like actors in a play). But although they are *in* the church, they are not *of* (part of) the church. (They are like gall stones which are in the body and are nourished by it, but do not belong to it). With the church, therefore, we must always look to Christ. He is its strength, its King. That is why, also for the church, we may expect all things from him, who has been given all power in heaven and on earth. We must always ask what his will is. If we do that, the church will be gathered and defended "automatically." If everyone did that, the unity of the church would be maintained properly. That unity is not maintained properly now, partly because of our defective insight into the truth, but more especially because men do not put their trust solely in Christ and do not seek exclusively what his Word demands.

The Catechism also says that Christ gathers a church "for Himself." He gathers it for his own, for the church is his. That is why we must always ask what the Lord's will is in all things concerning the church.

6. Christ gathers his church from the beginning of the world to its end. His church gathering work comprehends several dispensations (See Introduction, D, 4). Further, he gathers the church out of the whole human race, from all tribes and peoples and tongues (Rev 7:9). And he gathers it by his Spirit, who makes use of the Word (Acts 16:14). That is how he gathers the congregation which is chosen to everlasting life! The church's destination is life eternal. The church will reach that destination, because it was chosen for life eternal (Rom 8:29). The church's *source* is God's election.

7. Christ, who gathers his church, also *defends and preserves* it. That does not mean that it will always have a peaceful existence. The church has been called to struggle and to bear the cross and it was foretold the church that it would face persecution in the world. But despite all the fury of the enemy, Christ will not let it succumb (see BC, art. 27). Further, he will not neglect to provide the church with everything necessary to permit it to persevere in faith (2 Tim 4:17, 18).

8. In the last words of the answer the Catechism teaches us that there are two kinds of members, *living* and *dead* members. The latter, too, are members; otherwise they could not be excommunicated. They are dead branches on the vine. The last sentence of the answer, "And I believe that I am and forever shall remain a living member of it," makes it clear that this also forms part of our faith, just as much as the first sentence. That it why it repeats the words "I believe." Only in faith do I know that I am a living member of the church. And in that faith I also know that I shall forever remain a member of it. This knowledge should not lead us to complacency and carelessness, but is meant for our consolation and encouragement. (Read the fifth chapter of the CD carefully on this point).

9. The church is *one*. Article 27 of the BC says:

> . . . it is joined and united with heart and will, in one and the same Spirit, by the power of faith.

The Catechism says that the church is gathered "in the unity of the true faith" (Eph 4:4-6; Jn 17:21). The church EXISTS, in Christ, and through the Holy Spirit. And we are commanded to MAINTAIN the unity of the church. (See BC, art. 28). We may not be content to be by ourselves, but are obliged to join it and to submit ourselves to its instruction and discipline; we must bow our necks under Christ's yoke.

10. The church is *holy*. Article 27 of the BC says:

> . . . [its members] are washed by [Christ's] blood, and are sanctified and sealed by the Holy Spirit.

That does not mean that they are perfect. Article 29 of the BC says:

> Although great weakness remains in them, they fight against it by the Spirit all the days of their life. They appeal constantly to the blood, suffering, death, and obedience of Jesus Christ, in whom they have forgiveness of their sins through faith in Him.

(See also Eph 5:25-27).

11. The church is *catholic* (universal), for it is gathered out of all nations, and from all ranks and stations (Rev 7:9; BC, art. 27, penultimate sentence).

12. The church is *Christian*. Article 31 of the BC says that Christ is "the only universal Bishop and the only Head of the Church." (See further, Col 1:18; Eph 2:20-22). An assembly which does not recognize and maintain Christ's exclusive kingship, is not the church.

B. CROSS REFERENCES

1. CD II, 9, confesses that the church has always existed and will always exist.

2. See also the Form for the Public Profession of Faith, questions 1 and 4.

C. QUESTIONS

1. What do the words "church" and "congregation," respectively, mean? What is the difference between "I believe" and "I believe IN"? Why do we say, "I BELIEVE the church"?

2. What else must we distinguish concerning the church as it is described in Scripture?

3. What is God's promise for the church? What is his demand?

4. What aspect of the church does the Catechism address primarily? Which art. of the BC also confesses this? What is the subject matter of art. 28 and 29, respectively, of the BC?

5. Which two expressions does the BC use to describe the church? What is the distinction between them?

6. Who is the King of the church? Is true communion in the church possible if there is no communion with Christ?

7. What are hypocrites? Are they IN the church, or OF it? What is the difference?

8. During which time period does Christ gather his church? Out of what does he gather it? By what means does he gather it? What is the church's destination? What is its source?

9. What else does Christ do besides GATHERING his church? What does that mean?
10. What kinds of members are there? How do you know that you are a living member of the church and that you will forever remain a living member? Which chapter of the CD speaks about the perseverance of the saints?
11. What is the basis of the unity of the church? What is our duty with respect to this unity?
12. What does it mean that the church is holy? Is it also perfect?
13. What is the significance of calling the church "catholic"?
14. What does it mean that the church is called "Christian"?

Q. & A. 54 (Part II)
CHURCH AND CHURCHES?

A. NOTES

1. When people discuss the church, they are apt to use various terms which are *not used* by the confession, and which we should also avoid. For although each of these terms denotes something that is true about the church, their use has caused several misconceptions about the church. We shall discuss the terms here in order to point out and reject the errors connected with them.

2. For example, people speak of the church MILITANT, TRIUMPHANT and FUTURE. There is some truth in this distinction, provided one does not over emphasize it. The church does, indeed, have to FIGHT against Satan, the world and the corrupt nature of its members, but it is also already entitled to boast: "In all these things we are more than conquerors" (Rom 8:37). Further, the church in heaven is TRIUMPHANT, having CONQUERED, but also in heaven the members of the church continue to pray for Christ's *complete* victory (Rev 6:10). Speaking about the CHURCH TO COME also has merit, in that it reminds us of the fact that those already sanctified and those who presently believe do not together form the entire church. Others will still be added to it. That is why the Catechism says that the Son of God GATHERS, DEFENDS and PRESERVES his church, and uses the present tense for all three verbs. Christ does this today and continues to do it. Hence, the church is still NASCENT (in the process of becoming). No one can as yet survey it in its entirety. That will only be possible when the last of the elect has been glorified. For the time being, the church is still like a house that is being built. You can see part of it, but not the whole.

    The church MILITANT, TRIUMPHANT and TO COME are, therefore, not three churches, but three parts of the same church. No communion is possible between the first and the second, but the first must imitate the second's faith whereby it conquered. Further, the first must preserve this faith for the last.

3. Also used is the distinction between the VISIBLE and INVISIBLE church, and it has caused a lot of harm. It is true that there is much about the church that is INVISIBLE and much that is VISIBLE, just as a watch has an invisible part, the movement, and a visible, the face. Thus, *e.g.*, the church's extent and its faith are INVISIBLE, while its confession and walk of life are VISIBLE. The problem is that some people severed the one concept from the other to some extent. They would say, for example: What really counts is that we are members of the invisible

church. (This is, in fact, an absurdity. How can an *assembly of people* be invisible?) These people were of the opinion that the word "gathers" in the Catechism refers to the visible church, while the expression "forever shall remain a . . . member . . . " refers to the invisible church. But neither the Catechism, nor the BC recognizes the distinction.

4. Another distinction that is used is the one between the church as INSTITUTE and as ORGANISM. True, the church is a living organism. It is a BODY and we are its MEMBERS. But it also exists as an INSTITUTION, an established body. Thus, for example, it is governed by the established offices. But here, too, the problem was that some people severed the two concepts. Thus, it is sometimes said that although we are not one in the institute, we are one in the organism. But those who argue in that manner readily become apathetic toward the institute. That happens a lot, but is to be condemned.

5. Therefore (since the Confession does NOT teach it anywhere), we reject every distinction between THE CHURCH and *the churches*, by which is meant: THE CHURCH is spread over all *churches*, even though THE CHURCH may be represented to a greater or lesser degree in the different churches. This theory is called the doctrine of PLURIFORMITY,[8] which holds that THE CHURCH is revealed in MANY FORMS in all *churches*. It is true that the life of the church is pluriform. Thus, there are differences between city and country churches, large and small churches, rich and poor churches, and old and new churches. But when churches are not a unity, contradict each other, and refuse to enter into ecclesiastical fellowship with each other, there is not a pluriform manifestation of the one church.

   Dr. A. Kuyper, one of the most ardent defenders of this theory, acknowledged that the confession does not recognize it. The theory is particularly objectionable because it proceeds from the ACTUAL situation, instead of the Word only, and because it accords a certain legitimacy to the sin of disunity. That is why this theory is unable to promote the unity of the church and paralyses the church in the exercise of discipline. Further, the theory of pluriformity opened and continues to open the way to present-day ecumenism.

6. The confession does not speak of more or less pure churches like the theory of pluriformity, but speaks "of the body and the communion of the true Church which must be distinguished from all sects that call themselves the Church" (BC, art. 29). Article 29 of the BC also states:

   > We believe that we ought to discern diligently and very carefully from the Word of God what is the true Church, for all sects which are in the world today claim for themselves the name of Church.

   Article 29 further defines the marks of the true church as follows:

   a. "It practices the pure preaching of the gospel" [*i.e.*, without adding to it or subtracting from it];

---

[8]Transl. note: More commonly known as the doctrine of denominationalism on the North American continent.

b. "It maintains the pure administration of the sacraments as Christ has instituted them" [hence, in such a manner and to such persons as Christ commands]; and

c. "It exercises Church discipline for correcting and punishing sins."

In short, it governs itself according to the pure Word of God, *rejecting all things contrary to it* and regarding Jesus Christ as the only Head. (Emphasis supplied)

These marks can sometimes be applied in greater or lesser degree to groups which separate themselves improperly from the church and which are not, therefore, THE TRUE CHURCH, whilst they remain needlessly separate and apart and refuse to practice true communion. You should now look up the marks of the false church in art. 29.

There can be believers in the false church, as well as ministers who wish to preach the gospel. But art. 28 of the BC states that their calling, in accordance with the Word of God, then is to separate themselves from those who are not of the church and to join themselves to the true (faithful) church, wherever God has instituted it. When believers neglect to follow this prescribed course, they cause untold spiritual damage to themselves and confuse those of little faith who are blinded by the number of believers.

B. QUESTIONS

1. Can one recommend the use of the various terms people employ in speaking about the church which do not appear in the confessions? Why not?

2. What do the terms, church militant, triumphant and to come, mean? Can they be accepted as absolutes? Why not? What is the relationship between these three parts of the church? Can one survey the church?

3. What is visible of the church? What is invisible? Why is the term "invisible church" really an absurdity? What problem does the use of the terms "visible church" and "invisible church" cause?

4. What does it mean that the church is a living organism? What does it mean that it exists as an institution? What problem does the use of the terms "church as organism" and "church as institute" promote?

5. What does the doctrine of pluriformity teach? Does it derive from the confession? Is the life of the church not pluriform? In what way is it pluriform?

6. Does the confession speak about more or less pure churches? How does it distinguish between churches? What are the marks of the true church? What is the duty of those who are in the false church?

Q. & A. 54 (Part III)
HOW WE SHOULD CONDUCT OURSELVES IN GOD'S HOUSE

A. NOTES

1. Articles 30-32 of the BC speak about the government of the church. The only King of the church is Christ, who rules it by his Spirit and Word and by means of the offices in the church. Hence, the office bearers do not have a sovereign, but only a serving authority. They do not govern by force, but by instruction.

Their function is not to subject the believers to themselves, but to Christ and his Word.

2. The offices are:

   a. The EXTRAORDINARY offices of apostles, prophets and evangelists, which were instituted in the early years of the church for its establishment.

   b. the ORDINARY offices, which are still maintained and must continue (see LD 12, Q&A 32, Note 5.b):

     i. Ministers or pastors, who preach the Word of God and administer the sacraments (1 Tim 5:17).

     ii. Elders, who govern the church with the ministers (Acts 20:28).

     iii. Deacons, who practice the work of mercy.

3. The officers together form the council (or consistory) of the church (BC, art. 30; CO, art. 38). That is how Christ has regulated the *local* government of his church. (See Rev 1-3).

The consistory is the only *governing* authority in the church. The several local churches are required to enter into a federation with each other, but the major assemblies, that is, the *assemblies* in which delegates of local churches come together, are not higher forms of government. Nor are they meetings of officers of the church.

Two delegates (minister and elder) of each of a number of local churches meet as a Classis once every three months. Delegates of the classes meet as a Regional Synod once a year. Delegates of the regional synods meet as a General Synod once every three years. The decisions of a major assembly shall be considered settled and binding by the churches, UNLESS they are proved to be in conflict with the Word of God or with the Church Order (CO, art. 31). The Church Order, together with the Three Forms of Unity, form the accord for the federation of the churches.

4. Every active member of the church ought to be familiar with the Church Order. It is desirable that every member own a simple explanation of the Church Order.

B. CROSS REFERENCES

1. See the Forms for the Ordination (or Installation) of Ministers of the Word and of Missionaries, and for the Ordination of Elders and Deacons.

C. HERESIES

1. PLYMOUTH BRETHREN ("the Brethren," as they call themselves, or Darbyites, after their spiritual father, J.N. Darby). These do not accept the special offices in the church. Whoever of them feels moved (by the Holy Spirit, so they say), will lead in the preaching and the administration of the sacraments.

2. SALVATION ARMY. Apart from the fact that this sect promotes Arminian and other heresies, it is structured as a self-willed organization in which the sacraments are despised. The sect recognizes neither baptism nor the Lord's supper.

3. CATHOLIC APOSTOLIC CHURCH (or Irvingites). These believe that they must continue to maintain the office of apostle. Further, their most recent group (there

are three or four groupings within the sect) teaches that Christ has again appeared to their apostles in the flesh and that those apostles speak the word of God. (The Bible is a dated book for them).

4. HIERARCHY. This is found particularly in the Roman church. In that church, one office is subjected to the next, so that the offices form a pyramid which culminates in the Pope as the highest ruler of the church.

5. CAESAROPAPISM. This was found in the Greek church. In that church, Caesar (emperor, the worldly power) ruled as a pope.[9]

6. CONGREGATIONALISM (or independentism). It rejects a federation of churches. In so far as its adherents still have assemblies of delegates of the churches, they regard the decisions of the assemblies as having an advisory character only.

7. ECUMENICAL MOVEMENT. This movement accepts every organization which calls itself church and was established to organize all "churches" into a world church. (World Council of Churches (W.C.C.)). Other ecumenical organizations include the International Council of Christian Churches (I.C.C.C., which maintains that it is true to the Bible), and the Reformed Ecumenical Council (R.E.C., formerly, Reformed Ecumenical Synod).

D. COMMENTS: THE HISTORY OF THE CHURCH

The history of the church is a process of deformation and reformation. Under Rome's rule, the church became terribly deformed (adoration of the saints, papal mass, doctrine of good works, position of the pope). But in the beginning of the 16th century, God, in his faithfulness, granted the great Reformation (Luther, Calvin). In the Netherlands the Reformation achieved its zenith in the Synod of Dort of 1618-19. Thereafter, the church relapsed and degenerated. In 1816 King Willem I chained the church to the state. After that, people were free to teach what they wished in the church. The Lord gave a new Reformation in 1834 by means of the Secession, which began in Ulrum. Its leaders were: Hendrik de Cock, Simon van Velzen, Anth. Brummelkamp, H. Scholte. The Secession did not create a new church. Rather, it caused a return to the old doctrine and church polity and the church again became faithful, although many rejected the Secession. In 1886 a second secession, or "Doleantie," ocurred under the leadership of Dr. A. Kuyper and Dr. F.L. Rutgers. In 1892 the two groups united to form the Reformed Churches in the Netherlands. A small part of the church of 1834 did not join in the union, but continued as the "Christelijke Gereformeerde Kerk."[10] At first, the church flourished, but soon it again relapsed and deformed. The Synods of 1939-44 violated the principle of Christian freedom by binding the believers to a doctrine (presumptive regeneration) which cannot be proved from the Scriptures. Already in 1946 the so-called "Replacement Formula" was substituted for the doctrine. Synod no longer dared to accept the doctrine of presumptive regeneration, although it continued to impose it. Synod

---

[9]Transl. note: *Cf.* also the Church of England, of which the Queen is the titular head.

[10]Transl. note: The "Free Reformed Churches" on the North American continent.

"set aside" the Replacement Formula in 1959, but did not revoke it and continued to recommend it. Further, the Synods ascribed to themselves an authority which exceeded the authority of the Word (synodocracy).[11] In the Liberation of 1944, the Lord in his grace immediately granted repentance of these sins. Like the Secession, the Liberation did not establish a new church.[12] Everyone should make further study of the history of the church!

E. QUESTIONS

1. Who is the only King of the church? How does he govern it? What kind of authority do the office bearers have and how must they exercise it?

2. What do you know about extraordinary offices? Which are the ordinary offices?

3. How did Christ regulate the government of his church? Is it necessary that there be major assemblies? Which major assemblies do you know about? How often do they assemble? What authority do their decisions have?

4. What do the Plymouth Brethren, the Salvation Army, and the Catholic Apostolic Church, respectively, teach? What are hierarchy, caesaropapism and ecumenism?

5. What happened at the beginning of the 16th century? What happened, respectively, in 1618-19, 1834, 1886, 1892, and 1944? Who were the leaders of the Secession and of the Doleantie?

Q. & A. 55
YOU ARE EACH OTHER'S MEMBERS

A. NOTES

1. You must take careful note of the fact that the doctrine of the communion of "saints" is part of the doctrine of the church. In the Apostles' Creed you will not find a semicolon between the "church" and the "communion of saints," but a comma. These are two sides of the same coin. The church, which we believe, is the communion of saints.

2. The saints are the members of the church (see LD 21, Q&A 54, part I, note 10).

3. Their privilege is that they all share in Christ's TREASURES AND GIFTS. Their calling is to use those gifts READILY and CHEERFULLY for the BENEFIT and WELL-BEING of the other members.

4. He who thinks that the communion of saints can be practised properly whilst paying no heed to the church, is sorely misguided.

B. CROSS REFERENCES

1. Article 28 of the BC acknowledges that all and everyone are obliged to join the church and to

---

[11]Transl. note: The Christian Reformed Church in North America chose the side of these synodical churches.

[12]Transl. note: Immigrants from the liberated Reformed Churches in the Netherlands established the Canadian (American) Reformed Churches.

... serve the edification of the brothers and sisters, according to the talents which God has given them as members of the same body.

2. See also the Form for the Celebration of the Lord's supper (Fellowship).

C. QUESTIONS

1. Is the communion of saints something different than the church?
2. Who are the saints that are referred to?
3. What is their privilege? What is their duty?

Q. & A. 56
PEACE WITH GOD

A. NOTES

1. The Catechism discusses the forgiveness of sins in LD's 15, 23 and 51. In this Q&A this subject is portrayed especially as the benefit which God gives to his church. (See also the Compendium,[13] Q&A 42: "What benefits does God give to this congregation? He grants it forgiveness of sins, resurrection of the body and eternal life"). We can also point to art. 28 of the BC, which states that outside of the church there is no salvation. That does not mean that no one can be saved outside the church, but that SALVATION (health) is not found outside the church and no one may EXPECT it outside the church.

2. Only God can forgive sin. We will not get rid of it by discussing it with someone. That may give relief, but not forgiveness. You have to ask for and receive forgiveness of God!

3. When God forgives sin, he does not impute it to us and forgets it. Forgiveness is possible because he himself paid for the debt of sin through Christ, FOR THE SAKE OF CHRIST'S SATISFACTION.

4. God forgives ALL OUR SINS and *our sinful nature*, against which we have to struggle all our lives. There is no forgiveness without this struggle. For the struggle is the mark of our repentance and evidence of the genuineness of the prayer for forgiveness. Ps 32:2 says:

> Blessed is the man to whom the LORD imputes no iniquity, and in whose spirit there is no deceit.

B. QUESTIONS

1. Why is the forgiveness of sins discussed in this context? Where else does the Catechism discuss it? What does it mean that there is no salvation outside the church?
2. Who, only, can forgive?
3. What does the verb "to forgive" mean? How can the righteous God forgive sins?
4. What does God forgive?
5. What does Ps. 32:2 say?

---

[13]Transl. note: See LD 2, Q&A 4, footnote 2, *supra*.

57. *Q.* *What comfort does*
the resurrection of the body
offer you?

   A. *Not only shall my soul*
       after this life
       immediately be taken up
       to Christ, my Head,[1]
   but also this my flesh,
       raised by the power of Christ,
       shall be reunited with my soul
       and made like Christ's glorious body.[2]

      [1] Luke 16:22; 23:43; Phil. 1:21-23.
      [2] Job 19:25, 26; I Cor. 15:20, 42-46, 54; Phil. 3:21; I John 3:2.

58. *Q.* *What comfort do you receive*
from the article about
the life everlasting?

   A. *Since I now already*
   feel in my heart
   the beginning of eternal joy, [1]
   I shall after this life
   possess perfect blessedness,
   such as no eye has seen,
   nor ear heard,
   nor the heart of man conceived —
   a blessedness in which to praise God forever.[2]

      [1] John 17:3; Rom. 14:17; II Cor. 5:2, 3.
      [2] John 17:24; I Cor. 2:9.

A. NOTES

1. In this LD the church confesses the benefits which the Lord will give to it after this life. Hence, it is linked closely to the preceding LD.

2. At death, soul and body are separated. But this will not continue for ever. Hence, one can speak of an "interim state," *i.e.* for the period between death and resurrection. Scripture does not say much about this interim state. It directs our attention mostly to Christ's return. Then will come about that which will remain for ever. But we can say about the interim state that at death the soul receives a *preliminary* salvation or judgment, while the body will decompose.

3. The soul of the believer will IMMEDIATELY be taken up to Christ, our Head, after death. The child of the Lord closes his eyes here on earth when he dies, but re-opens them immediately in glory (see Lk 16:22, 23). Rev 14:13 says:

   Blessed are the dead who die in the Lord HENCEFORTH.

   My soul will then be taken up to Christ, MY HEAD. It was already joined to him. It already shared in his life and that will then continue fully. The dead-weight of sin of this life will fall away. The body of sin will fall away (Phil 1:23).

4. The body is committed to the grave. When Christ returns, he will raise it. (Jn 5:27-29). We are unable to comprehend the idea of the resurrection of the body. It has been denied and ridiculed from of old. The Catechism says that it happens "by *the power of Christ.*" That is our "explanation." His resurrection is our guarantee. (See LD 17, Answer 45, 3rd part). Our FLESH, our own bodies in which we lived, will rise (BC, art. 37), but with totally different, glorified qualities. Then it will be completely a suitable tool of the soul. In 1 Cor 15 Paul describes the difference between our present body and our glorified body in the following contrasting terms: perishable/imperishable; dishonour/glory; weakness/power; physical/spiritual; mortal/immortal. "Spiritual" does not mean that the resurrected body will not be physical, but that it will be completely subservient to the spirit, and be suited to the life of glory. Then it will no longer need food and there will be no marriage any more. For that which changes and grows will then be exchanged for that which is eternally complete. (1 Cor 6:13; Mt 22:30).

   Scripture also speaks about the resurrection of the ungodly. They shall awaken to shame and everlasting contempt (Dan 12:2), and to "the

157

resurrection of judgment" (Jn 5:29). The curse will then continue fully in their bodies. This resurrection is not "by the power of Christ," but in consequence of God's righteousness and truth. Through this resurrection they will not inherit eternal life, but eternal death.

B. COMMENTS

1. No serious person believes that everything is finished at death. The nature of our present life is too provisional to give such a belief credence.

2. Cremation, formerly forbidden, is of heathen origin and does not become those who live in the expectation of faith.

C. HERESIES

1. The doctrine of the sleep of the soul (psychopannychy).

2. The Roman Catholic doctrine of purgatory.

3. Spiritism.

4. Reincarnation.

D. QUESTIONS

1. What is the subject matter of this Lord's Day as compared to the preceding one?

2. What happens at death? Will that continue?

3. What do we know about the "interim state"?

4. Does the Bible say a lot about it? To what does it direct our attention principally? Why?

5. What happens to the soul of a believer when he dies?

6. How is that possible? What does Rev 14:13 say?

7. What happens to the body at death? What happens to the body when Christ returns?

8. What is our guarantee for the resurrection of the body?

9. How will our body be raised? What is a spiritual body?

10. What does the Bible say about the resurrection of the ungodly? Do they come to life through their resurrection?

Q. & A. 58
I LIVE AND YOU SHALL LIVE

A. NOTES

1. Life eternal is not the life of today extended in eternity. That would be "nothing less than a constant death" (Forms for the Baptism of Infants and of Adults, Prayer before Baptism). Rather, it is the *true*, the real life! It awaits us after this life. No one can describe what it will be. No eye has seen it, no matter how much beauty it has observed; no ear has heard it, even though it may have heard many beautiful sounds; and whatever the heart of man can conceive, it has not been able to comprehend life eternal (1 Cor 2:9). We can only say: No hunger, No thirst, No troubles, No sorrow. But what positive things can we say about it?

2. Immediately after death the soul enters eternal life. But it is received into that life only in a preliminary and interim way. Only when the body also receives eternal life and the number of the multitude of the redeemed is full, will eternal life commence in complete joy. Then it will be enjoyed on a new earth where the tabernacle of God will be with men (Rev 21:3). The Bible uses many metaphors to teach us something about the wonder of this bliss. Then we shall KNOW God. And then we shall know his works; no longer in part, but we shall see them in all their beauty. And it will be a state in which we shall praise and glorify God. That is also why we shall receive it.

3. Although all the redeemed will be saved, so that none of them will have any feelings of want, there will a difference in their glory. When we fill ten unequal glasses with water, then they are all full (saved), but one glass contains more water than the other (difference in glory). Thus, one person will have a wider and richer knowledge of God and his glory than the other. That is how God "rewards" (LD 24, Q. 63).

4. The believer already enjoys inexpressible joy in the service of the Lord in this life. This is a service of love for him and the gospel of the forgiveness of sins enlarges his heart and fills him with joy. Ps 26:5 (rhymed version) says:

> Thy praise will I record.
> I love Thy house, O LORD,
> The place where all Thy glories dwell. . . .

This joy is but a beginning. It will grow into the eternal joy. He who misses the beginning, will not inherit the fullness.

5. Holy Scripture also speaks about the eternal death of the wicked. (Mt 24:21; 25:30; Lk 13:28; Rev 19:20). Just as in the case of eternal life, so also in respect of eternal death, the Bible speaks in metaphors, such as "lake of fire" and "outer darkness." Also in this eternal death there will be differences in the degree of suffering. (Mt 11:20-24; and see especially Lk 12:47, 48; and LD 4, Q&A 11).

B. HERESIES

1. The doctrine of conditional immortality.

C. QUESTIONS

1. Is eternal life an everlasting continuation of this life?
2. What can you say about it?
3. When does the believer receive it initially? When completely? For what purpose does he receive it?
4. Will there be differences in life eternal? In what respect?
5. What does the believer enjoy already in this life?
6. How does the Bible speak about eternal death? Who will receive the heaviest punishment?

59. Q. *But what does it help you*
now that you believe all this?

    A. *In Christ I am righteous before God*
and heir to life everlasting.[1]
    [1] *Hab. 2:4; John 3:36; Rom. 1:17; 5:1, 2.*

60. Q. *How are you righteous before God?*

    A. *Only by true faith in Jesus Christ.*[1]
Although my conscience accuses me
    that I have grievously sinned
    against all God's commandments,
    have never kept any of them,[2]
    and am still inclined to all evil,[3]
yet God, without any merit of my own,[4]
    out of mere grace,[5]
    imputes to me
    the perfect satisfaction,
    righteousness, and holiness of Christ.[6]
He grants these to me
    as if I had never had nor committed
    any sin,
    and as if I myself had accomplished
    all the obedience
    which Christ has rendered for me,[7]
    if only I accept this gift
    with a believing heart.[8]
    [1] *Rom. 3:21-28; Gal. 2:16; Eph. 2:8, 9; Phil. 3:8-11.*
    [2] *Rom. 3:9, 10.*
    [3] *Rom. 7:23.*
    [4] *Deut. 9:6; Ezek. 36:22; Tit. 3:4, 5.*
    [5] *Rom. 3:24; Eph. 2:8.*
    [6] *Rom. 4:3-5; II Cor. 5:17-19; I John 2:1, 2.*
    [7] *Rom. 4:24, 25; II Cor. 5:21.*
    [8] *John 3:18; Acts 16:30, 31; Rom. 3:22.*

61. Q. *Why do you say*
that you are righteous
only by faith?

    A. *Not that I am acceptable to God*
    on account of the worthiness of my faith,
for only the satisfaction, righteousness,
    and holiness of Christ
    is my righteousness before God.[1]
I can receive this righteousness
    and make it mine my own
    by faith only.[2]
    [1] *I Cor. 1:30, 31; 2:2.*
    [2] *Rom. 10:10; I John 5:10-12.*

OUR JUSTIFICATION

A. NOTES

1. Question 59 asks about the benefit of faith. How does it help you? How does it benefit you? What advantage does it give you? This is not the same as the *fruit* of faith. The fruits of faith are good works. Our justification is not brought about by faith (fruit); it is the fruit of God's redemptive work in Christ, the fruit of the cross. But it is obtained in faith (benefit). Hence, faith is not in vain and is not worthless. But it does not give what the unrepentant sinner seeks: riches, pleasure and honour. That is why he regards it as worthless and says that it does not pay to serve God. But that is not true. Faith produces a rich benefit, namely, that IN CHRIST I AM RIGHTEOUS BEFORE GOD AND HEIR TO LIFE EVERLASTING.

2. To be righteous before God means that he holds us as righteous; we are accounted as righteous by him, and are regarded as such by him. In other words, it means that he acquits us and exonerates us of our guilt. To make righteous, therefore, does not mean that evil is made good and the crooked straight (sanctification). Rather, just as the verb "make" in the verbal phrase "to make great" means to recognise and praise someone as great, so also "to make righteous" (or, "just") means to recognize someone as righteous and declare him to be righteous or just. Thus, "to make righteous" is the opposite of to damn, or to judge. (See Prov 17:15). And it means to exonerate. God acquits us (that is the benefit of faith) of our guilt. And he makes us entitled to eternal life (as heirs). True, we do not yet enjoy eternal life, but our right to it is guaranteed and we shall in due course receive our inheritance. Thus, Ps 32:2 rightly says:

   BLESSED is the man to whom the LORD imputes no iniquity.

3. This benefit of the acquittal is a juridical act on God's part. It is easiest to understand if you think of a court of justice. That is how Answer 60 points out the benefit to us. And the entire Bible speaks about it in these terms. Zion is set free by justice. Justice saves!

   God is the Judge. The sinner is the accused. The prosecutors are the devil and the sinner's conscience. Christ is counsel for the defence (advocate). The law of the LORD is the applicable law (Criminal Code).

The prosecutor brings three counts against the accused:

a.   The accused has GRIEVOUSLY sinned against ALL God's commandments.

b.   He has kept none of the commandments.

c.   He is STILL INCLINED to ALL evil (he is a recidivist).

It can not be any worse. And we expect the strongest condemnation and judgment. That is what we deserve. But counsel for the defence now appears and he responds as follows to the three-fold accusation:

a.   I have borne ALL the punishment in the place of the accused.

b.   I fulfilled ALL commandments in his place.

c.   I place my holiness over against his evil and cover it thereby.

And then God grants us that completed work of Christ and imputes it to us. Thus we are acquitted and become entitled to eternal life. Now read that beautiful Answer 60 of the Catechism!

4.   This righteousness is complete. It is as if I had never had sin (original sin), nor committed any sin (actual sin). Indeed, it is as if I myself had accomplished all the obedience which Christ has rendered for me. And this happens without any merit on my part, solely out of grace. Rom 3:23, 24 says:

> Since all have sinned and fall short of the glory of God, they are justified by his grace as a gift, through the redemption which is in Christ Jesus.

And Rom 4:5 states:

> And to one who does not work but trusts him who justifies the ungodly, his faith is reckoned as righteousness.

5.   Already in Q. 59 and in Answer 60 faith was mentioned. Answer 60 said that we are righteous before God only by a true faith in Jesus Christ. And at the end, again, that we only receive this gift if we accept it with a believing heart. That is why Answer 61 continues the discussion. It says that we are not acceptable to God because of the worthiness of our faith. Faith is not an achievement on our part in consequence of which we become entitled to God's favour. There is nothing meritorious about faith. But it is the means whereby we accept the righteousness of Christ. That is how we are justified. Not BECAUSE OF, also not WITHOUT, but BY faith. Not our faith, but Christ is the basis of our acquittal.

6.   In order to see the entire work of the justification of sinners, one should note carefully:

a.   The eternal counsel of election in which God determined to justify those that are his through Christ (Eph 1:4, 5).

b.   The resurrection of Christ, when his satisfaction for our justification was approved (Rom 4:25).

c. Faith, by which we personally are justified in Christ in this dispensation (Phil 3:9).

d. The last judgment, when the justification will be announced publicly (Mt 25:23).

B. CROSS REFERENCES

1. Articles 22 and 23 of the BC confession speak extensively about justification by faith.

2. Also in the CD this benefit is spoken of more than once. See, *e.g.*, III/IV, 6.

3. Note also the Forms for the Baptism of Infants and Adults (Doctrine of Baptism):

> Thus we are freed from our sins and accounted righteous before God.

And see the Form for the Celebration of the Lord's Supper (Remembrance of Christ):

> He was innocently condemned to death that we might be acquitted at the judgment seat of God.

C. QUESTIONS

1. What is the fruit and what is the benefit of faith? What is the difference between benefit and fruit?

2. What does "to make righteous" mean? What is the opposite of this concept?

3. Who is the Judge? Who is the accuser? Who is the accused? What is the Criminal Code? What is the indictment (accusation)? Who is counsel for the defence? What does his defence consist of? Finally, what judgment does the Judge pronounce?

4. How complete is the justification? Does it happen in consequence of any merit of ours? If not, how does it happen? What do Rom 3:23, 24 and 4:5 say?

5. Is justification conferred BECAUSE of faith? Is it conferred WITHOUT faith? If neither, on what basis is it conferred? What word is used in art. 22 of the BC to describe the significance of faith?

6. Which four matters should we have regard to for a proper understanding of the work of justification?

62. *Q.* *But why can our good works not be*
    our righteousness before God,
    or at least a part of it?

   A. *Because the righteousness*
       which can stand before God's judgment
       must be absolutely perfect
       and in complete agreement
       with the law of God,[1]
       whereas even our best works in this life
       are all imperfect and defiled with sin.[2]

       [1] *Deut. 27:26; Gal. 3:10.*
       [2] *Is. 64:6.*

63. *Q.* *But do our good works earn nothing,*
    even though God promises to reward them
    in this life and the next?[1]

   A. *This reward is not earned;*
       it is a gift of grace.[2]

       [1] *Matt. 5:12; Heb. 11:6.*
       [2] *Luke 17:10; II Tim. 4:7, 8.*

64. *Q.* *Does this teaching not make people*
    careless and wicked?

   A. *No.*
       It is impossible
       that those grafted into Christ
       by true faith
       should not bring forth
       fruits of thankfulness.[1]

       [1] *Matt. 7:18; Luke 6:43-45; John 15:5.*

A. NOTES

1. This LD is closely related to the preceding one. In it we confessed that God justifies us BY FAITH. This LD states that this does NOT happen BECAUSE OF OUR WORKS. Logically, this addition is not necessary. But the guile of our sinful heart makes it necessary. And the Bible is our example in this respect. For after Paul states in Eph 2:8 that we are saved through faith, he adds in v. 9:

> NOT BECAUSE OF WORKS, lest any man should boast.

2. Question 62 shows why our good works can not bring about our righteousness, not even in part. The answer is entirely clear and scriptural. Isa 64:6 says:

> . . . all our righteous deeds are like a polluted garment.

3. Question 63 points to the reward that God nevertheless promises to give. And, indeed, Ps 19:12b says:

> . . . in keeping them [God's commandments] there is great reward.

So also Christ says in Rev 22:12:

> Behold, I am coming soon, bringing my recompense, to repay every one for what he has done.

Further, Mt 6 teaches that God will publicly reward the things that are done in secret. We are entitled to look to this reward, for God promised it to encourage us. Moses also looked to the reward (Heb 11:26). But none of this detracts from the principle "Not because of works." For the reward is not earned. What could we possibly earn?

The reward is out of grace, to show kindness towards us and because God has pleasure in his own work. The reward is like the reward a father gives to his child for something that the child has done; it is not like the salary an employer pays an employee.

4. God rewards in THIS life. His eye is on those who fear him. True, he will not always give prosperity and wealth, more often it will be the gift of peace of mind, confirmation of the hope that is in us, and other spiritual gifts. But in due course he will cause the righteous to inherit everything. In that LIFE TO COME God's reward will become apparent in differences in glory (see LD 22, Q. 58).

5. Some allege that the doctrine of justification WITHOUT MERIT on our part makes people careless and wicked. But that is not so, although the doctrine of free grace is misused. That happened already in Paul's time (Rom 6:1, 15). Rather, the doctrine of the Roman church that we earn our

165

righteousness through good works, causes a superficial life style. It causes one to believe that the outward actions are sufficient before God. Further, it causes people to do good works for fear of damnation and, thus, the works are done for oneself. But the doctrine of free grace causes one to do good works out of THANKFULNESS for the excellent grace which God freely gave us. Those good works follow as a matter of course. Is it possible that a tree fails to bear fruit? Even less is it possible that faith fails to produce its fruits, that is, good works.

B. COMMENTS

1. Paul's statement in Rom 3:28 that a man is justified BY FAITH APART FROM WORKS OF LAW, does not conflict with the statement in Jas 2:23 that a man IS JUSTIFIED BY WORKS AND NOT BY FAITH ALONE. Paul addresses those who think that a person is justified by his own works (the works of the law). James, on the other hand, addresses those who say that since it is all a matter of grace, good works are not required. James says to them that such a faith without works is dead! Justifying faith must BE APPARENT in its works (the works of faith).

C. CROSS REFERENCES

1. In the BC, art. 24, you will find each aspect of the subject matter of this LD discussed, including the unmeritoriousness of our works and the reward on our works, as well as the rejection of the accusation that this doctrine makes people careless and wicked.

2. The insufficiency of our works is also confessed in CD V, 1-3. Chapters I, 13 and V, 12 teach that the doctrine leads to thankfulness.

D. HERESIES

1. Pelagianism.

2. Antinomianism.

3. Perfectionism.

E. QUESTIONS

1. What is the relationship between this LD and the preceding one?

2. What does Isa. 64:6 say? Why can our good works not earn a reward?

3. Does God not reward good works? How does he reward them?

4. Why does the doctrine of the meritoriousness of good works make people superficial and selfish?

5. Explain why Rom 3:28 and Jas 2:24 do not conflict?

65. *Q.* *Since then faith alone*
makes us share in Christ and all His benefits,
where does this faith come from?

A. *From the Holy Spirit,[1]*
who works it in our hearts
by the preaching of the gospel,[2]
and strengthens it
by the use of the sacraments.[3]
[1] *John 3:5; I Cor. 2:10-14; Eph. 2:8; Phil. 1:29.*
[2] *Rom. 10:17; I Pet. 1:23-25.*
[3] *Matt. 28:19, 20; I Cor. 10:16.*

66. *Q.* *What are the sacraments?*

A. *The sacraments are holy, visible signs and seals.*
They were instituted by God
so that by their use
He might the more fully declare and seal to us
the promise of the gospel.[1]
And this is the promise:
that God graciously grants us
forgiveness of sins and everlasting life
because of the one sacrifice of Christ
accomplished on the cross.[2]
[1] *Gen. 17:11; Deut. 30:6; Rom. 4:11*
[2] *Matt. 26:27, 28; Acts 2:38; Heb. 10:10.*

67. *Q.* *Are both the Word and the sacraments*
then intended to focus our faith
on the sacrifice of Jesus Christ on the cross
as the only ground of our salvation?

A. *Yes, indeed.*
The Holy Spirit teaches us in the gospel
and assures us by the sacraments
that our entire salvation
rests on Christ's one sacrifice for us
on the cross.[1]
[1] *Rom. 6:3; I Cor. 11:26; Gal. 3:27.*

68. *Q.* *How many sacraments*
has Christ instituted in the new covenant?

A. *Two: holy baptism and the holy supper.[1]*
[1] *Matt. 28:19, 20; I Cor. 11:23-26.*

THE MEANS OF GRACE:
WORD AND SACRAMENTS
Lord's Days 25 - 30

FAITH COMES FROM WHAT IS HEARD

*.. NOTES

1. Lord's Days 25-30 deal with the means of grace. These are: *The Word and the Sacraments* (baptism and Lord's supper). The Catechism speaks extensively only about the sacraments. It discusses the Word as means of grace only briefly. This marks the time in which it was written. The reformers had to carry on a struggle about the sacraments. But the church of today must still do that! The Catechism has not become obsolete in this respect.

2. Just as food serves to sustain life and medicines to promote healing, the means of grace serve to work and strengthen God's gift of grace (*i.e.*, faith, by means of which we share in all Christ's benefits) in us. That is why the Catechism, when it begins to deal with the means of grace, first speaks about the origin and strengthening of faith. For the means of grace serve to work and strengthen FAITH. We must guard against underestimation of these means (like the mystics) and may not neglect the preaching and baptism by the argument: "What could the preaching and baptism possibly accomplish? God has to work faith!" By the same token, we have to guard against overestimation of these means (like the Roman Catholics). They teach that grace is inherent IN the sacraments, just like the power to heal is in medicine. If that were true, RECEIVING the means of grace would suffice. But the Catechism speaks of their USE. That involves more than merely receiving the means. Not the hearers, but the doers of the Word will be saved. We have to work with the sacrament. We must consider it, think about it, and seize hold of the promise which it signifies and seals. It is the Holy Spirit who WORKS faith and he is not confined to the means of grace. But we are bound to the means.

3. Where does faith come from? The Catechism has already spoken about the necessity (LD 20), nature (LD 21), content (LD 22, Q&A 58), and benefit (LD 23-24) of faith. Now it asks about its ORIGIN. Do we receive faith from our parents, or our teachers? Is it our own doing that we come to faith? NO! Eph 2:8 says:

> For by grace you have been saved through faith; and this is not your own doing, it is the gift of God.

The Holy Spirit works it in our hearts. We must pray for the Spirit. But we cannot understand how he works faith in our hearts (CD III/IV, 13).

4. The Holy Spirit works faith in our hearts BY THE PREACHING OF THE GOSPEL. The Catechism, thus, mentions the gospel and deliberately does not speak of "the Word of God," because the LAW does not work faith. The LAW (Law and gospel are the two parts of the Word which may be distinguished) judges; it does not call a person to God and does not work trust in him. The gospel does that. That is why it is referred to here. Further, the Catechism speaks of THE PREACHING. It pleases God to save those who believe through the folly of the preaching (1 Cor 1:21). True, faith can also be worked through the reading of the gospel, but the normal way is through the preaching. Rom 10:17 says:

> So faith comes from what is HEARD, and what is heard comes by the preaching of Christ.

5. Note carefully that the Catechism does not say that God *awakens* faith by the preaching of the gospel, but that he *works* faith thereby. The Holy Spirit does not work faith in us immediately (*i.e.*, without using means); he does not place the seed of faith in us in order to awaken it to growth by the preaching of the Word, as the sun does to seed that has been planted in the ground. Instead, the Holy Spirit *works* faith through the preaching. Jas 1:18 says:

> Of his own will he brought us forth by the word of truth.

6. Faith needs strengthening, because it constantly faces attacks by our sinful nature and the whole evil world, which contradict it. The Lord strengthens faith in different ways (*e.g.*, through testing and his guidance of our entire life) and as *means* to strengthen our faith he gave us the Word and the sacraments. When the Catechism says that the Holy Spirit WORKS faith in our hearts through the preaching of the gospel, it means that he works not only the beginning of faith, but also its preservation (by the means given to strengthen it). The Compendium[14] is clearer on this point.

7. The preaching strengthens faith. Despite all attacks on faith, the preaching constantly points us to God's promise and makes us understand that promise more and more broadly and fully. Think, for example of Abraham. God brought him on the way when he called him by the Word. And when Abraham might have given up hope because the waiting seemed endless, God STRENGTHENED him when he constantly addressed him by his Word.

---

[14]Transl. note: See LD 2, Q&A 4, footnote 2, *supra*.

8. Further, the Lord strengthens faith by the USE of the sacraments. The administration and receipt of the sacraments are not sufficient. We must use them. Otherwise they are useless, talents hidden in the ground.

B. CROSS REFERENCES

1. Article 22 of the BC says:

   . . . the Holy Spirit kindles in our hearts a true faith.

   (See also CD III/IV, 10).

2. Article 24 of the BC says:

   We believe that this true faith [is] worked in man by the hearing of God's Word and by the operation of the Holy Spirit.

   (See also CD III/IV, 17).

3. The CD V, 14 says:

   As it has pleased God to begin this work of grace in us by the preaching of the gospel, so he maintains, continues, and perfects it by the hearing and reading of His Word, by meditation upon it, by its exhortations, threats, and promises, and by the use of the sacraments.

C. QUESTIONS

1. How many means of grace are there? What is their purpose?
2. Which two misconceptions do we have to guard against in this context?
3. Is God confined by the means of grace? Are we bound to them?
4. Where does faith come from? What does Eph 2:8 say?
5. What is the means the Holy Spirit uses to work faith in us?
6. Which two parts can you distinguish in God's Word? Why does the Catechism speak of the gospel in this context? Why does it speak of preaching?
7. What does Rom 10:17 say? Can one say that the gospel awakens faith? Recite Jas 1:18.
8. Why does faith need strengthening? How does the Lord strengthen faith?
9. How is faith strengthened through the preaching of the gospel?
10. How do the sacraments strengthen faith?

D. QUESTIONS TO BE ANSWERED FROM THE CANONS OF DORT III/IV

1. Why can the "light of nature" left in man not give faith? (Art. 4).
2. Why can the Ten Commandments also not give faith? (Art. 5).
3. How then does God work faith? (Art. 6).
4. Why does God give faith to more people now than under the old dispensation? (Art. 7).
5. Are all who are called to faith called earnestly and sincerely? (Art. 8).
6. Why then do not all who are called come to faith? (Art. 9).
7. Why do others do come to faith? (Art. 10).
8. Is the preaching efficacious by itself? What else does God do to cause people to come to faith? (Art. 11).
9. How does God work regeneration? (Art. 12).
10. Is God required to give us faith? (Art. 15).
11. How are we to regard those who profess their faith? (Art. 15)

12. What should we do for those who have not yet come to faith? (Art. 15).
13. How does God not work in man? (A.: "Not as in . . . "). (Art. 16).
14. How is grace given to us? (A.: "Grace is given us through . . . "). (Art. 17).

Q. & A. 66
SIGN AND SEAL

A. NOTES

1. The word "sacrament" is not derived from the Bible, but from the Latin. In Roman society it denoted a sacred matter, a religious act. We use it to refer to baptism and the Lord's supper.

2. The sacraments are "HOLY, VISIBLE SIGNS AND SEALS . . . INSTITUTED BY GOD." They are not holy because the water of baptism, and the bread and wine of the Lord's supper are something special. They are only water and bread and wine. But they are SET APART for the service of God and, thus, holy. They are pledges of Christ's sacrifice and, thus, estimable, just as we esteem the value of a guarantee, even though it is just a piece of paper. The Catechism calls the sacraments VISIBLE. That is exactly how they differ from the Word. Christ enters our lives through our hearing by the Word and through our sight by the sacraments. We are allowed to SEE! Seeing gives more certainty than hearing. That is why people will ask someone who relates an event that has happened: "Did you *see* it?" For we will believe it more readily when he has seen what he reports than when he merely reports what he has heard.

    The sacraments are signs. A sign depicts something invisible. Clothes of mourning are a visible sign of the wearer's mourning, which is invisible. A teacher can make the invisible concept, 2 x 2 = 4, visible to young children on an abacus. The Lord gives VISIBLE instruction by the sacraments. They are "signs . . . INSTITUTED BY GOD. . . ." They are not natural, but created signs. Tears are a natural sign of mourning; clothes of mourning are an instituted sign. The phrase, "INSTITUTED BY GOD," teaches us who instituted the sacraments and who alone is able to do so. As signs the sacraments DECLARE to us the promise of the Gospel MORE FULLY.

3. Further, the sacraments are SEALS. A seal (such as a trade mark) serves to ensure the genuineness and trustworthiness of the object it seals. The sacraments are seals which are attached to the Word to guarantee to us the trustworthiness of the Word. This guarantee is necessary, not because of the untrustworthiness of the Word, but because of the weakness of our faith. As seals, the sacraments, therefore, guarantee the promise of the Gospel to us. Note that the Catechism says that GOD declares and seals the promise to us more fully by the sacraments. *He* does that. And note

that he does this "BY THEIR USE." (See Q. 65, Note 2).

4. What do the sacraments depict and seal? "THE PROMISE OF THE GOSPEL." This promise does speak of what God works in us. But it is not what God works in us or is presupposed to work in us,[15] but his promise that is depicted and sealed by the sacraments. They serve to direct our faith to the promise. And when we work faithfully with the promise in this way, God works in us through the power of the Holy Spirit by means of the sacraments (BC, art. 33).

B. CROSS REFERENCES

1. Article 33 of the BC speaks about the sacraments. It gratefully admits that "our gracious God" ordained the sacraments for us, because he was "mindful of our insensitivity and infirmity."

2. The same art. states that the sacraments serve "to seal His (*i.e.*, God's) promises to us and to be pledges to us of His good will and grace towards us."

C. HERESIES

1. The Roman Catholic doctrine, which invest the sacraments with magical power.

2. The belief that the sacraments seal grace already present in a person. It led to the distinction between a "real" and an "incomplete" baptism.[16]

D. QUESTIONS

1. What is the origin of the word, "sacrament," and what does it mean? How do we use it?

2. Why are the sacraments called holy signs? What is their function as signs? What purpose do they serve as signs?

3. Why are they called INSTITUTED signs? Who instituted them? Are they anything in addition to being signs?

4. What do they do as seals?

5. Why did God give the sacraments? (See BC, art. 33).

6. What do the sacraments depict and what do they seal? How does God work in us through the sacraments?

---

[15]Transl. note: The author refers here to a theory of Dr. A. Kuyper which was elevated to doctrine and imposed upon the churches by synods of the Gereformeerde Kerken in Nederland in 1939-44. This was one of the causes of the Liberation in 1944. The sacraments do not seal the regeneration as such, but the *promise* of forgiveness and regeneration. See further LD 26-27, Q&A 69-74, Note 4, *infra*.

[16]*Ibid.*

Q. & A. 67

WORD AND SACRAMENTS

A. NOTES

1. Here the Catechism points to the agreement between the Word and the sacraments. Their content is one and the same. The sacraments do not teach us anything that the Word does not impart. They may be compared to the illustrations in a book. The illustrations do not add anything to the story, but clarify it. Not only do the Word and the sacraments have the same content, *i.e.*, the promise of God, they also have the same origin, *i.e.*, both are given by God and both serve as means of grace.

2. But there are also differences between the Word and the sacraments:

   a. The Word is directed to our sense of hearing, the sacraments to our sense of sight.

   b. The Word works AND strengthens; the sacraments only strengthen faith.

   c. The Word is indispensable to salvation; the sacraments are not indispensable. But, since the Lord instituted them, no one may neglect them needlessly. They are necessary for us because of God's command.

   d. The Word analyses, *i.e.*, explains the content of the promise. The sacraments give the synthesis, *i.e.*, a brief summary of the promise.

3. Since the Lord gave us two means of grace, everyone who deems himself satisfied with one is culpable.

B. CROSS REFERENCES

1. Article 33 of the BC states that the sacraments were

   . . . added . . . to the Word of the gospel to represent better to our external senses both what He declares to us in His Word and what He does inwardly in our hearts.

C. QUESTIONS

1. Do the sacraments teach us anything that the Word does not inform us of? To what can we compare them?

2. How do the Word and the sacraments correspond?

3. How do they differ? Does it suffice if we come only to the preaching of the Word?

Q. & A. 68

TWO SACRAMENTS

A. NOTES

1. In the old dispensation there were two bloody sacraments: circumcision (instituted with Abraham) and Passover (instituted at the time of the exodus out of Egypt). Article 34 of the BC states:

> We believe and confess that Jesus Christ . . . has by His shed blood put an end to every other shedding of blood that one could or would make as an expiation or satisfaction for sins.

Hence, in the new dispensation the bloody sacraments were replaced by unbloody sacraments. Baptism came in the place of circumcision (Col 2:12), and the Lord's supper in the place of Passover (Lk 22:14ff). Article 33 of the BC states:

> Moreover, we are satisfied with the number of sacraments which Christ our Master has instituted for us, namely two. . . .

2. Also here, everyone should guard against separating what God has joined together. He who would use only baptism and not the Lord's supper is culpable before the Lord.

B. HERESIES

1. The Roman Catholic doctrine of the seven sacraments: Baptism (to confer grace through regeneration); Confirmation (to strengthen the believer in grace); Reconciliation ([formerly called Confession] to restore to grace); Communion ([formerly called Eucharist] to maintain grace); Sacrament of the Sick ([formerly called Extreme Unction, or Last Rites] to strengthen the believer for the struggle of death); Marriage; and Holy Rites (to ordain priests). Rome brags sometimes that it accompanies the believer from the cradle to the grave with the means of grace. But no one can receive all seven of the sacraments! The priest cannot receive the sacrament of marriage and the lay person cannot receive the sacrament of holy rites. The seven sacraments also serve to maintain the distinction between clergy and laity. God's Word does not support the institution of these sacraments other than baptism and communion.

C. QUESTIONS

1. Which sacraments existed in the old dispensation? When were they instituted?
2. Why were they replaced? Which sacraments of the new dispensation replace which sacraments of the old?
3. How many sacraments are there? How many do the Roman Catholics have?

69. Q. *How does holy baptism signify and seal to you*
    that the one sacrifice of Christ on the cross
    benefits you?

    A. *In this way:*
    Christ instituted this outward washing[1]
    and with it gave the promise that,
    as surely as water washes away
    the dirt from the body,
    so certainly His blood and Spirit
    wash away the impurity of my soul,
    that is, all my sins.[2]
    [1] *Matt. 28:19.*
    [2] *Matt. 3:11; Mark 16:16; John 1:33; Acts 2:38; Rom. 6:3, 4;*

    I Pet. 3:21.

70. Q. *What does it mean*
    to be washed with Christ's blood and Spirit?

    A. *To be washed with Christ's blood means*
    to receive forgiveness of sins from God,
    through grace, because of Christ's blood,
    poured out for us
    in His sacrifice on the cross.[1]
    To be washed with His Spirit means
    to be renewed by the Holy Spirit
    and sanctified to be members of Christ,
    so that more and more we become dead to sin
    and lead a holy and blameless life.[2]
    [1] *Ez. 36:25; Zech. 13:1; Eph. 1:7; Heb. 12:24; I Pet. 1:2;*
    Rev. 1:5; 7:14.
    [2] *John 3:5-8; Rom. 6:4; I Cor. 6:11; Col. 2:11, 12.*

71. Q. *Where has Christ promised*
    that He will wash us with His blood and Spirit
    as surely as we are washed
    with the water of baptism?

    A. *In the institution of baptism, where He says:*
    Go therefore and make disciples of all nations,
    baptizing them in the name of the Father
    and of the Son
    and of the Holy Spirit (Matthew 28:19).
    He who believes and is baptized
    will be saved,
    but he who does not believe
    will be condemned (Mark 16:16).
    This promise is repeated where Scripture calls
    baptism the washing of regeneration and the
    washing away of sins (Titus 3:5; Acts 22:16).

HOLY BAPTISM

A. NOTES

1. The Catechism devotes two Lord's Days to holy baptism. In them it discusses the following:

Q&A 69:   the sign and the promise which it signifies and seals;

Q&A 70:   the contents of the promise;

Q&A 71:   the texts where the promise can be found;

Q&A 72:   of what the connection between the sign and what is promised does not consist;

Q&A 73:   of what the connection between the sign and what is promised does consist;

Q&A 74:   that children of believers are entitled to Holy Baptism.

We shall summarize all of this in the following notes.

2. Lord's Day 25, Answer 66 taught us that the sacraments are SIGNS and SEALS. The SIGN of baptism is the water with which we are baptised in the name of the Father and the Son and the Holy Spirit. The Catechism calls it "this outward washing" in Answer 69. Ordinary, clean water should be used for this purpose. In early times it was customary to baptise by immersion. John the Baptist and the Apostles, for example, did this. Later (in colder climates and because of the baptism of infants!) sprinkling with water became the custom. Baptism by sprinkling is not wrong. The power of baptism does not lie in the amount of water used. Further, the Bible speaks about "the sprinkled blood" (Heb 12:24), and says, "I will sprinkle clean water upon you" (Ezek 36:25). Nevertheless, it is true that the symbolism is richer with immersion. With immersion the person receiving baptism disappears in the water; he is gone. He is, thus, buried with Christ into his death and becomes dead to sin. Thereafter he rises from the water as a new, cleansed person. That is how he is raised with Christ to newness of life (Rom 6:3, 4).

3. This sign was given to us so that we might the better understand the promise of the gospel (LD 25, Ans. 66). And that promise is, as stated in Answer 66:

> . . . that God graciously grants us
> forgiveness of sins and everlasting life
> because of the one sacrifice of Christ
> accomplished on the cross.

72. *Q.* *Does this outward washing with water*
    itself wash away sins?

   A. *No, only the blood of Jesus Christ*
       and the Holy Spirit
       cleanse us from all sins.[1]
       [1] *Matt. 3:11; I Pet. 3:21; I John 1:7.*

73. *Q.* *Why then does the Holy Spirit call baptism*
    the washing of regeneration
    and the washing away of sins?

   A. *God speaks in this way for a good reason.*
       He wants to teach us
           that the blood and Spirit of Christ
           remove our sins
           just as water takes away
           dirt from the body.[1]
       But, even more important,
       He wants to assure us
           by this divine pledge and sign
           that we are
           as truly cleansed from our sins spiritually
           as we are bodily washed with water.[2]
       [1] *I Cor. 6:11; Rev. 1:5; 7:14.*
       [2] *Mark 16:16; Acts 2:38; Rom. 6:3, 4; Gal. 3:27.*

74. *Q.* *Should infants, too, be baptized?*

   A. *Yes.*
       Infants as well as adults
           belong to God's covenant and congregation.[1]
       Through Christ's blood
           the redemption from sin
           and the Holy Spirit, who works faith,
           are promised to them
           no less than to adults.[2]
       Therefore, by baptism, as sign of the covenant,
           they must be grafted into the Christian church
           and distinguished from the children of
           unbelievers.[3]
       This was done in the old covenant by circumcision,[4]
           in place of which baptism was instituted
           in the new covenant.[5]
       [1] *Gen. 17:7; Matt. 19:14.*
       [2] *Ps. 22:11; Is. 44:1-3; Acts 2:38, 39; 16:31.*
       [3] *Acts 10:47; I Cor. 7:14.*
       [4] *Gen. 17:9-14.*
       [5] *Col. 2: 11-13.*

Thus, baptism instructs us visibly about the removal of our sins. For as water washes dirt from the body, so the blood and Spirit of Christ remove "the impurity of my soul, that is, all my sins" (A. 69). The blood of Christ denotes all his suffering, which culminated in the shedding of his blood. In this suffering he paid the punishment for our sins and thereby paid for our debt. Hence, we can say that his blood, that is, his suffering, cleanses us from sin, namely, from the *guilt* of sin (JUSTIFICATION). And the Spirit of Christ renews is. He releases us from the bonds of unrighteousness, causes us to become dead to sin and teaches us to lead a blameless life that is pleasing to God. More and more, he removes the *pollution* of sin (SANCTIFICATION). (See Ans. 70).

The water in baptism is, thus, sign of the blood and Spirit of Christ and the washing (sprinkling) with this water teaches visibly that the blood and the Spirit of Christ cleanse us of all our sins.

4. Baptism is also a SEAL on the same promise which it depicts for us as sign. It seals to us that the promise is true and trustworthy, and that it applies to ME; I am entitled to it. Baptism does not work forgiveness of sins. Only the blood of Christ and the Holy Spirit cleanse us from all sins (A. 72).

Roman Catholics, therefore, err in their doctrine that baptism causes regeneration and is, thus, essential to salvation. That is why they recognise lay baptism for children who are likely to die soon after birth and can not be brought to church for the sacrament.

Baptism also does not seal something that *is* already worked in us. It does not seal that we are already regenerated so that we must presume every baptised infant to have been regenerated. Prof. Lucas Lindeboom posited, *inter alia*, the following thesis, shortly before the General Synod of 1905: "Baptism does not sign and seal what IS PRESENT IN the person being baptised, or what IS PRESUPPOSED to be present, but the promises of the covenant of grace, revealed in the gospel." That is why the Form for the Baptism of Infants (Address to the Parents) also says that baptism is an ordinance of God to seal to us and our children *His covenant*, and why LD 25, Answer 66 says that the sacraments seal to us *the promise* of the gospel. So also, Answer 69 states clearly that Christ instituted this outward washing and with it *gave a promise*. It is the PROMISE which is sealed in baptism.

Baptism is a sign which *illustrates* that *promise* for us and *seals* it to us as trustworthy, in order to encourage and strengthen us in the acceptance of the promise in faith. Therefore, if one asks what baptism says to us as seal, the reply must be: The PROMISE (that God gives us forgiveness of sins out of grace, because of Christ's sacrifice) is true and trustworthy, and is meant for us; we are entitled to it. This is apparent also from Q. 71, which states that Christ has PROMISED that he WILL wash us with His blood and Spirit. Baptism, therefore, assures us that we may claim forgiveness of sins through faith in Christ. God assures us of *his grace toward us*.

Against this, some will say that baptism does not assure us that I am entitled to forgiveness of sins, but that I HAVE forgiveness. They point to the fact that the Catechism says in Answer 69 that water WASHES the dirt away, and in Answer 73 that we ARE cleansed from our sins spiritually. But we must not forget that those are the answers of a believing confessor, that is, someone who has accepted his baptism. Our entitlement to forgiveness of sins is like a cheque. When you have a cheque for $1,000, you do not have $1,000, but you are entitled to it. The cheque is evidence of your entitlement. The payee, who believes the cheque to be reliable, is apt to say, "I have $1,000." But the cheque is not the same as $1,000. Rather, it is the evidence and assurance of his right to the money.

5. What is important, therefore, is that we MAKE USE OF baptism. Just as not everyone who hears the gospel will be saved, so also, it can not be said of everyone who is baptised that he has or will receive forgiveness of sins. We must make use of baptism. We have to ACCEPT the PROMISE WHICH IS SIGNED AND SEALED to us, and cleave to God, "Father, Son, and Holy Spirit, . . . trust Him, and . . . love Him with our whole heart, soul, and mind, and with all our strength" (Forms for the Baptism of Infants and Adults, Doctrine of Baptism, third point). Otherwise, baptism, that cheque of God's grace, will make us the more guilty! Thus, baptism obliges us to profess the Lord's Name in our entire life and, therefore, also in the church (public profession of faith).

6. Yet baptism is called "the washing of regeneration and the washing away of sins" (see Q&A 73). We call this a SACRAMENTAL LOCUTION, in which the SIGN is spoken of as if it were the depicted matter itself. We also do that when we say that a bank note is $10, even though it only seals our entitlement to $10.

7. The INSTITUTION of baptism. Answer 69 says that Christ instituted baptism. This refers to its institution shortly before the Ascension (Mt 28:19, 20). Yet, John the Baptist already baptised people. And his baptism was in substance like the Christian baptism. They are both a baptism to repentance and of forgiveness of sins. But he baptised only in Israel and only those who came to him. Only after Pentecost could baptism be administered among all nations. See also Answer 71 about the institution of baptism and learn the texts in that answer.

    Mt 28:19: "IN THE NAME OF" means "to or in communion with" God. For his name is he himself, as he revealed himself to us. Baptism points to that communion and seals it.

8. Who must be baptised? The BC, art. 34 says: "For that reason He has

commanded all those who are His to be baptised." Hence, we should baptise all those who are sanctified in Christ, who belong to God's covenant and his congregation. That means: the believers, those who profess their faith, and their children. It is not permissible to baptise all who are presented for baptism in the hope that they will later learn to understand it and thereby to bind them to some extent to the church.

9. Answer 74 confesses separately that infants (*i.e.*, of believers) should (*i.e.*, must) also be baptised. For there have always been opponents of the baptism of infants. The Catechism says that they must be baptised because they "belong to God's covenant and congregation." (Learn Gen 17:7 and Acts 2:39). That is why they are entitled to the sign and seal of the covenant. Prof. Lindeboom, in the theses already referred to, therefore, said, correctly: "Baptism is administered, NOT on basis of presumed regeneration, BUT on the basis of the Lord's command, to those who profess their faith, and to their children because the promises of the covenant extend also to them." That is why the children must "by baptism, as sign of the covenant, . . . be grafted into the Christian church and distinguished from the children of unbelievers" (A. 74). They are not received into the covenant and the church by baptism. They ARE in them according to God's promise, but this is made VISIBLE in baptism. In baptism they receive the "mark and emblem" (BC, art. 34) of the Lord, to whom they belong.

This is the more so since baptism replaced circumcision (Col 2:11, 12). That is why the children must now be baptised, just as formerly they were circumcised. Were it not so, then infant baptism should have been forbidden in the NT. But since that is not the case, the rule which was established in the beginning of the OT, remains in force.

10. Opponents of infant baptism argue:

    a. *Holy Scripture does not command baptism.* But that was not necessary either (see above).

    b. *There is no example in the NT of infant baptism.* That is not surprising, for the church was being gathered by conversion from among the heathens at that time. Nonetheless, we always read in connection with such a conversion: he was baptised, with all his family (Cornelius, Acts 10:48; the jailer, Acts 16:33). Hence, these baptisms took place according to the rule of the covenant that when a father belongs to the congregation, his family also belongs.

    c. *They do not understand baptism.* But those who were circumcised did not understand their circumcision either and yet God required them to be circumcised. See also the Form for the Baptism of Infants (Doctrine of Baptism): "Although our children do not understand all this . . . ," *etc.*

    d. *We do not know whether the children believe.* But we do not baptise them on the basis of their faith, but on the basis of God's promise and command.

B. CROSS REFERENCES

1. The BC, art. 34 speaks extensively about baptism. Note that this article:

    a. points out that baptism replaced circumcision;

    b. explains that baptism does not work something in us, nor says anything about something which is supposedly worked in us, but speaks to us of what the LORD wants to be for us; it serves us as "a testimony that He will be our God and gracious Father for ever";

    c. clearly states that baptism is given to us to *signify* to us that, "As water . . . ," *etc.*

    d. point out that baptism benefits us throughout our whole life;

    e. gives detailed reasons why children also must be baptised.

2. Article 56 of the CO states that the sacraments must be administered in a public worship service. Further, art. 57 states:

> The consistory shall ensure that the covenant of God is sealed by baptism to the children of believers as soon as feasible.

It is not necessary to emphasize the phrase, "as soon as feasible," to such an extent that the mother is prevented from being present and acting as witness to the baptism of her child. But every unnecessary postponement of baptism is wrong.

3. The CD I, 17 says:

> God-fearing parents ought not to doubt the election and salvation of their children whom God calls out of this life in their infancy.

For God's covenant placed these children under the promise. The covenant also placed them under the obligation to accept the promise in faith when they grow up. But the Lord prevented their growing up and, thus, they were not faced with their obligation. Nevertheless, they have God's promise! However, it not permissible to draw the same conclusion for those who do grow up. The Lord chose a different route for them, in the course of which he causes them to be further instructed as they grow up.

C. FORM FOR THE BAPTISM OF INFANTS

1. *The Explanation of Baptism*

    a. Of our misery as children of wrath since baptism signifies the impurity of our souls;

    b. Of our deliverance through Jesus Christ, since baptism signifies and seals to us the washing away of our sins through his blood.

    i.   *The Father* testifies and seals to us that He establishes an eternal covenant of grace with us [and] adopts us for His children and heirs.

    ii.   *The Son* promises us that He washes us in his blood from all our sins and unites us with Him in His death and resurrection.

    iii.   *The Holy Spirit* assures us . . . that He will dwell in us and make us living members of Christ, imparting to us what we have in Christ.

  c.   Of the thankfulness to which baptism calls and obliges us.

2. *The Grounds for the Baptism of Infants*

  a.   Just as they share without their knowledge in the condemnation of Adam, so are they, without their knowledge, received into grace in Christ.

  b.   They are included in God's covenant and in his church (Gen 17:7).

  c.   The promise of the forgiveness of sins and of the Holy Spirit is made to them (Acts 2:39).

  d.   In the old dispensation children were circumcised.

  e.   Christ blessed the little children also.

3. *Prayer before Baptism*

This part of the Form, which is intended for the entire congregation, concludes with the prayer before baptism, after the admonition to the parents to instruct their children in the doctrine of baptism.

4. *Three Questions of the Parents*

  a.   Declaration of the parents concerning the children of the church as sanctified in Christ.

  b.   A repeated confession concerning the doctrine of Holy Scripture.

  c.   A promise to instruct their child in the doctrine of baptism and to cause him or her to be instructed therein (Reformed education, catechesis, and instruction in the home).

5. *Prayer of Thanksgiving*

D. QUESTIONS

1. What does the Catechism speak about in each of Q&A 69, 70, 71, 72, 73 and 74? Answer this question with the Catechism open in front of you.

2. What is the sign of baptism? Are there objections to sprinkling with water? Why not? Why did the church adopt sprinkling with water? Which form of administration has a greater symbolism? Why?

3. Why was the sign of baptism given? Of what is the water a sign? What is visually depicted by the sprinkling with water? Of which two acts of salvation does baptism therefore speak? What is signified by "Christ's blood"? How does it remove sin? How does Christ's Spirit remove sin?

4. Of what is baptism a seal? What do the Roman Catholics say about baptism? What do you know about lay baptism? Does baptism seal anything in the person being baptised? If not, what does it seal? What does baptism say as seal? To what can baptism be compared?

5. To what does baptism admonish and oblige us? How can the Bible speak of baptism as "the washing away of sins" and "the forgiveness of sins"?

6. Who instituted baptism? In what way should the baptism of John be distinguished from Christian baptism?

7. Who should be baptised?

8. Why should children also be baptised? On what basis are they therefore baptised? What did baptism replace? Which four objections are brought against infant baptism? How do you respond to each of them?

9. What do the CD say about children who die in infancy? Is it permissible to draw the same conclusion about children who are growing up? Why not?

10. List the main parts of the Form for the Baptism of Infants. What do the Father, the Son and the Holy Spirit, respectively, testify in baptism? What are the grounds which the Form gives for infant baptism? What are the questions posed to the parents?

75. Q. *How does the Lord's Supper signify and seal to you*
          that you share in Christ's one sacrifice on the cross
          and in all His gifts?

      A. *In this way:*
          Christ has commanded me and all believers to eat of this broken
          *   bread and drink of this cup in remembrance of Him.*
          With this command He gave these promises:[1]
    First,
          as surely as I see with my eyes the bread of the Lord broken for
          me and the cup given to me, so surely was His body offered for me
          and His blood poured out for me on the cross.
    Second,
          as surely as I receive from the hand of the minister and taste with
          my mouth the bread and the cup of the Lord as sure signs of
          Christ's body and blood, so surely does He Himself nourish and
          refresh my soul to everlasting life with His crucified body and shed
          blood.
          [1] *Matt. 26:26-28; Mark 14:22-24; Luke 22:19, 20; I Cor. 11:23-25.*

76. Q. *What does it mean to eat the crucified body of Christ*
          and to drink His shed blood?

      A. *First,*
          to accept with a believing heart all the suffering and the death
          of Christ, and so receive forgiveness of sins and life eternal.[1]
    Second,
          to be united more and more to His sacred body through the
          Holy Spirit, who lives both in Christ and in us.[2]
    Therefore, although Christ is in heaven[3] and we are on earth,
          yet we are flesh of His flesh and bone of His bones,[4]
          and we forever live and are governed by one Spirit,
          as the members of our body are by one soul.[5]
          [1] *John 6:35, 40, 50-54.*
          [2] *John 6:55, 56; I Cor. 12:13.*
          [3] *Acts 1:9-11; 3:21; I Cor. 11:26; Col. 3:1.*
          [4] *I Cor. 6:15, 17; Eph. 5:29, 30; I John 4:13.*
          [5] *John 6:56-58; 15:1-6; Eph. 4:15, 16; I John 3:24.*

77. Q. *Where has Christ promised that He will nourish and refresh*
          believers with His body and blood as surely as they eat of this
          broken bread and drink of this cup?

      A. *In the institution of the Lord's supper:*
          The Lord Jesus on the night when He was betrayed took
          bread, and when He had given thanks, He broke it and said,
          *   "This is My body which is for you. Do this in*
          *   remembrance of Me."*
          In the same way also the cup, after supper, saying,
          *   "Do this, as often as you drink it, in remembrance of Me."*
          For as often as you eat this bread and drink the cup, you
          proclaim the Lord's death until He comes (I Corinthians 11:23-26).
          This promise is repeated by Paul where he says:
          The cup of blessing which we bless, is it not a participation
          in the blood of Christ? The bread which we break, is it not a
          participation in the body of Christ?
          Because there is one bread, we who are many are one body,
          for we all partake of the one bread (I Corinthians 10:16, 17).

THE LORD'S SUPPER

LORD'S DAYS 28 - 30
Q. & A. 75 - 82
THE SUPPER OF OUR LORD

A. NOTES

1. The Catechism devotes three Lord's Days to its teaching about the second sacrament. In them it discusses the following:

Q&A 75: the sign and the promise which are signified and sealed in the Lord's supper;

Q&A 76: the content of the promise;

Q&A 77: the texts where the promise can be found;

Q&A 78: of what the connection between the sign and what is promised does not consist;

Q&A 79: of what the connection between the sign and what is promised does consist;

Q&A 80: the difference between the Lord's supper and the papal mass;

Q&A 81: for whom the Lord's supper is instituted and who are the desired guests;

Q&A 82: that the church must keep the Lord's supper holy and how it must do that.

Note that the Catechism's order of treatment of baptism and the Lord's supper is identical. (See LD 26-27, Note 1).

2. Holy Scripture refers to this sacrament by different names. Each of these names teaches us something about this sacrament. It is called the *Lord's Supper*, because Christ instituted it "on the night when he was betrayed" (1 Cor 11:23). In Acts 2:42, it is called the *Breaking of Bread*, thereby referring to what happens in this sacrament; in 1 Cor 10:16, it is called *Participation in the Body and Blood of Christ*, thereby pointing out what this sacrament signifies and seals; and 1 Cor 10:21 speaks of the *Table of the Lord*, for the Lord instituted this table and is the host.

3. Christ instituted the Lord's supper in the circle of his disciples "on the night when he was betrayed," while sitting at the Passover table. The old Passover was fulfilled when he, the Lamb of God, went to his sacrifice. That is why that old bloody sacrament was replaced with the unbloody supper, which is called holy, because it is the "table of the Lord" (see above). It is a meal of remembrance, for Christ said in Lk 22:19: "Do this in remembrance of me."

78. *Q.* *Are then the bread and wine*
       changed into the real body and blood of Christ?

  A. *No.*
       Just as the water of baptism
           is not changed into the blood of Christ
           and is not the washing away of sins itself
           but is simply God's sign and pledge,[1]
       so also the bread in the Lord's supper
           does not become the body of Christ itself,[2]
           although it is called Christ's body[3] in keeping
           with the nature and usage of sacraments.[4]

   [1] *Eph. 5:26; Tit. 3:5.*
   [2] *Matt. 26:26-29.*
   [3] *I Cor. 10:16, 17; 11:26-28.*
   [4] *Gen. 17:10, 11; Ex. 12:11, 13; I Cor. 10:3, 4; I Pet. 3:21.*

79. *Q.* *Why then does Christ call the bread His body*
       and the cup His blood,
       or the new covenant in His blood,
       and why does Paul speak of a participation
       in the body and blood of Christ?

  A. *Christ speaks in this way for a good reason:*
       He wants to teach us by His supper
           that as bread and wine sustain us
           in this temporal life,
           so His crucified body and shed blood
           are true food and drink for our souls
           to eternal life.[1]
       But, even more important,
       He wants to assure us by this visible sign and pledge,
           first,
               that through the working of the Holy Spirit
               we share in His true body and blood
               as surely as we receive with our mouth
               these holy signs in remembrance of Him,[2]
           and, second,
               that all His suffering and obedience
               are as certainly ours
               as if we personally
               had suffered and paid for our sins.[3]

   [1] *John 6:51, 55.*
   [2] *I Cor. 10:16, 17; 11:26.*
   [3] *Rom. 6:5-11.*

The fourth part of the Form for the Celebration of the Lord's Supper (Remembrance of Christ) describes the manner in which we should remember Christ in a very beautiful way. Read it! Article 35 of the BC states that we receive this sacrament "in the congregation of the people of God" (no communion for the sick!). The Lord did not give us a rule about the frequency of celebration. It is possible that the first congregation of Christians celebrated the supper every Sunday. Article 60 of the CO says:

> The Lord's Supper shall be celebrated at least once every three months.

Our infrequent celebration of the Lord's supper is evidence of a low level of spiritual life.

4. Article 35 of the BC says that we receive the Lord's supper

    > . . . as we together commemorate the death of Christ our Saviour with thanksgiving and we confess our faith and Christian religion.

    For Christ said: "Do this in remembrance of me." That is why young children are not admitted to the supper. They must first be instructed so that they may be able to discern the body of the Lord (1 Cor 11:29). Hence, the Catechism says in Answer 75 that Christ has commanded "me and all *believers*" to maintain this sacrament. It is instituted, says art. 35 of the BC, for

    > . . . those whom He has already regenerated and incorporated into His family, which is His Church.

    The word "regenerated" here means: brought to faith and repentance.

5. The signs are:

    a. *bread and wine*, signifying the body and blood of the Lord;

    b. *broken and poured out*, signifying that the body of the Lord was broken and his blood was shed;

    c. *distributed and apportioned*, signifying that the sacrifice of Christ was made for us;

    d. *eaten and drunk*, signifying that just as bread and wine become permanently united with our bodies when we eat and drink them, so also we are united with Christ by faith and are entitled to the benefit of the payment made by his suffering and to renewal by his Spirit; and that he nourishes us just as bread and wine nourish and refresh our bodies.

    Hence, the Lord's supper speaks about what Christ did for (*i.e., on behalf of*) us: His sacrifice, completed on the cross; and about what he does *in* us by his Spirit: He nourishes and refreshes us, strengthens us, and renews us to eternal life.

80. *Q.* *What difference is there*
    between the Lord's supper and the papal mass?

  A. *The Lord's supper testifies to us,*
      first,
          that we have complete forgiveness of all our sins through the
          one sacrifice of Jesus Christ, which He Himself accomplished
          on the cross once for all;[1]
      and, second,
          that through the Holy Spirit we are grafted into Christ,[2]
          who with His true body is now in heaven at the right hand of
          the Father,[3] and this is where He wants to be worshipped.[4]
      But the mass teaches,
      first,
          that the living and the dead do not have forgiveness of sins
          through the suffering of Christ unless He is still offered for
          them daily by the priests;
      and, second,
          that Christ is bodily present in the form of bread and wine,
          and there is to be worshipped.
      Therefore the mass is basically nothing but a denial
          of the one sacrifice and suffering of Jesus Christ,
          and an accursed idolatry.
      [1] *Matt. 26:28; John 19:30; Heb. 7:27; 9:12, 25, 26; 10:10-18.*
      [2] *1 Cor. 6:17; 10:16, 17.*
      [3] *Joh. 20:17; Acts 7:55, 56; Heb. 1:3; 8:1.*
      [4] *John 4:21-24; Phil. 3:20; Col. 3:1; I Thess. 1:10.*

81. *Q.* *Who are to come to the table of the Lord?*

  A. *Those who are truly displeased with themselves*
          because of their sins and yet trust that these are forgiven
          them and that their remaining weakness is covered by the
          suffering and death of Christ,
      and who also desire more and more to strengthen their faith
          and amend their life.
      But hypocrites and those who do not repent
          eat and drink judgment upon themselves.[1]
      [1] *I Cor. 10:19-22; 11:26-32.*

82. *Q.* *Are those also to be admitted to the Lord's supper who by their*
    confession and life show that they are unbelieving and ungodly?

  A. *No, for then the covenant of God would be profaned and His*
          wrath kindled against the whole congregation.[1]
      Therefore,
          according to the command of Christ and His apostles, the
          Christian church is duty-bound to exclude such persons by
          the keys of the kingdom of heaven,
          until they amend their lives.
      [1] *Ps. 50:16; Is. 1:11-17; I Cor. 11:17-34.*

The supper speaks about the forgiveness of sins (Mt 26:27-28) and eternal life (Jn 6:54). It also speaks about the communion of saints (1 Cor 10:17), for just as we all partake of the same bread, so we all partake of the same Christ; just as one bread and one wine become part of us through the celebration of the Lord's supper, so also is there one life in all believers through Christ, and they are members of each other. The bread and wine are not themselves spiritual food; Christ is. But Christ gave us the bread and wine as a sacrament to "represent to us the spiritual and heavenly bread" (BC, art. 35). Thus, there is also no *ex opere operato* here (*cf.* Lord's Days 26-27, Note 5). We must accept in faith what the bread and wine signify and seal to us.

Also with the Lord's supper we come across the sacramental locution which identifies the sign with that which it portrays, so that the bread is called his body and the wine his blood (*cf.* Lord's Days 26-27, Note 6, and Q. 79).

6. Article 35 of the BC states that what we eat and drink is the true body and true blood of Christ. Q&A 76 explains what this means. Eating is that action by which I make something a part of myself in such a way that no one can take it away. That which I ate has become part of me. In the same way the crucified body and shed blood of Christ become part of us, entirely ours. Their worth and significance are given to us, so that we have forgiveness of sins. The Catechism states that this being united with Christ is such that we are one body with him. We are not united with the Lord by eating with our mouths, but by our faith, in the spirit. For faith is "the hand and mouth of our soul" (BC, art. 35). The manner in which this occurs is beyond our understanding and comprehension (*ibid.*).

This communion in faith, this "eating of Christ" is something which we may and must do every day. But we receive the external and visible signs and seals of it at the Lord's supper. And the true and natural body and blood of Christ are pledged, and in that pledge also given, to us with the signs and seals, just as a cheque for $10 pledges and gives to us ten dollars. But he who fails to cash the cheque does not receive and obtain the $10, through his own foolishness. So also, he who does not use the pledge in faith and does not desire that which is pledged by it in faith, does not receive what is pledged and given. BC, art. 35 says:

> Although the sacrament is joined together with that which is signified, the latter is not always received by all.

One should, therefore, distinguish between giving and receiving.

7. Thus, in the Lord's supper, the bread remains bread and the wine remains wine. There is no change in their substance (transsubstantiation), as the Roman Catholics claim. They believe that although the attributes (taste,

smell, *etc.*) of the bread and wine remain the same, their essence is changed into the essence of Christ's body. This is nonsensical. If the essence changes, then the attributes must change as well. When Christ says, "This Is my body," it is clear that that has the same connotation as when I point to a dot on the map of Canada and say, "This is Ottawa." The Lutherans taught co-existence of substance (consubstantiation). They believed that the essence of Christ's body was present in (under, with and in) the signs. Thus, in respect of the question: HOW IS CHRIST PRESENT IN THE LORD'S SUPPER, there are these differences:

a. ROMAN CATHOLICS: *Bodily* and *materially* (transsubstantiation). He is eaten with the mouth.

b. LUTHERANS: Also *bodily* (consubstantiation) and eaten with the mouth.

c. ZWINGLIITES: *Not present.* The Lord's supper is solely a meal of remembrance.

d. REFORMED: Really present, but only *spiritually.* He is eaten with the mouth of faith (see Ans. 78).

8. The Roman Catholics call the sacrament of the Lord's supper the mass. In the early church it was the (wrong) custom for the baptised members to leave the church after the sermon, when the Lord's supper was about to be celebrated. The minister would then say: *Ite, concio missa est* (*i.e.,* Go, the meeting has ended), or simply: *missa est.* This was misinterpreted and the name "mass" came to be used for the Lord's supper. The papal mass is something entirely different than the Lord's supper. The mass is not celebrated as a meal at table, but as a sacrifice at an altar. The papal mass is not a *remembrance* of the sacrifice at Golgotha, but a *repetition* of that offer. According to Rome, in the mass there is an unbloody repetition of Christ's sacrifice when the priest breaks the host (the body of Christ, according to them, by transsubstantiation). They believe that without this repetition "the living and the dead do not have forgiveness of sins" (A. 80). Further, they worship Christ in the mass in the appearance of the bread. Hence, when the Geuzen called the Roman Catholics "worshippers of the bread-god," they were correct.[17] Further, Answer 80 does not put it too strongly when it says: "the mass is basically nothing but a denial of the one sacrifice and suffering of Jesus Christ." For in the mass man does not confess redemption through the

---

[17]Transl. note: The word, *Geuzen*, derives from the French *gueux* or *gueuses*, meaning "beggars." It was the name first given contemptuously to Dutch Protestant nobles when they presented a petition to the the the Spanish Regent of the Netherlands, Margaret of Parma. The name was subsequently adopted by partisans, mostly seafarers, in the 80-Years' War, the Dutch war of independence and for religious freedom against Spain.

Lord's one sacrifice (Heb 10:11, 14), but thinks that he can obtain his own redemption through the service of the priest. Moreover, the worship of what is in reality just matter is "an accursed idolatry." How poor in all its pomp is the papal mass! There, man has to do it all himself. How rich in its simplicity is the Lord's supper. There is the preaching that our redemption is complete. A simple celebration of the Lord's supper in a barn is richer than a pontifical high mass in a cathedral.

9. For whom is the Lord's supper instituted? That is a burdensome question for some people. They almost do not dare to come to the supper. It is hardly a question at all for others; they come to the holy table without much thought. Both are wrong, as pointed out in Answer 81. The Lord's supper is not only for those who are certain of their faith, but also for those who are weak in faith. It is for those "who are truly displeased with *themselves* because of their sins and yet trust that these are forgiven them" for Christ's sake, and who desire "to strengthen their faith and amend their life."

But hypocrites, those who pretend, those who outwardly enter into the life of the church and speak its language, but who deny their hearts to the Lord and do not heartily turn to him, "eat and drink judgment upon themselves" when they come to the supper. This judgment is not THE judgment. Repentance remains possible. But if we celebrate the Lord's supper in an unworthy manner, our consciences will be hardened and we shall more and more be caught up in sin. Also believers can eat and drink judgment and bring God's wrath upon themselves, if they eat and drink in an unworthy manner (*i.e.*, unseemly manner, without exercise of faith). Some people, therefore, say: "Let us never celebrate the Lord's supper, for then we can not profane it." But thereby it is also profaned, not through misuse, but through non-use. We "must examine ourselves and so eat of the bread" (1 Cor 11:29).

10. This *self*-examination does not consist of answering the question: Should I go or not? The command is to go! But it is ensuring that we do not go to the Lord's table unworthily, *i.e.*, in an unworthy manner, a manner not suited to the Lord's supper. This examination is not designed to make us worthy for the Lord's supper. We are always unworthy, but the Lord makes us worthy. The self-examination serves to make us enjoy the Lord's supper TO OUR COMFORT (and not to our judgment). It consists of three parts:

a. the consideration of our sins and accursedness, so that we humble ourselves before God; also, so that we remove sin from us and make straight what is wrong between us and brothers and sisters;

b. the acceptance in faith of the promise of forgiveness of sins; and

c. the renewed desire to serve the Lord according to his Word and to love our neighbour as ourselves.

In this connection, read the beginning of the Form for the Celebration of the Lord's Supper (Self-examination).

11. Apart from this personal discipline, church discipline is also necessary. We do not know the hypocrites; God does! And they can know themselves. But if those who are guilty of *public* sins wish to attend the Lord's supper, they must be prevented from doing so. If the seals of the covenant were to be administered to public sinners, the covenant would be dishonoured and God's wrath would be kindled over the *whole* congregation.

B. COMMENTS

1. There is no principial objection to the use of separate cups, but it is not to be recommended.

2. The Roman Catholic practice of not giving the cup to the believers is contrary to Christ's command: "Drink from it, all of you."

3. Paedocummunion (admission of children to the table) is contrary to the injunction of 1 Cor 11:29. Postponing admission to the table until after age 20 betrays a wrong attitude to the Lord's supper (*cf.* Ex 30:14).

C. CROSS REFERENCES

1. Several quotations from the broad explanation of the Lord's supper in BC, art. 35 have been given. It is impossible to reproduce the entire contents of this article. Read it carefully in its entirety!

D. FORM FOR THE CELEBRATION OF THE LORD'S SUPPER

1. *The Doctrinal Part.*

It comprehends:

a. the institution according to 1 Cor 11:23-29;

b. the description of the self-examination in three parts;

c. exercise of the disciplinary power in which abstention is commanded to those who "persist in such sins," but in which also those of broken and contrite hearts are encouraged.

d. consideration of the purpose of the institution of the Lord's supper:

   i.   celebration in remembrance of Christ's atoning death;

   ii. assurance of faith; and

   iii. strengthening of brotherly love.

2. *The Liturgical Part.*

It consists of:

a. the prayer before the supper;

b. the *sursum corda* (let us lift our hearts on high) and the celebration (communion);

c. the call to thankfulness in accordance with Ps 103 and Rom 8; and

d. the prayer of thanksgiving.

E. QUESTIONS

1. What does the Catechism speak about in each of Q&A 75, 76, 77, 78, 79, 80, 81, and 82? Answer this question with the Catechism open in front of you.

2. What names does the Bible use for the second sacrament and what do each of them mean?

3. When did Christ institute the Lord's supper? What sacrament did it replace? Why?

4. What kind of meal is it? How must we remember Christ at it? Where must it be celebrated? How often?

5. What do we do when we celebrate the Lord's supper? Why are young children not admitted to it? What must they first do?

6. What are the signs of the Lord's supper, what happens to them and what does that signify? Of what does the Lord's supper speak?

7. Are bread and wine our spiritual food? If not, what is their purpose? What is sacramental locution? How can Holy Scripture call bread and wine the body and blood of the Lord?

8. What does eating and drinking the body and blood of the Lord mean? Do we do that with the mouth? If not, how? Do we do this only at the Lord's supper? Are the body and blood of Christ given to everyone who receives the bread and wine? Are they received by everyone? What, therefore, do we have to distinguish?

9. Is the essence of the bread changed into the body of Christ? Who teach that it is? What do the Lutherans teach?

10. How is Christ present in the Lord's supper according to the Roman Catholics, the Lutherans, the Zwinglians and the Reformed confession?

11. What is the origin of the word "mass"? What does the mass purport to be of Christ's sacrifice? How do we obtain forgiveness of sins according to the Roman Catholics? How is Christ worshipped in the mass? What is the mass in essence?

12. For whom is the Lord's supper? What are hypocrites? What do they do when they come to the Lord's supper? Is repentance of that action possible? Can believers eat and drink judgment unto themselves? What, therefore, must we do?

13. Why is self-examination necessary? Of what parts does it consist?

14. To whom does church discipline extend? Why is it necessary?

83. *Q.* *What are the keys of the kingdom of heaven?*

A. *The preaching of the holy gospel and church discipline.*
By these two the kingdom of heaven is opened to believers
and closed to unbelievers.[1]

[1] *Matt. 16:19; John 20:21-23.*

84. *Q.* *How is the kingdom of heaven opened and closed*
by the preaching of the gospel?

A. *According to the command of Christ,*
the kingdom of heaven is opened
when it is proclaimed and publicly testified to each and every
believer that God has really forgiven all their sins
for the sake of Christ's merits, as often as they by true faith
accept the promise of the gospel.
The kingdom of heaven is closed when it is proclaimed and
testified to all unbelievers and hypocrites that the wrath of
God and eternal condemnation rest on them
as long as they do not repent.
According to this testimony of the gospel, God will judge both in
this life and in the life to come.[1]

[1] *Matt. 16:19; John 3:31-36; 20:21-23.*

85. *Q.* *How is the kingdom of heaven closed and opened*
by church discipline?

A. *According to the command of Christ, people who call themselves*
Christians but show themselves to be unchristian in doctrine
or life are first repeatedly admonished in a brotherly manner.
If they do not give up their errors or wickedness, they are
reported to the church, that is, to the elders.
If they do not heed also their admonitions, they are forbidden the
use of the sacraments, and they are excluded by the elders
from the Christian congregation, and by God Himself from
the kingdom of Christ.[1]
They are again received as members of Christ and of the church
when they promise and show real amendment.[2]

[1] *Matt. 18:15-20; I Cor. 5:3-5; 11-13; II Thess. 3:14, 15.*
[2] *Luke 15:20-24; II Cor. 2:6-11.*

A. NOTES

1. This LD speaks about the "keys of the kingdom of heaven," which were referred to in the previous LD. A key enables one to unlock or open and to lock or close something. This LD tells us about the admission to and the exclusion from the kingdom of heaven. (On this point, see also LD 48, Q&A 123, Note 1). He who is admitted to this "kingdom of heaven" or "kingdom of God" is entitled to share in its goods, *viz.*, forgiveness of sins, renewal of life, and eternal glory. The discussion, therefore, concerns the granting of these goods, or their denial. The One who makes that decision is Christ. He is, says Rev 3:7:

> ... the holy one, the true one, who has the key of David, who opens and no one shall shut, who shuts and no one opens.

2. Christ exercises this power through his church. He gave the keys of the kingdom of heaven, *i.e.*, the authority to open this kingdom and to close it, to the church. He did not merely give it to Peter (Mt 16:19) and to the apostles (Jn 20:23), but to HIS CHURCH. See Mt 18:17-18:

> ... TELL IT TO THE CHURCH ... Truly, I say to you, whatever you bind on earth shall be bound in heaven, and whatever you loose on earth shall be loosed in heaven.

3. The church may not leave this power unused. It must use it,

   a. to save sinners (Excommunication is the "ultimate remedy" to bring about repentance. Note that the Catechism discusses church discipline in the part on our *deliverance* (1 Cor 5:5).);

   b. to save the congregation from the possibility that the evil may conquer the hearts of all; and

   c. to keep the name of the Lord holy.

   The church must also ensure that it does not misuse church discipline. It may only be exercised in accordance with the command of Christ. He has indicated clearly in his Word who must be admitted to and who must be excluded from the kingdom in Isa 3:10, 11:

   > Tell the righteous that it shall be well with them. . . .Woe to the wicked! It shall be ill with him. . . .

   Christ has also commanded the *manner* in which the power must be exercised. There are two keys:

   a. the preaching of the holy gospel; and

   b. church discipline.

Q. & A. 84
SON OF MAN, I HAVE MADE YOU A WATCHMAN

A. NOTES

1. The preaching of the holy gospel is a key of the kingdom of heaven. By the preaching it is openly proclaimed who is entitled to share in this kingdom and who is excluded from it. This teaches us the great significance of the preaching. For in accordance with its testimony God will judge, both in this life and in the life to come.

    The preaching must, therefore, proclaim the eternal weal and woe. It may not degenerate into a genial talk about religious topics. Nor is its message concerned with interpersonal relationships, to which many restrict it nowadays.

2. The preaching OPENS the kingdom of heaven. It points to it and acquaints one with it. Further, it shows the way (Jesus Christ) to this kingdom. Not only that, but it also proclaims, in the Lord's Name, to everyone who enters upon that way and believes in Christ that his sins are forgiven. That is how it opens the kingdom to us and ushers us in into the joy of the Father.

3. The preaching CLOSES the kingdom of heaven. For the gospel does not only speak about salvation, but also about condemnation and say of him who does not obey the Son that the wrath of God rests upon him (Jn 3:36). This must be proclaimed openly to unbelievers, so that they may be shaken out of their false security and learn to ask for grace.

Q. & A. 85
LEAD THE SINNER TO REPENTANCE

A. NOTES

1. Scripture clearly teaches church discipline or excommunication. 1 Cor 5:13 says:

    > Drive out the wicked person from among you.

    (See also Mt 18:18; Rom 16:17; 1 Cor 5:1, 2; Tit 3:10; 2 Thess 3:6, 14).

2. The exercise of Christian discipline is concerned with those who "call themselves Christians but show themselves to be un-christian in doctrine or life." It is concerned with those who belong to the *congregation.* God will judge those who are outside (1 Cor 5:13). And it is concerned with "doctrine and life." Article 66 of the CO states:

... the consistory shall ensure that church discipline is used to punish sins against both the purity of doctrine and the piety of conduct.

(See also Gal 6:2; Tit 3:11).

3. The first step in discipline is *brotherly* admonition. The keys of the kingdom were not given to one person or to a board (the consistory), but to the CONGREGATION. That is why the congregation is involved in every step of censure. And it is the congregation which begins all discipline. Good administration of discipline is impossible unless the congregation is faithful in this respect. Relaxation of church discipline (which is the beginning of the destruction of the church!) is always the fault of the congregation! Mt 18:15-17 says:

> If your brother sins against you, go and tell him his fault, between you and him alone. If he listens to you, you have gained your brother. But if he does not listen, take one or two others along with you, that every word may be confirmed by the evidence of two or three witnesses. If he refuses to listen to them, tell it to the church.

(The witnesses serve as witnesses of the PUNISHMENT, not of the SIN which was committed).

4. After investigating the accusation and finding it correct, the consistory begins with the admonition. Article 68 of the CO then provides:

> Anyone who obstinately rejects the admonition by the consistory or who has committed a public sin shall be suspended from the Lord's Supper.

This is the so-called silent censure. If the sinner does not repent after continued admonition, this is followed by:

THE FIRST PUBLIC ANNOUNCEMENT. In it the *sin* is made known and the congregation is encouraged to pray for the sinner, whose name is not yet mentioned, and for the work of the elders. If the sinner still does not repent after continued admonition, this is followed by:

THE SECOND PUBLIC ANNOUNCEMENT. In it the sin, as well as the name and address of the sinner are made known to the congregation, so that it will not only pray for the sinner, but will also admonish him or her. This second public announcement is made only after the advice of classis has been obtained, so that everything is done as justly as possible. If this also does not bear fruit, it is followed by:

THE THIRD PUBLIC ANNOUNCEMENT. In it the date when excommunication will take place unless the sinner repents is made known, again with the advice of classis.

The EXCOMMUNICATION takes place in accordance with the applicable form. Read it! In the excommunication it is declared officially, in the words of the Form for the Excommunication of Communicant Members (The Excommunication), that the sinner

. . . is now excluded from the fellowship of Christ and from His kingdom. He (she) may no longer use the sacraments. He (she) has no part any more in the spiritual blessings and benefits which Christ bestows upon His Church.

(See also the Form for the Excommunication of Non-Communicant Members).

This shows the seriousness of the matter!

5. If the excommunicated person should afterwards repent and he PROMISES and shows real amendment, he will be readmitted into the communion of the church in accordance with the Form for Readmission into the Church of Christ. Read this form, in the back of your Book of Praise, too!

6. When you publicly profess your faith, you place yourself under the supervision and discipline of the consistory. You are then asked (in the Form for the Public Profession of Faith, Profession, Fourth Question):

Do you promise to submit willingly to the admonition and discipline of the Church, if it should happen, and may God graciously prevent it, that you become delinquent in doctrine or in conduct?

Many violate this promise when they are admonished, to their destruction. We must consider it a privilege that God wants to watch over our salvation also in this way.

B. CROSS REFERENCES

1. The CD V, 14 also states that God maintains, continues and perfects his word of grace, *inter alia*, by exhortations and threatenings.

2. Article 30 of the BC states that evil men are to be disciplined in a spiritual way and restrained.

3. Artcile 32 of the BC states:

. . . discipline and excommunication ought to be exercised in agreement with the Word of God.

4. Apart from the forms for excommunication and readmission, reference should be made also to the Form for the Ordination (or Installation) of Ministers of the Word, Form for the Ordination (or Installation) of Missionaries, and Form for the Ordination of Elders and Deacons. Further, also to the Form for the Celebration of the Lord's Supper (as well as the Abbreviated Form for the Celebration of the Lord's Supper), in which the power to close and open the kingdom of heaven is practised especially.

C. COMMENTS

1. Non-Communicant members are also subject to the discipline of the congregation. The General Synod of Sneek-Utrecht gave guidelines for the exercise of discipline over non-communicant members in 1940. This

matter had been addressed at many previous synods.[18]

2. When office bearers "have committed a public or otherwise gross sin, or refuse to heed the admonitions by the consistory with the deacons," they must be suspended from office. (CO, art. 71. And see art. 72).

3. In earlier times a general pronouncement of forgiveness of sins (absolution) was made in the public worship service after the reading of the law and a general confession of sins.

D. HERESIES

1. The idea of the state, or national church.

2. The denial of the necessity and possibility of discipline in matters of doctrine.

3. Labadism.

E. QUESTIONS (Q&A 83-85)

1. What is a key? What is being discussed here, therefore? What is the kingdom of heaven? What do those who are admitted to it have?

2. Who, alone, can give admission to this kingdom? Through whom does he exercise this power?

3. Prove from Scripture that Christ gave the power to open and close the kingdom of heaven to the church.

4. For what purpose must the church exercise discipline? To what must it have regard when it exercises discipline?

5. What are the two keys?

6. What is the purpose of the preaching of the gospel in this respect? How does it open? How does it close?

7. Give a couple of Scripture references to church discipline.

8. Over whom is church discipline exercised? About what is it exercised?

9. With what does church discipline begin? How does the brotherly admonition progress?

10. How does the exercise of church discipline by the consistory progress?

11. From what is a person excluded when he is excommunicated?

12. Can an excommunicated person be readmitted? When and how?

13. Is it proper for a person to withdraw himself from church discipline? Why not?

14. Are non-communicant members subject to church discipline? What about office bearers?

---

[18]Transl. note: See now the Form for the Excommunication of Non-Communicant Members.

PREDESTINATION

A. NOTES

1. In the Second Part of the Catechism, about our deliverance, we referred a couple of times to election or predestination. Lord's Day 21, Answer 54 spoke of "a church chosen to everlasting life," and LD 19, Answer 52 confessed that Christ "will take me and all His chosen ones to Himself into heavenly joy and glory." Thus, the Catechism does confess predestination, although this manual for the youth of the church does not give a broad exposition of this doctrine. Article 16 of the BC is more detailed, while ch. I of the CD gives the most ample discussion.

2. The CD I, 7 states:

   Election is the unchangeable purpose of God whereby, before the foundation of the world, out of the whole human race, which had fallen by its own fault out of its original integrity into sin and perdition, He *has, according to the sovereign good pleasure of His will, out of mere grace, chosen in Christ to salvation a definite number of persons, neither better nor more worthy than others,* but with themselves involved in a common misery. He has also from eternity appointed Christ to be the Mediator and Head of all the elect and the foundation of salvation.

   Memorize the parts in italics!

3. The CD I, 15 states concerning Reprobation:

   . . . not all men are elect but . . . some have not been elected or have been passed by in the eternal election of God. Out of His most free, most just, blameless, and unchangeable *good pleasure, God has decreed to leave them in the common misery into which they have by their own fault plunged themselves,* and not to give them saving faith and the grace of conversion. These, having been left in their own ways and under His just judgment, God has decreed finally to condemn and punish eternally, not only on account of their unbelief but also on account of all their other sins, for the declaration of His justice. This is the decree of reprobation, which by no means makes God the author of sin (the very thought is blasphemous!), but rather declares Him an awesome, blameless, and just judge and avenger thereof.

   Memorize the parts in italics!

4. The reason for election and reprobation is not a foreknowledge of faith and good works, or of a person's unbelief and irredeemability. It occurs "without any consideration of their works" (BC, art. 16). The reason for election and reprobation is solely and exclusively God's mercy. Rom 9:16 says:

So it depends not upon man's will or exertion, but upon God's mercy.

It is not *out* of faith, but *to* faith. Eph 1:4 says:

> Even as he chose us in him before the foundation of the world, that we should be holy and blameless before him.

5. One cannot call this predestination unjust, for, as CD I, 1 states:

   > God would have done injustice to no one if He had willed to leave the whole human race in sin . . . *into which they plunged themselves*.

6. This election does not make us careless, for it does not exclude our responsibility. For it is an election to faith. And the Lord *calls* us to this faith by the preaching of his holy gospel (LD 25, Ans. 65). It is necessary to distinguish between the *decree* of predestination and its *execution*. God carries out his decree in such a way that our responsibility is not excluded. (See also CD I, 13; LD 24, Ans. 64). He who is lost is not lost because he was rejected, but because of his own sin.

7. To become certain of one's election is a fruit of faith (CD I, 6). We must, therefore, work on that. 2 Pet 1:10 says:

   > Therefore, brethren, be the more zealous to confirm your call and election, for if you do this you will never fall.

8. The doctrine of predestination has not been revealed to us in order to alarm us (CD I, 16), but in order that we might give honour to God for our salvation (CD I, 13, 18; Rom 11:33-36), and in order to comfort us (CD I, 14).

B. COMMENTS

1. Infralapsarianism and Supralapsarianism. These doctrines are concerned with the order of the decrees in God's eternal counsel. The infralapsarians placed the decree of predestination under the decree of the fall. The supralapsarians reversed the order.[19]

C. HERESIES

1. Fatalism.

2. Remonstrantism (Arminianism).

3. General atonement.

4. Universalism.

---

[19]Trans. note: Supralapsarians begin with and reason out of God's eternal election in explaining the covenant. Infralapsarians, on the other hand, begin with the chronological facts of man's history as revealed in Scripture in explaining the covenant, but ultimately they rely for the deepest ground of their salvation on God's sovereign grace and eternal election. Our confessions speak in an infralapsarian manner, although they cannot be said to have adopted that approach as a system.

D. QUESTIONS

1. Does the Catechism discuss predestination? Does it confess this doctrine? Where? Where is it confessed in greater detail in the Three Forms of Unity?
2. What is election? What is reprobation?
3. What is not the reason for election? What is the reason? What do Rom 9:16 and Eph 1:4 say?
4. May one call predestination unjust? Why not?
5. Does it make one careless? Why not?
6. How do we become certain about our election?
7. Why was predestination revealed to us?

OUR THANKFULNESS

Lord's Days 32-52

DIVISION

Lord's Day 32:	The Necessity of thankfulness.
Lord's Day 33:	The Nature of thankfulness (conversion).
Lord's Days 34-44a:	The Rule of thankfulness (the law of the Lord).
Lord's Day 44b:	The Imperfection of our thankfulness.
Lord's Days 45-52:	The Power of thankfulness (prayer).

86. Q. Since we have been delivered
from our misery
by grace alone through Christ,
without any merit of our own,
why must we yet do good works?

A. Because Christ,
having redeemed us by His blood,
also renews us by His Holy Spirit
to be His image,
so that with our whole life
we may show ourselves thankful to God
for His benefits,[1]
and He may be praised by us.[2]
Further, that we ourselves
may be assured of our faith
by its fruits,[3]
and that by our godly walk of life
we may win our neighbours for Christ.[4]

[1] Rom. 6:13; 12:1, 2; I Pet. 2:5-10.
[2] Matt. 5:16; I Cor. 6:19, 20.
[3] Matt. 7:17, 18; Gal. 5:22-24; II Pet. 1:10, 11.
[4] Matt. 5:14-16; Rom. 14:17-19; I Pet. 2:12; 3:1, 2.

87. Q. Can those be saved
who do not turn to God
from their ungrateful and impenitent
walk of life?

A. By no means.
Scripture says that no unchaste person,
idolater, adulterer,
thief, greedy person,
drunkard, slanderer,
robber, or the like
shall inherit the kingdom of God.[1]

[1] I Cor. 6:9, 10; Gal. 5:19-21; Eph. 5:5, 6; I John 3:14.

THE GOOD TREE BRINGS FORTH GOOD FRUIT

A. NOTES

1. We should note that in this first Q. of the third part, the Catechism ties the third part to the first and the second parts. We cannot show ourselves thankful to the Lord unless we acknowledge our *sins and misery* and accept our *deliverance* through Christ in faith. Ps 51:17 says:

> The sacrifice acceptable to God is a broken spirit; a broken and contrite heart, O God, thou wilt not despise.

This forecloses any notion of legalism and the meritoriousness of good works.

2. In this Answer the Catechism once again exposes the folly of the accusation of the Roman Catholics that the Reformed doctrine makes people careless and wicked. (See also LD 24, Q&A 64). It also rejects the heresy of the antinomians, who suppose that we are no longer subject to the law because Christ has redeemed us from it. But Christ does not redeem us from the law, but from the curse of the law (Gal 3:13).

3. The necessity of good works becomes apparent when we pay attention to their purpose, which is three-fold:

a. for *God*: so that he may be praised by us;

b. for *us*: so that we may be assured of our faith by its fruits;

c. for our *neighbours*: so that they may be won for Christ by our godly walk of life.

4. Good works are necessary because of the purpose of the redemption in Christ. 1 Pet 2:9 says:

> But you are a chosen race, a royal priesthood, a holy nation, God's own people, that you may declare the wonderful deeds of him who called you out of darkness into his marvellous light.

Tit 2:14 says:

> Who gave himself for us to redeem us from all iniquity and to purify for himself a people of his own who are zealous for good deeds.

The purpose of the creation of man was that he should praise God. (See also LD 3, Ans. 6). Christ restores this purpose. The highest goal of our redemption is not our salvation, but the honour of God! This Answer does not say: so that we may show thankfulness to God, but SO THAT . . . WE MAY SHOW OURSELVES THANKFUL TO GOD. Our thankfulness is not that we give something to the Lord while remaining unchanged. Rather, it is that we offer *ourselves* to the Lord, in reciprocal love.

We must do this *with our whole life.* Our entire life must be service to the Lord. He bought us and we are his possession. 1 Cor 10:31 says:

> So, whether you eat or drink, or whatever you do, do all to the glory of God.

5. The second purpose of good works is that each person may be assured of his faith by its fruits. This assurance is not the result of an arithmetical sum: I do good works, therefore I believe. Rather, it is a gift of the Holy Spirit. He gives it by means of good works. His light does not shine in the life of a person who is careless and disobedient. But he who lives a sanctified life discovers therein the fruit that he may be assured of his faith. If I never skate, or only rarely, I am no longer certain that I can do so. But if I do it regularly, I am certain that I can. (See 2 Pet 1:10).

6. The third purpose of good works is that our neighbours may be won for Christ. Jesus says in Mt 5:16:

> Let your light so shine before men, that they may see your good works and give glory to your Father who is in heaven.

We must confess the Lord's Name. But those who do not listen to it, must be drawn by our walk of life. (See 1 Pet 3:1, 2). That is the best form of evangelism. Without it no evangelism amounts to anything. Those who are Christian in name only are a great detriment to the kingdom of God. But a God-fearing walk of life will: (a) strengthen our brothers and sisters in the good fight (many a person has been led to the zealous and conscientious service of the Lord through the good example of another person!); and (b) show the power of godliness to those who are outside. Doing good works is not a burden to the believer, but a delight. Would it be a burden for a flower to bloom and display its beauty? For it is Christ who works all of this in us. Eph 2:10 says:

> For we are his workmanship, created in Christ Jesus for good works, which God prepared beforehand, that we should walk in them.

He renews us by his Holy Spirit in his image.

Doing good works is not: "You're never allowed to do anything." Rather, it is that we again become normal people. For we were created to the end that we should do good works. And in doing them is life. Ps 119:60 (rhymed version) says:

> Behold, O LORD, Thy precepts I revere;
> I love Thy law, I scorn the wicked's railing.
> Preserve my life, O LORD, and persevere
> According to Thy mercy never failing. . . .

B. CROSS REFERENCES

1. In article 24 of the BC we confess that true faith makes man "live a new life and frees him from the slavery of sin." (See the entire article).

2. The CD V, 10, acknowledges that we are assured that we are children and heirs of God "by the serious and holy pursuit of a good conscience and good works." (See also CD I, 9, 12 and 13).

C. QUESTIONS

1. What subject matter does the third part of the Catechism discuss? Which Lord's Days does this part encompass?

2. How is the third part divided?

3. What does Ps 51:17 say? Can we show ourselves thankful to the Lord without knowing our sins and misery? Which sacrifices does the Lord delight in?

4. Which two heresies does the Catechism reject in this A.? What do the antinomians teach?

5. What is the three-fold goal of good works?

6. What does 1 Pet 2:9 say? What is restored through Christ's redemptive work? What is the highest purpose of the redemption? Is it sufficient if we give the Lord a lot? With what must show ourselves thankful? What does 1 Cor 10:31 say?

7. Who assures us of our faith? What means does he use to do this?

8. What is the purpose of good works toward those who do not yet know Christ? What is their purpose toward those who do belong to him?

9. Does the doing of good works restrict our lives? Is it a burden to believers to do good works?

Q. & A. 87
FAITH WITHOUT WORKS IS DEAD

A. NOTES

1. Good works do not earn salvation. Eph 2:8 says:

> For by grace you have been saved through faith; and this is not your own doing, it is the gift of God.

But they are indispensable to salvation. No one shall see the Lord unless he is sanctified. (See Heb 12:14; Mt 3:10; Rev 21:27; Jas 2:20, 26).

2. This does not mean that only sinless people are saved. Such people do not exist. Also believers sometimes fall into serious sins. (Read CD V, 4-7). But although they sometimes *act* sinfully, they do not *walk* in sin. They do not *continue* in an ungrateful and impenitent life. They rise again from their fall into sin through God's grace and turn to him in repentance (Ps 51). But if repentance is lacking and we continue to live in ingratitude, there is no redemption.

3. And yet a light shines for those who are evil and ungrateful. The Q. speaks about those who do not repent. If those who are evil repent, there is salvation for them! Isa 55:7 says:

> Let the wicked forsake his way, and the unrighteous man his thoughts; let him return to the LORD, that he may have mercy on him, and to our God, for he will abundantly pardon.

B. QUESTIONS

1. Do we earn salvation by doing good works? Can we, then, do without good works?
2. Are only sinless people saved? If not, what kind of person does the Catechism refer to?
3. Is there any hope for godless people?

88 *Q.* *What is the true repentance or conversion of man?*

    A. *It is the dying of the old nature*
      and the coming to life of the new.[1]

> [1] *Rom. 6:1-11; I Cor. 5:7; II Cor. 5:17; Eph. 4:22-24;*
> *Col. 3:5-10.*

89. *Q.* *What is the dying of the old nature?*

    A. *It is to grieve with heartfelt sorrow*
      that we have offended God by our sin,
      and more and more to hate it
      and flee from it.[1]

> [1] *Ps. 51:3, 4, 17; Joel 2:12, 13; Rom. 8:12, 13; II Cor. 7:10.*

90. *Q.* *What is the coming to life*
      of the new nature?

    A. *It is a heartfelt joy*
      in God through Christ,[1]
      and a love and delight
      to live according to the will of God
      in all good works.[2]

> [1] *Ps. 51:8, 12; Is. 57:15; Rom. 5:1; 14:17.*
> [2] *Rom. 6:10, 11; Gal. 2:20.*

91. *Q.* *But what are good works?*

    A. *Only those which are done*
        out of true faith,[1]
        in accordance with the law of God,[2]
        and to His glory,[3]
      and not those based
        on our own opinion
        or on precepts of men.[4]

> [1] *Joh. 15:5; Rom. 14:23; Heb. 11:6.*
> [2] *Lev. 18:4; I Sam. 15:22; Eph. 2:10.*
> [3] *I Cor. 10:31.*
> [4] *Deut. 12:32; Is. 29:13; Ezek. 20:18, 19; Matt. 15:7-9.*

A. NOTES

1. At the end of the previous LD we already described the nature of a life of thankfulness as "repentance." For LD 32, Q. 87 said of those who are UNgrateful that they do NOT repent. This LD now tells us what repentance is and, thus, describes the nature of thankfulness. The Catechism does not describe the manner in which repentance occurs. That differs substantially from person to person. Lydia's repentance was different from that of the jailer. But the *essence* of repentance is the same for everyone. And it is the essence that is important. The question is not when or how, but *whether* we *live a life of repentance*. We must ensure that we do that!

2, The Catechism asks about THE repentance or conversion. We do speak about an initial and a continuing repentance, but these are one. They are the beginning and continuation of one and the same thing. Further, the Catechism mentions the TRUE repentance. For there is also a sham conversion which is a turning from sin to virtue. But that is only a superficial change in which man does not turn to GOD. Repentance is a complete reversal. Man, who lived his life turned away from God and disregarded him, is turned around, converted to God, so that he begins to live for God. (See 1 Thess 1:9). Moreover, the Catechism asks about the conversion of MAN. Not only the serious sinners, but EVERYONE is in need of repentance. For it is true of everyone, as Ps 14:3 says:

   . . . there is none that does good, no, not one.

3. The Answer says that conversion consists of two parts. These are two sides of the same coin. The one does not follow the other; they always occur together. The old nature dies as the new comes to life.

4. The expressions "old nature" and "new nature" are scriptural (see Eph 4:22-24; and Col 3:9, 10). The term "old nature" denotes man born in sin, who says no to God and his Word. The term "new nature" denotes man as renewed by Christ and who is continually being renewed more and more by his Spirit and Word; it is regenerate man, who says yes to God and his Word.

   The terms "old nature" and "new nature" do not, therefore, describe two persons, but two *ways of life* of one and the same person. We call the first way of life "old," because it is decayed and corrupt, and because it was the first state of life of the converted person. But it must yield more and more to the other state of life which comes into existence, the "new" nature. When we speak about the old and new nature of MAN,[20] we indicate thereby that sin affected our entire human nature, but that it is also entirely renewed in conversion or regeneration. This is not something that occurs at one moment of time. Man's old nature still lives in regenerate man and continues to act accordingly. (See Rom 7:18-21; CD V, 1). The Catechism also speaks of a dying of the old nature, which connotes a continuing process, not a concluded one. But the old nature does not govern the life of regenerate man any more. On the contrary, it has to yield. What is sinful is pushed back and dies, and the new nature rises and begins to conquer. The Holy Spirit works this in us by the Word. Hence, our responsibility is not excluded. The Bible says as often that we convert ourselves, as that the Lord converts us. Both are true. Phil 2:12, 13 says:

> ... work out your own salvation with fear and trembling; For God is at work in you, both to will and to work for his good pleasure.

B.   CROSS REFERENCES

1.   The CD III/IV, 12 says:

> ... Therefore the will so renewed is not only acted upon and moved by God but, acted upon by God, the will itself also acts. Hence, also man himself is rightly said to believe and repent through the grace he has received.

Q. & A. 89
THE DYING OF THE OLD NATURE

A.   NOTES

1.   The original languages of both the Old and New Testament use two words for "repentance." One connotes primarily a change in insight and inclination, while the other connotes primarily a change in behaviour and way of life. Thus, Scripture identifies conversion as a matter of our inner self: we begin to think differently about things and nourish other desires; *and* as a matter of our actions: we begin to speak and act in a different manner. You will find both elements in this Answer of the Catechism. It speaks about a heartfelt sorrow *and* a fleeing from sin. But we should not suppose that the one without the other is sufficient. A mere external change does not amount to conversion. So also, it is foolish to say about a careless life style that everything is fine on the inside!

---

[20]The Dutch version of the Catechism, consonant with the Dutch Bible translations, uses the terms "old man" and "new man." These terms, which are also used in the KJV and were used in earlier English versions of the Catechism, are not subject to the same misunderstanding in Dutch as they are in English.

2. Conversion is, in the first place, a heartfelt regret: a sorrow towards God! (2 Cor 7:10). Ps 51:4 says:

> Against thee, thee only, have I sinned, and done that which is evil in thy sight. . . .

It is not a sorrow about the consequences of sin, but because we have angered God by our sin. This sorrow is not more genuine the more troubled you feel and the more tears you shed, but because it is directed to GOD.

3. Further, conversion is a hating of sin. We no longer justify and cover up sin. We are its enemy and flee from it. It is a hero's flight! This flight is the only way to win. He who believes that he can remain close to sin and the places where sin is powerful, because he knows how far he can go, does not know himself. He is like the moth which circles around a flame!

4. The Catechism says that we do this "more and more." For there is growth in conversion. We begin to hate sin more and more, because we begin to see more and more that its nature is hateful and dishonours God.

B. CROSS REFERENCES

1. Note also the Form for the Celebration of the Lord's Supper (Self-examination, First Part).

Q. & A. 90
THE COMING TO LIFE OF THE NEW NATURE

A. NOTES

1. This Answer, too, describes conversion in accordance with its internal ("heartfelt joy in God . . . and a love and delight") and its external ("live") aspects. It is a heartfelt joy in God through Christ. Joy in him, who so exceedingly loved us and showers us with his blessings day in day out. And it is a love and delight to live according to the will of God in all good works.

B. CROSS REFERENCES

1. Note here also the Form for the Celebration of the Lord's Supper (Self-examination, Third Part).

C. QUESTIONS (Q&A 88-90)

1. What is the nature of a life of thankfulness? Is it important how and when our conversion began? If not, what should we pay attention to?

2. Why does the Catechism ask about TRUE repentance or conversion? What is a sham conversion? What is repentance or conversion? Who needs to be converted?

3. Of how many parts does conversion consist? Does the one follow the other?

4. What is the "old nature"? What is the "new nature"? Do these terms describe two persons? If not, what then? Why is the old nature called "old"? Why is the new nature called "new"? Why do we speak of the old and new nature of MAN?

5. Does the old nature still exist in the regenerate person? But what happens to him?

6. Who works conversion? Are we converted, or do we also convert ourselves?

7. How many words does the Bible use for conversion? What is the difference between them?

8. About what is there sorrow in conversion? What determines the genuineness of conversion? What is the position of generate man towards sin?

9. Is conversion something that occurs at one moment of time? Is there progression in conversion?

10. About what is there joy in conversion? What is the position of regenerate man toward the will of the Lord?

Q. & A. 91
THAT WHICH IS NOT DONE OUT OF FAITH IS SIN

A. NOTES

1. The previous Answer stated that conversion motivates us to do good works. It is natural, therefore, that this Q. now asks what good works are. The Catechism does not answer by giving a list of certain works. For good works are not separate works of prayer and charity. Good works are all those works to which the Lord calls us by his Word and in the way he directs our lives. So long as they correspond to what the Catechism says in this Answer. Many a Christian home maker, who is unknown to the world, does more good works than any number of persons whose "good works" are common knowledge!

2. The Catechism points to the SOURCE, the RULE and the PURPOSE of good works.

   The SOURCE is true faith. Rom 8:8 says:

   > . . . those who are in the flesh cannot please God.

   Rom 14:23 says:

   > . . . for whatever does not proceed from faith is sin.

   We cannot do anything unless we abide in Christ (Jn 15:4).

3. The RULE is God's law. The Catechism makes it explicit that we are not to be guided by human rules. We do that readily. But Jesus says in Mt 15:9:

   > In vain do they worship me, teaching as doctrines the precepts of men.

   Self-willed religion is always impressive, but it is worthless.

4. The PURPOSE of good works is the glory of God.

   Mt 6:1:

> Beware of practicing your piety before men in order to be seen by them; for then you will have no reward from your Father who is in heaven.

5. None of our works is perfect. (See LD 24, Ans. 62 (conclusion), and LD 44, Ans. 114). But we also confess in the BC, art. 24:

> These works, proceeding from the good root of faith, are good and acceptable in the sight of God, since they are all sanctified by His grace.

B. HERESIES

1. Antinomianism.

2. Barthianism.

C. QUESTIONS

1. Are "good works" special works which only certain people can do?

2. What does the Catechism point out about good works? What is the source of good works?

3. According to what rule must they be done? What should we guard against?

4. What is the purpose of good works? Are they perfect? Does God delight in them? Why?

5. Where does the Catechism speak about the unmeritoriousness of and the reward for works?

92. Q.   What is the law of the LORD?

A.   God spoke all these words, saying: I am the LORD your God, who brought you
out of the land of Egypt, out of the house of bondage.
1. You shall have no other gods before Me.
2. You shall not make for yourself a graven image, or any likeness of anything
that is in heaven above, or that is in the earth beneath, or that is in the
water under the earth; you shall not bow down to them or serve them; for
I the LORD your God am a jealous God, visiting the iniquity of the fathers
upon the children to the third and fourth generation of those who hate Me,
but showing steadfast love to thousands of those who love Me and keep My
commandments.
3. You shall not take the Name of the LORD your God in vain; for the LORD
will not hold him guiltless who takes His Name in vain.
4. Remember the sabbath day, to keep it holy. Six days you shall labour, and do
all your work; but the seventh day is a sabbath to the LORD your God; in
it you shall not do any work, you, or your son, or your daughter, your
manservant, or your maidservant, or your cattle, or the sojourner who is
within your gates; for in six days the LORD made heaven and earth, the
sea, and all that is in them, and rested the seventh day; therefore the
LORD blessed the sabbath day and hallowed it.
5. Honour your father and your mother, that your days may be long in the land
which the LORD your God gives you.
6. You shall not kill.
7. You shall not commit adultery.
8. You shall not steal.
9. You shall not bear false witness against your neighbour.
10. You shall not covet your neighbour's house; you shall not covet your
neighbour's wife, or his manservant, or his maidservant, or his ox, or his
ass, or anything that is your neighbour's.[1]
   [1] Ex. 20:1-17; Deut. 5:6-21.

93. Q.   How are these commandments divided?

A.   Into two parts.
The first teaches us how to live in relation to God;
the second, what duties we owe our neighbour.[1]
   [1] Matt. 22:37-40.

94. Q.   What does the LORD require in the first commandment?

A.   That for the sake of my very salvation I avoid and flee all idolatry,[1] witchcraft,
superstition,[2] and prayer to saints or to other creatures.[3]
Further, that I rightly come to know the only true God.[4] trust in Him alone,[5]
submit to Him with all humility[6] and patience,[7] expect all good from Him
only,[8] and love,[9] fear,[10] and honour Him[11] with all my heart.
In short, that I forsake all creatures rather than do the least thing
against His will.[12]
   [1] 1 Cor. 6:9, 10; 10:5-14; 1 John 5:21.
   [2] Lev. 19:31; Deut. 18:9-12.
   [3] Matt. 4:10; Rev. 19:10; 22:8, 9.
   [4] John 17:3.
   [5] Jer. 17:5, 7.
   [6] 1 Pet. 5:5, 6.
   [7] Rom. 5:3, 4; 1 Cor. 10:10; Phil. 2:14; Col. 1:11; Heb. 10:36.
   [8] Ps. 104:27, 28; Is. 45:7; James 1:17.
   [9] Deut. 6:5; (Matt. 22:37).
   [10] Deut. 6:2; Ps. 111:10; Prov. 1:7; 9:10; Matt. 10:28; 1 Pet. 1:17.
   [11] Deut. 6:13; (Matt. 4:10); Deut. 10:20.
   [12] Matt. 5:29, 30; 10:37-39; Acts 5:29.

95. Q.   What is idolatry?

A.   Idolatry is having or inventing something in which to put our trust instead of, or
in addition to, the only true God who has revealed Himself in His Word.[1]
   [1] 1 Chron. 16:26; Gal. 4:8, 9; Eph. 5:5; Phil. 3:19.

THE TEN WORDS

A. NOTES

1. Lord's Day 2 already taught us the summary of the law. Now all the ten commandments will be discussed separately. They constitute the rule of thankfulness. That they were given for this purpose, is apparent from the introduction. The law was not given to enable us to attain our own salvation by observing it. For the Lord says that he freed us. The introduction says that he adopted us as his people. And now he gives us the law as the rule of his house so that we may know how we should live in it.

2. The law does, indeed, display the characteristics of a document peculiarly applicable to the Israelites. (See commandments 4, 5 and 10). However, it is valid for all time, in fact for eternity. Jesus did not come to abolish the law, but to fulfil it (Mt 5:17). And he summarized it again in Mt 22:37-40.

3. We find the law in Ex 20:1ff and in Deut 5:6ff. There are minor differences between these two versions. These occur, *inter alia*, in the motivation for the fourth and in the order and contents of the tenth commandment.

4. We should not view the law as having to do solely with matters external to us. The tenth commandment shows clearly that it has relevance also to what takes place in our hearts. We must understand the law in a spiritual sense. In the explanation of the law you must have regard to the following:

   a. Each commandment names the worst of a particular type of sin and thereby comprehends the whole type.

   b. The opposite of what is *forbidden* is *required*.

   c. The law is directed not only to our actions, but also to our inner being, our deliberations, desires and thoughts.

5. The first nine commandments respectively demand love for: 1. God's person, 2. God's service, 3. God's name, 4. God's day, 5. parents, 6. the neighbour's life, 7. the neighbour's wife, 8. the neighbour's property, and 9. the neighbour's reputation. The 10th commandment demands that we have this hearty love and show it.

Q. & A. 93
GOD AND THE NEIGHBOUR

A. NOTES

1. The law is a unit. Jas 2:10 says:

   > For whoever keeps the whole law but fails in one point has become guilty of all of it.

   Nevertheless, we can divide it into two parts. Jesus himself also spoke of two commandments. The first part, which comprises the first four commandments, tells us what we owe to God, while the second part, commandments five to ten, informs us what we owe to our neighbour. (See the Notes to LD 2, Q&A 4 about the neighbour and about the relationship between the first and second parts of the law).

Q. & A. 94 and 95
GIVE ME YOUR HEART

A. NOTES

1. This is the root commandment, the basis of the law. That is why it is the first. The phrase "no other gods" does not mean that there are any, but that people act as though there are. The phrase "before Me" also refers to what goes on in your heart!

2. The commandment FORBIDS idolatry, that is, putting your trust in something or someone instead of or in addition to God. In other words, it means giving the honour which belongs only to God to something or someone else. There are many sins in which this happens. Some examples are:

   WITCHCRAFT, *i.e.*, the expectation of a work of God from something which is not God.

   FORTUNE-TELLING, *i.e.*, the expectation that something which is not God will reveal what is hidden.

   SUPERSTITION, *i.e.*, the expectation that something which is not God will do something which only God can do. Amulets and mascots fall into this category.

   For the sake of your very salvation you must *avoid* and *flee* these!

3. The commandment REQUIRES us to come to know the only true God, and to trust, love, fear (*i.e.*, respect, esteem) and honour him. In short, our hearts must be so devoted to him that we would rather forsake all creatures than do the least thing against his will. Ps 73:25 says:

Whom have I in heaven but thee? And there is nothing upon earth that I desire besides thee.

B. HERESIES

1. The principial equation of Christianity with other religions, such as spiritualism.

C. QUESTIONS (Q&A 92-95)

1. Was the law given us so that, by keeping it, we could earn eternal life ourselves? If not, why was it given? How is that apparent?

2. Was the law meant only for Israel? Why does it appear that way?

3. Where do we read the law in the Bible? Are there differences between the two versions? What are they?

4. What must we have regard to in the explanation of the law? Recite the rules for its explanation. For what do the respective commandments demand love?

5. Into how many parts do we divide the commandments? What is the difference between them?

6. Are there "other gods"? What does the phrase "before Me" mean?

7. What is forbidden in the first commandment? What are witchcraft, fortune-telling and superstition?

8. What does the commandment require?

LORD'S DAY 35

96. Q. What does God require
in the second commandment?

A. We are not to make an image of God in any way,[1]
nor to worship Him in any other manner
than He has commanded in His Word.[2]

> [1] Deut. 4:15-19; Is. 40:18-25; Acts 17:29; Rom. 1:23.
> [2] Lev. 10:1-7; Deut. 12:30; I Sam. 15:22, 23; Matt. 15:9;
> John 4:23, 24.

97. Q. May we then not make
any image at all?

A. God cannot and may not
be visibly portrayed in any way.
Creatures may be portrayed,
but God forbids us
to make or have any images of them
in order to worship them
or to serve God through them.[1]

> [1] Ex. 34:13, 14, 17; Num. 33:52; II Kings 18:4, 5; Is. 40:25.

98. Q. But may images not be tolerated
in the churches
as "books for the laity"?

A. No, for we should not be wiser than God.
He wants His people to be taught
not by means of dumb images[1]
but by the living preaching of His Word.[2]

> [1] Jer. 10:8; Hab. 2:18-20.
> [2] Rom. 10:14, 15, 17; II Tim. 3:16, 17; II Pet. 1:19.

A. NOTES

1. A "graven image" is any image made of wood or stone. "Any likeness" means any conceivable representation of something.

These images or representations may be of beings in heaven above (birds), or in the earth beneath (a calf), or in the water under the earth (a fish, or crocodile).

To "bow down" and to "serve" means to offer the honour of worship and sacrifice. The LORD is a jealous God. His relationship to his people is so close that he does not tolerate a rival (*cf.* the marriage relationship). Those who hate him bring upon themselves a punishment which affects not only themselves but, in accordance with the nature of their offence, also their descendants. But there is grace for the descendants when they repent. We may not use the threat of the second commandment wrongly. (See Ezek 18).

He who loves the LORD is blessed by him so liberally that this blessing makes its influence felt to thousands. Here we see the blessing of the true and the curse of the false religion.

The addendum to the second commandment belongs also to the first, to which the second is closely connected. Moreover, because the first and second commandment together form the root of the law, the penal provision contained in the second applies to the whole law.

2. The first commandment requires us to serve God. Therein it directs itself against the worship of idols and demands that the *heart* worship God only.

The second commandment charges us how we must serve God. It directs itself thereby against the worship of images and requires of us the true *worship*. The worship of idols (idolatry) and the worship of images (iconolatry) are not the same. Idolatry is the worship of someone who, or something that is NOT God. Iconolatry is worship of GOD in a wrong way (*e.g.* the golden calf; Judg 17 and 18).

3. The commandment FORBIDS all self-willed religion by which we disobey God, and all religion in which only the form is observed but the heart does not love God.

The commandment REQUIRES us to worship God in the manner he commands in his Word. We must serve him by being like him. Eph 5:1 says:

> Therefore be imitators of God. . . .

Mt 5:48 says:

> You, therefore, must be perfect, as your heavenly Father is perfect.

4. This LD refers to God's image. In Paradise, man himself was God's image. There he existed and lived in such a way that one recognized God in him. The Fall changed that entirely. Now we see in man the image of the evil one. Jesus said (Jn 8:44):

> You are of your father the devil, and your will is to do your father's desires.

The true worship of God is not that we make an image of him and prostrate ourselves before it, but that, through the renewal of the Holy Spirit, we again become his image, *i.e.*, that we live in such a way that God may be seen in us again and that we are his followers and are perfect as he is. In order to be strengthened in this true worship, the service of God night and day, we need *formal* worship. But we must always remember that *formal* worship is not the only, or even the most important service that the LORD requires of us. It will not exist any more in heaven. Then we shall serve God day and night and the entire creation will be his temple again.

5. FORMAL WORSHIP is:

a. PUBLIC. People, being created of one blood, are communal beings. Only in communion with others does man's humanity truly become apparent. In his redemptive work Christ, therefore, unites us into a people, the communion of saints. This has consequences for all of life. Also for the worship service. We must worship commun' y That happened already in the days of Enosh (Gen 4:26b); it happened also in Israel in the tabernacle and temple and on the several feasts. And it continued after Pentecost (Acts 2:42, 46).

Christ's injunction in Jn 4:23, that the true worshippers must worship the Father in spirit and truth, applies also to the worship service. The worship service is not restricted to a particular place (such as the temple and the holy city in the OT), and it m .' .er consist of empty, formal actions in which the worshipper does not give his heart. It must be truthful, *i.e.*, it must express publicly what lives in the heart.

This public worship service is characterized by the meeting of God with his covenant people. The tabernacle was called of old "the tent of meeting."

Hence, in the public worship service we distinguish two actions:

i.   *on God's part:* salutation, the ten words of the covenant, reading of the holy Scripture, ministry of the Word, administration of baptism and celebration of the Lord's supper.

ii. *on the congregation's part:* votum, congregational singing, offertory and prayer (Acts 2:42).

b. FAMILIAL. The family is a God-given unit. He gave it to man in creation and renews it in his covenant of grace, wherever he unites parents and children. Therefore, also the family must honour the LORD. Familial worship consists of reading of holy Scripture, prayer and singing. It takes place thrice daily in accordance with the division of the day which God assigned in creation. We find examples of this in Daniel (Dan 6:11) and Ps 55:18. The father or, in his absence, the mother or one of the adult children must lead the others in the worship.

c. PERSONAL. Since the service of the LORD is ultimately a bond of a single person to his God, the Christian is also bound to worship him personally. This consists in reading and pondering the Scriptures and in silent prayer. Everyone must make time for this every day. Carelessness in this matter leads to untold harm.

6. The second commandment does not proscribe the fine arts and does not forbid all making of images. This is apparent from the commandment itself. It forbids the making of images for worship. (See also Deut 4:15-18).

7. The Roman Catholic church wanted to use images as "books for the laity" in order thereby to instruct the ignorant. But we must not be wiser than God. He wants his Christians to be taught by the living preaching of his Word.

B. CROSS REFERENCES

1. Note also what the BC, art. 7, says about the "manner of worship which God requires of us."

C. QUESTIONS

1. What is a "graven image"? What is a "likeness"? What does it mean that the LORD is "a jealous God"? To what does the penal provision of the second commandment belong? Can children of those who hate the LORD not share in his grace?

2. What is the difference between the first and second commandments? What do the first and second commandments, respectively, forbid? What is the difference between idolatry and iconolatry?

3. What does the second commandment forbid? What is self-willed religion? What is religion in which the form only is observed? What does the commandment require? What do Eph 5:1 and Mt 5:48, respectively, say?

4. What is true worship? What is the goal of formal worship?

5. How do we classify formal worship? Why is communal worship necessary? Give examples from the Bible. What is its nature? Which two kinds of action do we recognize in the public worship service? List what belongs to each.

6. Why is family worship necessary? Of what does it consist? Who must lead it?

7. Why is personal worship necessary? Of what does it consist?
8. Does the second commandment forbid all making of images?
9. Is it a good idea to use images as "books for the laity"? Why not? What does the expression "books for the laity" mean?

99.   Q.   *What is required*
              in the third commandment?

       A.   *We are not to blaspheme or to abuse the*
              Name of God
                      by cursing,[1] perjury,[2] or unnecessary oaths,[3]
                      nor to share in such horrible sins
                      by being silent bystanders.[4]
              In short, we must use the holy Name of God
                      only with fear and reverence,[5]
                      so that we may rightly confess Him,[6]
                      call upon Him,[7]
                      and praise Him in all our words and
                      works.[8]

              [1] *Lev. 24:10-17.*
              [2] *Lev. 19:12*
              [3] *Matt. 5:37; James 5:12.*
              [4] *Lev. 5:1; Prov. 29:24.*
              [5] *Ps. 99:1-5; Is. 45:23; Jer. 4:2.*
              [6] *Matt. 10:32, 33; Rom. 10:9, 10.*
              [7] *Ps. 50:14, 15; I Tim. 2:8.*
              [8] *Rom. 2:24; Col. 3:17; I Tim. 6:1.*

100.   Q.   *Is the blaspheming of God's Name*
              by swearing and cursing
              such a grievous sin
              that God is angry also with those
              who do not prevent and forbid it
              as much as they can?

       A.   *Certainly,[1] for no sin is greater*
                      or provokes God's wrath more
                      than the blaspheming of His Name.
              That is why He commanded it to be punished
                      with death.[2]

              [1] *Lev. 5:1.*
              [2] *Lev. 24:16.*

A. NOTES

1. "The name of the LORD" is everything which God made known about himself, his entire revelation in nature and Scripture, our knowledge of him (Ps 8:2; Jn 17:6). We may not take this name "in vain," *i.e.*, use it in a frivolous manner. Literally, the commandment says that we may not raise it as false, useless, vain, mendacious. Thus, we may not use the Name for sinful or useless purposes, or thoughtlessly. The LORD adds a special announcement of punishment to this commandment. This proves that Answer 100 is not too strong. (See also Lev 24:10-16). He who profanes God's name, profanes God himself!

2. FORBIDDEN are:

   a. The ungodly curse, *i.e.*, calling upon God's name improperly in order to call evil upon others. Cursing is the opposite of blessing; thus, it amounts to praying for evil from God upon a person.

   b. Profanity, *i.e.*, the ungodly and thoughtless misuse of God's name for "amusement," or as expletive.

   c. Blasphemy, *i.e.*, the hellish ignition of hate towards God.

   d. Perjury, *i.e.*, calling upon God's name to cover up a lie.

   e. Unnecessary oaths, *i.e.*, calling upon God's name for trivial matters.

   A person who silently condones these horrible sins shares in the guilt of the offender. Further, all neglect of God's Word is forbidden. The unbeliever who knows nothing better than bread and games does this, but also he who strives for something better and neglects God's name in the pursuit of knowledge. The commandment, therefore, prohibits "neutrality" in education and in societal organizations.

   COMMANDED are:

   f. To hallow the name of the LORD, *i.e.*, to use his name only with respect and to his praise; hence, to confess his name. We must do this always and everywhere, even at the cost of our lives.

   g. To call upon the name of the LORD, for that is why his name was given to us.

   h. Diligently to probe God's revelation in Scripture, nature and history, and to praise and magnify his name which is written in them.

101.   Q. *But may we swear an oath*
            by the Name of God
            in a godly manner?

        A. *Yes, when the government demands it*
                of its subjects,
                or when necessity requires it,
                in order to maintain and promote
                fidelity and truth,
                to God's glory and for our neighbour's
                good.
            Such oath-taking is based on God's Word[1]
                and was therefore rightly used
                by saints in the Old and the New
                Testament.[2]

            [1] *Deut. 6:13; 10:20; Jer. 4:1, 2; Heb. 6:16.*
            [2] *Gen. 21:24; 31:53; Josh. 9:15; I Sam. 24:22;*
                I Kings 1:29, 30; Rom. 1:9; II Cor. 1:23.

102.   Q. *May we also swear by saints*
            or other creatures?

        A. *No.*
            A lawful oath is a calling upon God,
                who alone knows the heart,
                to bear witness to the truth,
                and to punish me if I swear falsely.[1]
            No creature is worthy of such honour.[2]

            [1] *Rom. 9:1; II Cor. 1:23.*
            [2] *Matt. 5:34-37; 23:16-22; James 5:12.*

3. It is necessary to speak about the oath in this context. The oath is a special invocation of the name of God. In the oath we call God to witness to the truth of what we declare or promise. In it we pray that he, who is holy, omniscient and all-powerful, will punish us if we speak a lie, but will bless us if we speak the truth. When we use the oath, therefore, we purposely place ourselves before God as our witness. This was unnecessary in Paradise, for man was always aware that he walked with God. But in a sinful world the oath is necessary to confirm fidelity and truth. But it is intolerable in the church. The believers are expected always to associate with each other in God's presence. Among them, each word and promise must be the equivalent of an oath!

We may not take unnecessary oaths, nor commit perjury. That would be a misuse of God's name. Nor may we swear by something or someone other than the only God. He, only, is omniscient and holy. He, only, is entitled to receive the honour of being the witness accepted by all, and who will reveal the truth now or on the last day.

Some persons are of the view that one may not take the oath and refer to Mt 5:33-37 and Jas 5:12 in support. But in those places Scripture prohibits the misuse of God's name and unnecessary oaths. Moreover, Jesus does not say in Mt 5:37 that the oath is evil, but that it exists because of sin and that, for that reason, it is no longer appropriate among those who are his, who have been delivered from sin and who flee from sin. In fact, taking the oath is based on Scripture, which shows us how God's children use it correctly (*e.g.*, Gen 22:16; Ps 110:4; 2 Cor 1:23; Jesus' oath before the Sanhedrin). We may use the oath when the government demands it of us, or when necessity requires it. And then we must use in accordance with Jer 4:2a (KJV): *in truth, i.e.*, speaking just as one thinks; *in judgment, i.e.*, knowing what one does (hence, not by children or those who are mentally incapacitated); and *in uprightness, i.e.*, not in unjust and evil matters.

B. COMMENTS

1. The government, as God's servant (Rom 13:4), which exercises judgment over public life, has the duty to punish all public misuse of God's name.

C. HERESIES

1. All kinds of substitutes for religion, such as Spiritism, Theosophy, and Scripture criticism.

2. The Anabaptist rejection of the oath and avoidance of the world.

D. QUESTIONS

1. What does the phrase, "the Name of God," denote? What does the separate declaration of punishment that accompanies the commandment indicate?

2. What does the commandment forbid? What does it command?

3. What do we do when we swear an oath? Did the oath exist already in Paradise? May we use it in our association with other believers? How should that association be governed? May we swear by anything or anyone other than God? Why not?

4. Which texts do people appeal to in support of their objection to the oath? Do the texts support their position?

5. Prove that the use of the oath is based on Scripture. By whom and when may the oath be demanded? How must it be used when it is demanded?

103.   Q.   *What does God require*
       in the fourth commandment?

       A.   *First,*
         that the ministry of the gospel and the schools
         be maintained[1]
         and that, especially on the day of rest,
         I diligently attend the church of God[2]
            to hear God's Word,[3]
            to use the sacraments,[4]
            to call publicly upon the LORD,[5]
            and to give Christian offerings for the
            poor.[6]
         Second,
            that all the days of my life
            I rest from my evil works,
            let the LORD work in me through His Holy
            Spirit,
            and so begin in this life
            the eternal sabbath.[7]

[1] *Deut. 6:4-9; 20-25; I Cor. 9:13, 14;*
   II Tim. 2:2; 3:13-17; Tit. 1:5.
[2] *Deut. 12:5-12; Ps. 40:9, 10; 68:26; Acts 2:42-47;*
   Heb. 10:23-25.
[3] *Rom. 10:14-17; I Cor. 14:26-33; I Tim. 4:13.*
[4] *I Cor. 11:23, 24.*
[5] *Col. 3:16; I Tim. 2:1.*
[6] *Ps. 50:14; I Cor. 16:2; II Cor. 8 and 9.*
[7] *Is. 66:23; Heb. 4:9-11.*

A. NOTES

1. The commandment says: *Remember* the sabbath day. It was already known, for the LORD had instituted it in Paradise. The duty to maintain and hallow the sabbath was, therefore, not merely part of Israel's ceremonial law, but applies for all time. It is a religious duty to rest on the sabbath, but it is not the highest goal; rather, it is the means to keep this day holy, *i.e.*, the means to devote this day especially to the LORD. The LORD coupled a convincing reason to the commandment: We must observe this day of rest after six days of labour because God did so. Deut 5:14 gives another reason as well:

> . . . that your manservant and your maidservant may rest as well as you.

(See also Ex 2:12).

Deut 5:15 adds yet another reason:

> You shall remember that you were a servant in the land of Egypt, and the LORD your God brought you out thence with a mighty hand and an outstretched arm; therefore the LORD your God has commanded you to keep the sabbath day.

Scripture, therefore, gives three reasons for keeping the sabbath: (a) to imitate God; (b) to rest and to allow one's employees to rest; and (c) to remember the deliverance from Egypt.

2. The reason that God instructed Adam to rest on the *seventh* day and that he commanded Israel accordingly is because for them the rest could come only *after* their labour. For Adam this was after completion of the demand of the covenant of works; for Israel it was when the Messiah should have come. All this is now past. We celebrate the sabbath on the first day of the week. For Christ brought rest. We may now look back on Christ's completed work. The apostles began to keep the sabbath on the first day of the week (see Acts 20:7; 1 Cor 16:2). The first day is hallowed by Christ's resurrection and is, thus, called the Lord's day (Rev 1:10).

3. The purpose of this day is to devote it to God for his service. It is pre-eminently the day for the *formal* and *public* worship service. Refer, in this connection, to the first part of Answer 103 and pay attention to the duty to attend diligently!

Everything on the day of rest must accommodate the worship service. That is the purpose of the day. All labour in the home and in one's business that is avoidable must be left undone. We may seek recreation and relaxation on the day of rest, but those may not interfere with the character of the day.

4. The fourth commandment has a spiritual tenor. The second part of Answer 103 points to it. We must be imitators of God: that is the deepest meaning of the commandment about the sabbath. Sin disturbed our ability to imitate God. But Christ restores this ability in all who are his by the Holy Spirit. Accordingly, the commandment requires us, ALL THE DAYS OF OUR LIVES, to rest from our evil works and to let the LORD work in us through his Holy Spirit. That is why the eternal sabbath already begins in this life.

5. The purpose of maintaining the *weekly* sabbath is to strengthen us in this *spiritual* celebration of the sabbath all the days of our lives. The Lord has also promised salutary consequences for the keeping of the weekly sabbath: he blessed and hallowed this day. Through it he offers refreshment to man and beast and guards against the complete materialization of life. The conversion of the Sunday into a day of sin, which happens more and more, is therefore very disturbing. A nation which no longer keeps the Sunday holy will soon cease to be holy itself.

B. COMMENTS

1. The government has the duty to ensure that the Sunday is maintained as day of rest in public life. Further, it must forbid everything that can hinder or harm the worship service.

2. Works of mercy and those which promote the worship service are permitted on Sunday.

C. HERESIES

1. Sabbattarianism.

2. Celebrating the Lord's Day in a legalistic manner.

3. The belief that the commandment to celebrate the sabbath every week has been abolished.

D. QUESTIONS

1. When was the sabbath instituted?

2. Is it concerned with resting? If not, what then? What is that?

3. Which reasons does Scripture advance for keeping the sabbath?

4. Why did the people of the OT rest on the seventh day of the week, and why do we rest on the first day? When did the first day of the week become the day of rest?

5. What is the purpose of the sabbath day? May we seek recreation on this day? What must we constantly keep in mind in our recreation on the Lord's Day?

6. What is the spiritual tenor of the commandment? What is the relationship between the spiritual celebration of the sabbath and the weekly sabbath?

7. Which salutary consequences did the Lord add to the keeping of the sabbath?

LORD'S DAY 39

104.   Q.   *What does God require*
                  in the fifth commandment?

           A.   *That I show all honour, love, and faithfulness*
                  to my father and mother
                  and to all those in authority over me,
             submit myself with due obedience
                  to their good instruction and discipline,[1]
             and also have patience with their weaknesses
                  and shortcomings,[2]
             since it is God's will
                  to govern us by their hand.[3]

[1] *Ex. 21:17; Prov. 1:8; 4:1; Rom. 13:1, 2;*
   Eph. 5:21, 22; 6:1-9; Col. 3:18-4:1.
[2] *Prov. 20:20; 23:22; I Pet.2:18.*
[3] *Matt. 22:21, Rom. 13:1-8; Eph. 6:1-9; Col. 3:18-21.*

A. NOTES

1. The verb, "honour," in the original, shows that it is directed to the individual. To honour is more than to obey. It means to regard the object of one's honour as important, to esteem the object. Further, it speaks about loving the object. We must remember that the Bible also gives the name of father and mother to prophets, teachers and rulers (see Gen 45:8; Judg 5:7; 2 Kings 2:12; 13:14). The commandment applies not only to our parents, but to everyone God has placed over us.

2. The law speaks about *authority* in this commandment. Authority differs from power. Power implies strength. The powerful person can assert himself. Authority, on the other hand, implies the right to command. He who has authority can command, even though he is not able to assert himself for lack of power. God, who is everyone's Creator, has absolute authority, and he never abdicates it.

   But God in his providence does not exercise his authority directly and immediately, but mediately, *i.e.*, through the interposition of, by means of, others, to whom he grants authority. Even then, these bearers of authority do not act in God's stead. They are his servants. Article 36 of the BC speaks very clearly about the task of the civil government in this respect.

   This is true of all authority that exists. It does not come from the people (*sovereignty of the people*), as if the government could only give effect to the will of the people. Nor does it come from the strong (*despotism*). Authority comes from God. He has it and he confers it. Hence, we must recognize God in the authorities which are placed over us. And he who resists those in authority resists God (Rom 13:2). That is why Scripture says: Fear God; honour the king. These are the same in principle.

3. The most natural form of authority, clearly established in life, is the authority of parents over their children. Everyone is met first with this form of authority and the resistance to parental authority is often the most intense. That is why the commandment is expressed with reference to parental authority. But, as mentioned under Note 1 above, it has wider application.

4. In human society we distinguish between the authority of:

   the husband over the wife in marriage;

   the parents over their children in the family;

   the employer over the employee in society;

the government over the subject in the state; and

the office bearer over the member of the congregation in the church.

5. The husband has authority over the wife in marriage (Eph 5:22). Its nature was persuasive in Paradise, but it became coercive because of sin. This authority is recognized in Christian marriage (Eph 5:22-24; Col 3:18), in which its persuasive nature is again recognized (Eph 5:24ff). It does not demean a woman to submit herself to this authority, for it conforms with her nature to do so and she does it for the Lord's sake.

In the family the parents have authority over the children. This is not because they are wiser or more powerful, for they have the authority even if they lack wisdom and power, because God has placed them over their children (Eph 6:1, 2). That is why you must show honour, love, and faithfulness to them. When the children become independent and leave the family, the duty to be obedient ends, but the duty to show honour and love remains.

In society the housewife has authority over the maid and the employer over his employee (Eph 6:5-8; Col 3:22ff; 1 Pet 2:18). The employment relationship is established freely by the parties. They enter into a contract. But in the relationship the employer has authority with respect to the employee's work.

In the state the government (king, president, college of rulers — Scripture does not prescribe the correct form of government) has authority over the subject (Rom 13).

In the church the "overseers" or elders have authority over the members. However, this authority is not coercive in nature, but has the character of service (see LD 21, Q&A 54).

6. All earthly authority is limited. No one has authority over all aspects of the lives of those subject to his authority. Each authority limits the next. For example, the government must respect the authority of the parents over their children. Thus, it may not interfere in the upbringing of the children. But the parents must respect the authority of the government and must, therefore, permit their children to fulfil their military service if that is obligatory. Further, all authority is limited by God's authority. Only he may require what he commands; only he may ask for a response from those whom he made responsible.

All those who exercise authority must remember this. They must require obedience; they may even enforce it if necessary, but only for GOD'S SAKE! And they may never misuse their authority. Nor may they neglect to use it as Eli did. Further, they must exercise their authority with dignity and be followers of God.

7. We must show honour, love and faithfulness to all whom God placed in authority over us (parents, teachers, employer, governments, *etc.*), not because and to the extent that we find them agreeable, but because it is God's will to govern us by their hand. In doing so, we must submit ourselves with due obedience to their good instruction and discipline. This is subject to only one exception, *viz.*, that we obey God rather than man (Acts 5:29). Further, we must have patience with the weaknesses and shortcomings of those who exercise authority over us ("office bearers"). Often as not, they have to have more patience with us! Eph 6:5, 6 teaches us that our obedience must be:

> ... in singleness of heart, as to Christ; not in the way of eyeservice, as men-pleasers, but as servants of Christ, DOING THE WILL OF GOD FROM THE HEART.

8. God added a promise of long life in the land which he was going to give to this commandment. Thereby the LORD promises that everyone who complies with this commandment shall share in the blessing of the covenant already in this life.

B. CROSS REFERENCES

1. Article 36 of the BC confesses the Word of God about the governing authorities in detail and states that everyone must subject himself to them and pray for them. In 1905 the General Synod of the Reformed Churches in the Netherlands amended the article by deleting the words: "all idolatry and false worship may be removed and prevented, the kingdom of the antichrist may be destroyed."

C. HERESIES

1. Anarchism.
2. Despotism.
3. The idea that love can take the place of authority.
4. The denial of the duty of children to maintain their parents.
5. Sharing authority with the subject.
6. Rejection of authority in society.
7. Strikes in which the employment contract is breached.
9. Sympathy strikes.
10. Emancipation (feminism).
11. Independentism (congregationalism).
12. Hierarchy.
13. The class struggle (Marxism).

D. QUESTIONS

1. What does "honour" mean? Who must we honour?
2. What is the distinction between authority and power? Who has absolute authority? How does he exercise his authority? Whom do we oppose when we resist authority?
3. How many kinds of authority do we recognize?
4. Who has authority in marriage? How and why must it be honoured?
5. Who has authority in the family? Why do they have it? Do adult children still owe duties toward their parents? Which ones?
6. Who has authority in society? What is the extent of the employer's authority?
7. Who has authority in the state? What form of government is the correct one?
8. Who exercises authority in the church? What is the nature of this authority?
9. What limits authority? Why must those who exercise authority require obedience?
10. How must we conduct ourselves toward those who stand in authority over us? What is the limit of the duty of obedience?
11. What promise did God add to this commandment?

105.   Q. *What does God require*
            in the sixth commandment?

        A. *I am not to dishonour, hate, injure,*
                or kill my neighbour
                by thoughts, words, or gestures,
                and much less by deeds,
                whether personally or through another;[1]
            rather, I am to put away
                all desire of revenge.[2]
            Moreover, I am not to harm or recklessly
                endanger myself.[3]
            Therefore, also, the government bears the sword
                to prevent murder.[4]
            [1] *Gen. 9:6; Lev. 19:17, 18; Matt. 5:21, 22; 26:52.*
            [2] *Prov. 25:21, 22; Matt. 18:35; Rom. 12:19; Eph. 4:26.*
            [3] *Matt. 4:7; 26:52; Rom. 13:11-14.*
            [4] *Gen. 9:6; Ex. 21:14; Rom. 13:4.*

106.   Q. *But does this commandment*
            speak only of killing?

        A. *By forbidding murder God teaches us*
            that He hates the root of murder,
            such as envy, hatred, anger, and desire of
            revenge,[1]
            and that He regards all these as murder.[2]
            [1] *Prov. 14:30; Rom. 1:29; 12:19; Gal. 5:19-21;*
                James 1:20; I John 2:9-11.
            [2] *I John 3:15.*

107.   Q. *Is it enough, then,*
            that we do not kill our neighbour
            in any such way?

        A. *No.*
            When God condemns envy, hatred, and anger,
            He commands us
                    to love our neighbour as ourselves,[1]
                    to show patience, peace, gentleness,
                        mercy, and friendliness toward him,[2]
                    to protect him from harm as much as
                    we can, and to do good even to our
                    enemies.[3]
            [1] *Matt. 7:12; 22:39; Rom. 12:10.*
            [2] *Matt. 5:5; Luke 6:36; Rom. 12:10, 18; Gal. 6:1, 2;*
                Eph. 4:2; Col. 3:12; I Pet. 3:8.
            [3] *Ex. 23:4, 5; Matt. 5:44, 45; Rom. 12:20.*

A. NOTES

1. Life is entirely God's gift; it belongs to him. He breathed the breath of life into man's nostrils. Of him it is said: "in whose hand is your breath" (Dan 5:23). Man is a most miraculous and priceless creature of God! That is why the LORD requires us to respect the life of our neighbour.

   By forbidding homicide (*i.e.*, *wrongful killing*) the Lord *forbids* all harm to the life of the neighbour. Further, we may not cause his life to be endangered (see Deut 22:8). Nor may we do this by others, not even by words (and words can harm terribly!), or gestures.

2. Life is not only a physical phenomenon, it is also spiritual. That is why we may not dishonour, hate or injure the neighbour either. Nor may we desire to do so. Further, in the sixth commandment God forbids all envy and desire for revenge.

3. The Answer explains that we are commanded to seek good for the life of the neighbour in every respect. We must love him and must show patience, peace, gentleness, mercy and friendliness towards him; and we must protect him from harm as much as we can. We must even do good to our enemies.

4. This applies also to our own lives. We may not deliberately and unnecessarily endanger our lives through intemperance (eating, drinking, smoking, lewdness, excessive exertion, sports mania).

   Every form of suicide (truly a form of cowardice) is forbidden.

5. We must care for ourselves, both physically and spiritually. We must also use the gift of life to God's honour through faith in Christ Jesus.

6. Self defence and war are commanded in extreme situations when there is no other solution. So also capital punishment is commanded for those who took the lives of their neighbours (or who caused the death of the neighbour by betrayal, *e.g.*, in time of war). These are not attacks on life, but are for the protection of life. Hence, they are not murder. It is the duty of the government to carry out capital punishment, since it does not bear the sword in vain (Rom 13:4).

7. Sometimes the Lord requires a person to sacrifice his own life in obedience to him in order to save the life of another person, or to remain faithful to him (martyrdom).

B. HERESIES
1. Glorification of war.
2. Anti-militarism (pacifism).
3. Rejection of capital punishment.
4. The doctrine of defencelessness (unilateral disarmament).
5. Asceticism.
6. Rejection of the duty of military service other than on the ground that one must "obey God rather than men" (Rom 5:29).

C. QUESTIONS
1. To whom does life belong? What, therefore, must we do with our lives.
2. Does God only forbid homicide in the sixth commandment? What else does he forbid?
3. What does the commandment require in respect of the neighbour?
4. What does the commandment forbid regarding one's own life? What does it require in this respect?
5. Is capital punishment forbidden? What about war?
6. When may one sacrifice one's own life?

108.   Q.   *What does the seventh commandment teach us?*

        A.   *That all unchastity is cursed by God.[1]*
              We must therefore detest it from the heart[2]
                  and live chaste and disciplined lives,
                  both within and outside of holy marriage.[3]

              [1] *Lev. 18:30; Eph. 5:3-5.*
              [2] *Jude 22, 23.*
              [3] *I Cor. 7:1-9; I Thess. 4:3-8; Heb. 13:4.*

109.   Q.   *Does God in this commandment*
              forbid nothing more than adultery
              and similar shameful sins?

        A.   *Since we, body and soul,*
                  are temples of the Holy Spirit,
                  it is God's will
                  that we keep ourselves pure and holy.
              Therefore He forbids all unchaste acts,
                  gestures, words, thoughts, desires,[1]
                  and whatever may entice us to unchastity.[2]

              [1] *Matt. 5:27-29; I Cor. 6:18-20; Eph. 5:3, 4.*
              [2] *I Cor. 15:33; Eph. 5:18.*

A. NOTES

1. God created man male and female. This distinction concerns not just their physical nature, but their entire manner of existence. And God gave a beautiful gift to man in this distinction. He made it possible by this distinction that those who were two should become one. The Lord gave this distinction for that purpose as well. He gave it for the marriage state.

2. Marriage is an institution of God (Gen 1:28). It is the alliance for life of one man and one woman in spiritual and physical communion. Divorce is permissible only in case of adultery (Mt 5:32).

3. Marriage is designed to provide mutual help and assistance in all things that belong to temporal and eternal life. It also serves the reproduction of mankind in the fear of God. That is why it must always be "in the Lord" (1 Cor 7:39b). Marriage to an unbeliever is expressly forbidden (2 Cor 6:14). Only when husband and wife are one in the Lord can they, in their marriage, fulfil its purpose. That is impossible when the parties are not members of the same church.

4. We must keep the gift of sexual distinction pure both before and in marriage. Boys and girls may not make lascivious sport of the gift which God gave them as boys and as girls. Frivolous association, flirtation, caressing without love, filthy language, *etc.*, are forbidden, together with everything that can induce one to engage in such things, such as: titillating reading materials; going to movies; and provocative clothing and manners of association, which fail to take our sinful nature into account. The commandment also forbids pre-marital sex, *i.e.*, taking already during one's engagement that which is allowed only in marriage. He who breaks the vial of love prematurely, will find it empty later in marriage.

   Also in marriage we must avoid all unchastity and live holy lives. For our bodies are temples of the Holy Spirit. And he who profanes God's temple, profanes God.

5. We must keep ourselves free from unchastity, not only in words and deeds, but also in our thoughts and desires. We must have regard to what is pure and lovely and good.

6. God's anger over all unchastity is very severe, because of the filthiness of this sin and the depravity of those who commit it, and also because of the sad consequences of it. All unchastity is cursed by God (1 Thess 4:3-5; Rev 21:8).

B. HERESIES

1. Polygamy.
2. Permitting divorce whenever the parties wish it.
3. "Free love."
4. Neo-malthusianism.

C. QUESTIONS

1. How did God create man? What was his purpose in doing that?
2. What is marriage? Is divorce permissible?
3. What is the purpose of marriage? What condition must it satisfy, therefore?
4. What does the commandment forbid? What does it require?
5. How does God judge unchastity?

110.   Q.   *What does God forbid*
            in the eighth commandment?

       A.   *God forbids not only outright theft and robbery[1]*
            but also such wicked schemes and devices as
            false weights and measures,
            deceptive merchandising,
            counterfeit money,
            and usury;[2]
            we must not defraud our neighbour in any way,
            whether by force or by show of right.[3]
            In addition God forbids all greed[4]
            and all abuse or squandering of His gifts.[5]

            [1] *Ex. 22:1; 1 Cor. 5:9, 10; 6:9, 10.*
            [2] *Deut. 25:13-16; Ps. 15:5; Prov. 11:1; 12:22;*
                Ezek. 45:9-12; Luke 6:35.
            [3] *Mic. 6:9-11; Luke 3:14; James 5:1-6.*
            [4] *Luke 12:15; Eph. 5:5.*
            [5] *Prov. 21:20; 23:20, 21; Luke 16:10-13.*

111.   Q.   *What does God require of you*
            in this commandment?

       A.   *I must promote my neighbour's good*
            wherever I can and may,
            deal with him
            as I would like others to deal with me,
            and work faithfully
            so that I may be able to give
            to those in need.[1]

            [1] *Is. 58:5-10; Matt. 7:12; Gal. 6:9, 10; Eph. 4:28.*

A. NOTES

1. Stealing is the wrongful taking and appropriation of another person's goods. The command, "You shall not steal," therefore, presupposes that the other person has something that is *his*; it presumes *ownership*. Many persons today dispute the right to call an object one's own to the exclusion of others. But they are wrong.

2. The Lord is the absolute owner of everything. Ps 24:1 says:

> The earth is the Lord's and the fulness thereof, the world and those who dwell therein.

(See also Acts 17:24).

But God created man so that he had need of possessions. Man cannot fulfil his life and calling without any possessions. He needs at least a minimum number. The Lord, therefore, gave material goods to man (Gen 1:29; Ps 8:7). Article 12 of the BC says of God's providence toward all creatures:

> We believe that He also continues to sustain and govern them . . . in order to serve man, to the end that man may serve his God.

In his providence, God gave each person his share (Acts 5:4a). And we must be satisfied with his ordinance.

We must, therefore, not speak or think disparagingly about material things and possessions. They are, if lawfully obtained, God's gifts. But we should also not assume that our possessions are everything. Mt 16:26 says:

> For what will it profit a man, if he gains the whole world and forfeits his life?

We must use our material goods properly, as stewards, in such a manner that it pleases God (Lk 16:1-13). Then it will earn profit for eternity!

3. The Lord protects lawful ownership in his law. He forbids the most extreme sin, *i.e.*, theft, but thereby he also forbids all attacks upon and violation of property rights.

The commandment FORBIDS:

a. The unlawful *acquisition* of another's goods (by theft, robbery, fraud, usury, deceptive merchandise, false weights and measures, counterfeit money, failure to put in a good day's work, black market activities, non-payment of debts, *etc.*).

and

    b.   The wrongful *use* of our property (as when we withhold it from the Lord, his church, our family, or society; greed; and dissipation)

The commandment REQUIRES:

    a.   The lawful *acquisition* of possessions. (Pray and work [2 Thess 3:10-12; Eph 4:28]).

    and

    b.   The lawful *use* of our property. We must show love by means of our possessions too, and promote our neighbour's good wherever we can and may. We must deal with him as we would like others to deal with us. Further, we must serve the cause of the gospel in this world by giving our gifts for church, school and mission. And we may use our possessions to show love to poor family members. Christ says, in Mt 25:40:

> Truly, I say to you, as you did it to one of the least of these my brethren, you did it to me.

B. HERESIES

1. The "liberal" rejection of the Christian social calling toward society.
2. Communism.
3. Socialism.
4. Materialism.

C. QUESTIONS

1. What is stealing? What does the eighth commandment presuppose?
2. Who is the absolute owner? What does Ps 24:1 say? To whom did God give material goods? To what end did he do so? How must we use our goods?
3. What does the eighth commandment forbid? What does it require?
4. What should be our conduct toward the neighbour?

112.   Q.   *What is required*
            in the ninth commandment?

       A.   *I must not give false testimony against anyone,*
                twist no one's words,
                not gossip or slander,
                nor condemn or join in condemning anyone
                rashly and unheard.[1]
            Rather, I must avoid all lying and deceit
                as the devil's own works,
                under penalty of God's heavy wrath.[2]
            In court and everywhere else,
            I must love the truth,[3]
                speak and confess it honestly,
                and do what I can
                to defend and promote
                my neighbour's honour and reputation.[4]

       [1] *Ps. 15; Prov. 19:5, 9; 21:28; Matt. 7:1; Luke 6:37;*
           Rom. 1:28-32.
       [2] *Lev. 19:11, 12; Prov. 12:22; 13:5; John 8:44; Rev. 21:8.*
       [3] *I Cor. 13:6; Eph. 4:25.*
       [4] *I Pet. 3:8, 9; 4:8.*

A. NOTES

1. The ninth commandment is concerned with the neighbour's name, that is, what people think of him, his reputation. Scripture says, in Ecc 7:1, of a person's name:

> A good name is better than precious ointment.

A person's name determines his standing in society (see, *e.g.*, Lk 7:4-5). He who attacks a person's name attacks his standing among men. The most serious sin against a person's name is perjury, *i.e.*, false testimony before a judge (1 Kings 21:13). By forbidding the most serious sin, God forbids every sin of this type.

2. The commandment FORBIDS: Twisting someone's words by adding something to or deleting something from them; gossip and slander; and condemning someone rashly and unheard, or joining in doing so.

Also, we must not immediately repeat everything that we hear, even if it is true. 1 Pet 4:8 says:

> . . . love covers a multitude of sins.

And James says in 1:19:

> Let every man be quick to hear, slow to speak. . . .

The commandment also forbids all lying and deceit whereby we deliberately misrepresent things in order to gain advantage or to hurt another person. These include lies to prevent loss to yourself and to further your business, as well as the white lie.

3. The Catechism calls lying and deceit the devil's own work. Those are the only things the evil one does himself. He does not steal or kill, he lies only (Jn 8:44). That is how he destroys God's whole creation.

God hates all lies. Prov 12:22 says:

> Lying lips are an abomination to the LORD, but those who act faithfully are his delight.

4. The commandment REQUIRES: That I defend and promote my neighbour's honour and good reputation; and that, in court and in all other situations, I love the truth and speak and confess it uprightly.

B. HERESY

The Jesuits' doctrine of mental reservation.

257

C. QUESTIONS

1. What does the ninth commandment deal with? What does Ecc 7:1 say? What does a person's name denote? What significance does a person's name have among men?

2. What does the commandment forbid? May we repeat everything we hear? What does Jas 1:19 say? What else does the commandment forbid?

3. What does the Catechism call lying and deceit?

4. What does the commandment require?

113. Q. *What does the tenth commandment require of us?*

  A. *That not even the slightest thought or desire contrary to any*
    of God's commandments should ever arise in our heart.
    Rather, we should always hate all sin with all our heart,
    and delight in all righteousness.[1]

  [1] *Ps. 19:7-14; 139:23, 24; Rom. 7:7, 8.*

114. Q. *But can those converted to God keep these commandments*
    perfectly?

  A. *No.*
    In this life even the holiest have only a small beginning
    of this obedience.[1]
    Nevertheless, with earnest purpose they do begin to live not
    only according to some
    but to all the commandments of God.[2]

  [1] *Eccles. 7:20; Rom. 7:14, 15; I Cor. 13:9; I John 1:8.*
  [2] *Ps. 1:1, 2; Rom. 7:22-25; Phil. 3:12-16.*

115. Q. *If in this life no one can keep the ten commandments*
    perfectly, why does God have them preached so strictly?

  A. *First,*
    that throughout our life
    we may more and more become aware of
    our sinful nature,
    and therefore seek more eagerly
    the forgiveness of sins and righteousness in Christ.[1]
    Second,
    that we may be zealous for good deeds
    and constantly pray to God
    for the grace of the Holy Spirit,
    that He may more and more renew us
    after God's image,
    until after this life we reach
    the goal of perfection.[2]

  [1] *Ps. 32:5; Rom. 3:19-26; 7:7, 24, 25; I John 1:9.*
  [2] *I Cor. 9:24; Phil. 3:12-14; I John 3:1-3.*

A. QUESTIONS

1. The tenth commandment occupies a special place. We sometimes call it the key to the law. For this commandment gives us clear insight into the demand of the law. It speaks about the same matters as the seventh and eighth commandments. But those words of the covenant forbade a particular sinful deed. This might give the impression that the Catechism is concerned solely with our actions. But that impression is radically rejected in this Q&A. It states that not even the slightest thought or desire contrary to any commandment may arise in our hearts.

2. The tenth commandment, therefore, deals with desire. Desire can be natural, such as hunger and thirst. It can also be spiritual, such as that described in Ps 84:2:

   My soul longs, yea, faints for the courts of the LORD. . . .

   This kind of desire is not sinful; God himself put it in man.

   Desire is sinful when it is contrary to God's commandment or his direction for my life.

3. The commandment FORBIDS: All sinful desire. It is not sufficient to suppress our sinful desires as soon as they arise in our hearts (as the Roman Catholic church teaches). Not even the least desire contrary to any of God's commandments may arise in us. For therein already our depravity through sin is evident. The commandment also forbids all apathy and passivity.

4. The commandment REQUIRES: That we have delight in all righteousness. Further, that we desire to attain a richer development of the talents given to us.

B. HERESIES

1. The Buddhist doctrine of the extinguishment of all desire.

2. The class struggle (Marxism).

C. QUESTIONS

1. What do we sometimes call the tenth commandment? What does it teach us?
2. What does this commandment deal with? Are all desires sinful? When is desire sinful?
3. What does the commandment forbid?
4. What does the commandment require?

Q. & A. 114
THE CONVERTED AND THE LAW

A. NOTES

1. We already confessed in LD 2, Q&A 5, that those who are not converted cannot keep the law. How about those who are converted to God? Can they keep the law perfectly? Scripture teaches clearly that also these cannot do so. Jas 3:2 says:

> For we all make many mistakes. . . .

1 Jn 1:8 states:

> If we say we have no sin, we deceive ourselves, and the truth is not in us.

And Paul says in Phil 3:12:

> Not that I have already obtained this or am already perfect. . . .

(See also CD V, 1-8).

2. Is there, then, no distinction between the converted and the unconverted? Yes, there is! In fact, the difference between them is greater than that between night and day. For the unconverted say: Depart from me; I have no delight in knowing thy ways. But the converted say: I take delight in the law of God in my inmost self (*cf.* Rom 7:22; Ps 119:47).

3. There are differences among the converted. The one loves the Lord more and serves him with greater zeal than the other. There are those who are holiest! Think, for example about Abraham, who sacrificed Isaac, and of Job's patience. But not even Abraham was sinless, and at the end Job cursed the day of his birth. Even the holiest have only a small beginning of the obedience which God demands. Gal 5:17 says:

> For the desires of the flesh are against the Spirit . . . to prevent you from doing what you would.

4. But it is true of the converted that they, with earnest purpose (*i.e.*, they have set their whole heart to do this!), begin to live according to God's commandments. Paul says in Phil 3:12:

> . . . I press on to make it my own. . . .

That is why they do their utmost to keep not only some, but all the Lord's commandments. For although they are still imperfect, the Lord perfects them.

B. HERESIES

1. Perfectionism.
2. Antinomianism.
3. Barthianism.

C. QUESTIONS

1. Can those who are converted keep the law perfectly? What do Jas 3:2 and 1 Jn 1:8 say?
2. Is there no difference between the converted and the unconverted? What is the difference?
3. Are there distinctions among the converted? What is true of the holiest?
4. What is true of all the converted?

Q. & A. 115
THE PURPOSE OF PREACHING THE LAW

A. NOTES

1. God has the law preached to us. The books of the prophets and the letters of the apostles, as well as Christ's instruction, clearly show this. Further, he causes the law to be preached "strictly," *i.e.*, accurately and precisely, as well as rigorously and seriously. The preaching of the law in the church may never take the form of a broad outline, or be superficial. It must call a spade a spade! But one might object: What benefit does that have? For we cannot keep the law perfectly anyway. Why, then, is it necessary to have it preached so "strictly"?

2. That is how the Lord works our salvation. We become aware of our sinful nature (not just our sins, but our sinful nature) more and more through the preaching of the law. The Lord works this in us so that we might the more eagerly seek forgiveness of our sins and righteousness in Christ. That is how the Lord teaches us to say with Paul in Rom 7:24-25:

> Wretched man that I am! Who will deliver me from this body of death? Thanks be to God through Jesus Christ our Lord!

3. The Lord also wants us to understand what pleases him through the preaching of the law, so that we may be zealous to do those things. This zeal can only be effected by praying for the grace which the Holy Spirit confers; such prayer must always be accompanied by works.

That is how the Lord wants to fulfil the promise of Jer 31:33, which is still being fulfilled:

> I will put my law within them, and I will write it upon their hearts.

The CD V, 2, state that through this preaching of the law the saints learn

> . . . to flee to the crucified Christ, to put the flesh to death more and more through the Spirit of prayer and by holy exercises of godliness, and to long for the goal of perfection until at last, delivered from this body of death, they reign with the Lamb of God in heaven.

B. QUESTIONS

1. Does God have the law preached? How does he have this done?
2. What do we learn more and more through the law? Why does this happen?
3. What else does the Lord want to work through the preaching of the law?
4. What does Jer 31:33 say?

116.   Q.   *Why is prayer necessary for Christians?*

       A.   *Because prayer is the most important part*
             of the thankfulness which God requires of us.[1]
        Moreover, God will give His grace and the Holy Spirit
             only to those who constantly and with heartfelt longing
             ask Him for these gifts and thank Him for them.[2]

         [1] *Ps. 50:14, 15; 116:12-19; I Thess. 5:16-18.*
         [2] *Matt. 7:7, 8; Luke 11:9-13.*

117.   Q.   *What belongs to a prayer which pleases God*
            and is heard by Him?

       A.   *First,*
             we must from the heart call upon the one true God only,
             who has revealed Himself in His Word, for all that He
             has commanded us to pray.[1]
        Second,
             we must thoroughly know our need and misery, so that
             we may humble ourselves before God.[2]
        Third,
             we must rest on this firm foundation that, although we
             do not deserve it, God will certainly hear our prayer for
             the sake of Christ our Lord, as He has promised us in
             His Word.[3]

         [1] *Ps. 145:18-20; John 4:22-24; Rom. 8:26, 27; James 1:5;*
            I John 5:14, 15; Rev. 19:10.
         [2] *II Chron. 7:14; 20:12; Ps. 2:11; 34:18; 62:8; Is. 66:2; Rev. 4.*
         [3] *Dan. 9:17-19; Matt. 7:8; John 14:13, 14; 16:23; Rom. 10:13; James 1:6.*

118.   Q.   *What has God commanded us to ask of Him?*

       A.   *All the things we need for body and soul,[1]*
        as included in the prayer
        which Christ our Lord Himself taught us.

         [1] *Matt. 6:33; James 1:17.*

119.   Q.   *What is the Lord's prayer?*

       A.   *Our Father who art in heaven,*
        Hallowed be Thy Name.
        Thy kingdom come,
        Thy will be done, On earth as it is in heaven.
        Give us this day our daily bread;
        And forgive us our debts,
             As we also have forgiven our debtors;
        And lead us not into temptation,
             But deliver us from the evil one.
        For Thine is the kingdom, and the power,
             and the glory, for ever. Amen.[1]

         [1] *Matt. 6:9-13; Luke 11:2-4.*

PRAYER

Lord's Days 45 - 52

A. NOTES

1. The Catechism does not begin its instruction about prayer by asking what prayer is; it will tell us that in due course. Rather, it asks the question why prayer is necessary for Christians. For this necessity is denied by all kinds of pseudo-scientific arguments. Moreover, our own slow and evil heart often whispers to us that prayer is not necessary! It is that, especially, which our text book wants to disabuse us of. For although prayer is "the breath of the soul," in the sense that we cannot do without it, just like we cannot do without our breath, prayer is not something that comes naturally to a Christian. We have had to learn and must learn again and again how to pray. That is what the Catechism is concerned with. Not that we shall know a lot about prayer, but that we shall be persons *who pray*. And nothing can move us to become such persons than to know the necessity of prayer.

2. Prayer is necessary because:

    a. GOD DEMANDS IT OF US. 1 Thess 5:17 says:

    > Pray constantly.

    (See also Mt 7:7; Lk 18:1-8; Phil 4:6; Ps 50:14, 15; and note the first, third and fourth commandments!)

    God's commandment, not our need is what matters. Saying that one must pray only when one feels the need is a hypocritical suggestion of the evil one to break us of the habit of praying. We must have fixed times for our prayer (*cf*. Daniel and read Ps 5:4; and 55:18).

    b. IT IS THE MOST IMPORTANT PART OF THANKFULNESS. It is not all the thankfulness which God demands of us, but it is the most important part. A life without prayer is like perfume without scent. What is the place of prayer in your life?

    c. THE LORD WILL GIVE HIS GRACE AND THE HOLY SPIRIT ONLY TO THOSE WHO ASK FOR THEM IN PRAYER. We are readily inclined to query this. Does God not first have to give his Spirit before we can pray? How can the Catechism then say that he gives us his Spirit only if we ask in prayer? But it is clear that the Catechism speaks here about the continuing gift of the Spirit! The only way to continue to receive the Spirit, who has been vouchsafed us in God's promise, is in the way of prayer.

3. The Catechism says that we must pray "with heartfelt longing." Our prayer may not be superficial, the work of our lips only. It must come from inside us, like a sigh, full of honest desire. And we must pray "constantly," *i.e.*, without ceasing, without giving up. If we do not receive what we pray for immediately, we should not stop praying. The Lord sometimes tests us by making us wait (Lk 18:1-8).

B. COMMENTS

1. Some people say: You do not have to pray, for God knows what you need. It is, indeed, not necessary for God, but is necessary for us. People also say: Prayer makes no difference, since everything has been fixed in God's counsel. Or they will say: God is too exalted to concern himself with us. But God has taken account of our prayer in his counsel (*cf.* Hezekiah). And the exalted God wants to be our Father and listen to us. However, we do better not to refute the arguments of unbelief, but to keep the commandment of the Lord!

C. QUESTIONS

1. Does a Christian know how to pray automatically? What does his evil heart sometimes whisper to him? What must he first learn about prayer? What is the point of the Catechism in this respect?

2. Why is prayer necessary? What do 1 Thess 5:17 and Phil 4:6, respectively, say? Is it correct to pray only when we feel the need to do so?

3. How must we pray?

Q. & A. 117
HEAR MY PRAYER, SPOKEN WITH SINCERE LIPS

A. NOTES

1. Praying is a holy art which must be learned. Not everything is prayer which is presented as such. The Catechism teaches us to recognize true prayer when it asks: "What belongs to a prayer which pleases God and is heard by Him?" The first question is not: Will we receive what we desire? But: Does our prayer please God? Prayer is giving thanks! It is serving the Lord! It magnifies him! And we do not have to be unsure about what pleases him. He has revealed it to us. He has given us a rule for it. That is why the Catechism is able to ask: What belongs . . . , *i.e.*, what is prescribed for, what is the rule of prayer?

2. The Lord hears prayer which pleases him. That is why the Catechism does not asks: What belongs to a prayer which pleases God and has a

chance of being heard, but: What belongs to such a prayer which IS HEARD. In fact, there are not really any unheard prayers. Prayers which are not heard are not true prayers. The Lord says in Hos 7:13-14:

> . . . I would redeem them, but they speak lies against me. They do not cry to me from the heart. . . .

(See also Amos 5:21-24). Further, Jas 4:3 says:

> You ask and do not receive, because you ask wrongly, to spend it on your passions.

3. In order to pray in a manner pleasing to the Lord, we must (a) know God, (b) know ourselves, and (c) know Christ.

   a. *We must know God.* For we must "call upon the one true God, who has revealed Himself in His Word" in our prayer. We may not call upon idols. We do this easily and more often than we realize. And this becomes apparent when we read the Answer of the Catechism as follows: "the one true God only, As He has revealed Himself in His Word." But we sometimes act in our prayer as if that good and trustworthy God is callous and unreliable! Then we pray to a God which consists of an image which we have formed of him in our minds, instead of to the one true God!

      Further, we must pray to this one true God only "for all that He has commanded us to pray." True prayer is not the presentation of a wish list. Rather, it is a presentation to God of his promises as empty vessels, so that he might fill them. In order to be able to pray properly, we must first listen to him. Therefore, do not forget to read your Bible when you pray! For, as Rom 8:26 says:

      > . . . for we do not know how to pray as we ought. . . .

   b. *We must know ourselves.* We must know our need, that is, our dependence on God. Adam already knew this need before the fall. And we must know our misery, that is, our guilt before God, and our depravity. We must know this thoroughly, so that, in our prayer, we assume the proper attitude and, being fully cognizant of our dependence and guilt, we "humble ourselves before God." We may not pray like the Pharisee! Isa 66:2 says:

      > But this is the man to whom I will look, he that is humble and contrite in spirit, and trembles at my word.

      Let this humbleness, this admission of guilt and insignificance before the Lord determine our posture! That posture is deferential. Kneeling is, therefore, the best posture.

   c. *We must know Christ.* Our prayer may not be a risky enterprise. We may not, in our prayer, just try something out. For, "we must rest on this firm *foundation* that, although we do not deserve it, God will certainly hear our prayer for the sake of Christ our Lord, as He has promised us in His Word." We must always pray in the confidence and in the certainty that God certainly hears us. The Lord promised in Mt 7:8:

> For every one who asks receives. . . .

And Jas 1:6-7 says:

> But let him ask in faith, with no doubting, for he who doubts is like a wave of the sea that is driven and tossed by the wind. For that person must not suppose that a double-minded man, unstable in all his ways, will receive anything from the Lord.

And John writes in his first letter (1 Jn 5:14-15):

> And this is the confidence which we have in him, that if we ask anything according to his will he hears us. And if we know that he hears us in whatever we ask, we know that we have obtained the requests made of him.

We HAVE received in the promise what we prayed for in accordance with God's will! And God gives it to us, but only in his time! Our prayer must be based on that confidence. And then we shall no longer wait in uncertainty about what may happen, but we shall wait patiently on the Lord, who will hear our prayer.

B. QUESTIONS

1. Is every prayer good? What is of prime importance in our prayer? Why? How do we know this?

2. What does Jas 4:3 say? What are prayers that are unheard? Why do we not always receive what we ask for?

3. What do we need to know in order to pray in a manner that pleases God? To whom, only, may we pray? What may we pray? What must always accompany our prayer?

4. What is our need? What is our misery? How must we approach God? Is our physical posture significant in this respect? What should that posture be?

5. What must be our firm foundation in our prayer? What does Mt 7:8 say?

Q. & A. 118
OPEN YOUR MOUTH WIDE AND I WILL FILL IT

A. NOTES

1. We have already seen that we must pray for what God has commanded us to pray. This is explained further in this Answer. And it becomes immediately apparent that we are allowed to pray for a lot, *viz.*, all the things we need for body and soul. "Need" is that which we lack. Hence, God commands us to pray for what we need. Not for what we might deem necessary, but what is necessary for the proper fulfilment of the charge the Lord has given us. And this includes things both for body and

soul. We may ask for that which is necessary for us and our family, for the church and the nation, to serve the Lord. That includes everything, for the Catechism says: ALL the things we need. Not just the big things, but also the little ones. He who does not desire EVERYTHING from the Lord, will soon no longer desire anything from him.

2. The Catechism teaches us also the order in which we should pray: First for the spiritual things, then for the bodily things. This is in accordance with the rule of Mt 6:33: "Seek first his kingdom."

3. Finally, the Answer points us to the "sample" prayer which Christ himself taught us. It includes (*i.e.*, summarizes) everything for which God commanded us to pray.

B. QUESTIONS

1. What must we pray for? What is need? May we pray only for important things?
2. What order should our prayer follow?
3. What is the example that we should follow in our prayer?

Q. & A. 119
PRAY THEN LIKE THIS

A. NOTES

1. We find the perfect (not the most perfect) prayer in Mt 6:9-13 and Lk 11:2-4. There are minor differences between these two renditions. Christ did not intend that we should only use that form in our prayer. It is an example. Nevertheless, respect for this example should cause us to use it every day in our prayers.

2. In this example we distinguish:

    a.   The address: Our Father who art in heaven.

    b.   Six petitions: Three "Thy" petitions, in which we ask that God fill our *spiritual* need in order that we may rightly serve him; and

                                  three "our" petitions, in which we ask that the Lord fill our *temporal* need in order that we may rightly serve him.

    c.   The doxology.

    d.   The word, Amen.

B.   HERESIES

1.   The use of the "pater noster" in the Roman church.

2.   The complete rejection of formulary prayers and collects.

C.   QUESTIONS

1.   What do we call the Lord's Prayer? Where do we find it in Scripture? May we only use its words when we pray? How did the Saviour intend that it be used?

2.   How is the perfect prayer divided? What do the first three petitions ask? What do the last three ask?

120.   *Q.*   *Why has Christ commanded us*
           to address God as Our Father?

       A.   *To awaken in us*
                at the very beginning of our prayer
                that childlike reverence and trust
                toward God
                which should be basic to our prayer:
           God has become our Father
                through Christ
                and will much less deny us
                what we ask of Him in faith
                than our fathers would
                refuse us earthly things.[1]

        [1] *Matt. 7:9-11; Luke 11:11-13.*

121.   *Q.*   *Why is there added,*
           Who art in heaven?

       A.   *These words teach us*
           not to think of God's heavenly majesty
           in an earthly manner,[1]
           and to expect from His almighty power
           all things we need
           for body and soul.[2]

        [1] *Jer. 23:23, 24; Acts 17:24, 25.*
        [2] *Matt. 6:25-34; Rom. 8:31, 32.*

TO THEE I LIFT UP MY EYES,
O THOU WHO ART ENTHRONED IN THE HEAVENS!

A. NOTES

1. Christ teaches us, by means of the address, "Our Father, who art in heaven," to speak to God in our prayers. Ps. 25:1 says:

   To thee, O LORD, I lift up my soul.

   Praying is not daydreaming, a reverie, being lost in yourself, but speaking to the Lord. That is why we must begin our prayer with an address. We do not always have to use the words with which Christ prompts us. We may also address the Lord in other ways. But in doing so, we must use sober and simple language, which is what Christ teaches us in this address.

2. The address is so important because thereby we express the relationship between the addressee and ourselves. Christ teaches us in the address of the perfect prayer to approach God with "childlike reverence and trust." Thus, we must (that is childlike reverence) approach God not with servile fear, but with childlike, loving and respectful awe, and with childlike trust. This "reverence" and "trust" are strengthened by the added words, "who art in heaven." Thereby the Lord forbids us "to think of God's heavenly majesty in an earthly manner." Our intimate relationship may not degenerate into a pedestrian familiarity. This happens readily if our prayers become routine and habitual! Also in our trust and our expectation we may not think of God in an earthly or petty manner. Our need will never exceed the power of the Helper!

3. This childlike reverence and trust together "should be basic to our *prayer.*" They are not the basis upon which our prayer is *heard.* It lies solely in God's grace and Christ's sacrifice. But they are basic to our prayer. *Prayer* is impossible without reverence and trust.

4. When we call upon "our Father," by Christ's command, we plead the work of the Saviour. God became our Father through him. There is an old question whether every person may call upon God as "Father." Must we not be quite sure before we do this and, therefore, before we place a childlike trust in God, that we are believers? But God allows us to call upon him as our Father in his covenant. We do not do that because we are so sure of ourselves, but because we do not doubt the Lord's promises and because we are certain that he is the Father!

5. The Lord teaches us to pray, "OUR Father," for we approach him as members of the church. Hence, in our prayer, we may not act as if we are alone, but we must pray for each other.

B.   QUESTIONS

1. What is praying? May we address the Lord only as "our Father"? What must we be conscious of in our address?
2. What do we express in the address? How must we approach God? What is childlike reverence? What is childlike trust?
3. What is the basis upon which our prayer is answered? What is basic to our prayer?
4. Upon whose work do we plead when we call upon the Father? May all persons call upon God as Father? How do we get the confidence to do so?
5. Why did Christ teach us say "OUR Father"?

122.   Q.   *What is the first petition?*

A.   *Hallowed be Thy Name.*
That is:
Grant us first of all
that we may rightly know Thee,[1]
and sanctify, glorify, and praise Thee
in all Thy works,
in which shine forth
Thy almighty power,
wisdom, goodness, righteousness,
mercy, and truth.[2]
Grant us also
that we may so direct our whole life —
our thoughts, words, and actions —
that Thy Name is not blasphemed
because of us
but always honoured and praised.[3]

[1] *Jer. 9:23, 24; 31: 33, 34; Matt. 16:17; John 17:3.*
[2] *Ex. 34:5-8; Ps. 145; Jer. 32:16-20; Luke 1:46-55, 68-75;*
Rom. 11: 33-36.
[3] *Ps. 115:1; Matt. 5:16.*

A. NOTES

1. God's name is God himself, as he has revealed himself. When we pray, "*Hallowed* be Thy Name," we do not make a wish that God's name be hallowed, but we formulate a prayer in which we ask that God will grant us that we hallow his name. The Catechism, therefore, begins the explanation in a beautiful way by stating, "That is: *Grant us.*"

   The person who prays does not mention the manner and the means by which the Lord will grant this petition at all. He leaves that entirely up to God. "To hallow" means to acknowledge and esteem as holy and to keep holy. The hallowing of God's name comes first in the perfect prayer. For this is the highest goal in heaven and on earth. This petition received a preliminary answer in Christ's coming. The answer continues in the humble acknowledgement and obedience of the believers and will be completed in Christ's return.

2. The form of the Answer is itself a prayer. You can pray it yourself! For the point is not that we need to learn to speak a lot about the name of the Lord, but that we should learn to pray for the hallowing of that name!

3. In explanation of the word, HALLOWED, the Catechism states that the first thing necessary is that we rightly *know* God. And that is what we pray for. For God has made himself clearly known in his Word (BC, art. 2), but he also has to grant us the ability to understand that Word.

4. When I know someone, such as a writer, well, I can recognize him in his works. I need to read only a couple of pages before I can say, that is his work! In the same way, we must recognize and notice God in his works, that is, in all that he does. We must see his hand in all that happens, so that, both in the blessings which gladden us and the judgments which strike us, we can say, "It is the Lord!" We must say that too, in order to praise and glorify him. We may not be ashamed of the Lord. We must *acknowledge* him. The hallowing of his name requires that we publicly (*i.e.*, in our speaking with others) acknowledge his name in all that happens! Sadly, this is missing so often. If only we asked it, as the Lord taught it to us.

5. Finally, we ourselves must live in such a manner, that is, we must so order our lives (all our thoughts, words and actions must be so directed) that God's name is not blasphemed because of us, but is honoured and praised instead.

B. QUESTIONS

1. What is God's name? Is the first petition a wish on our part, directed to God? What is it, then? Why is the hallowing of God's name mentioned first in the prayer? Does the Lord answer this petition? How?

2. What is the form of this Answer of the Catechism? Why?

3. What is necessary for the hallowing of God's name in the first place? When must we pray that God give this? What else is necessary for the hallowing of God's name? And what in addition?

LORD'S DAY 48

123.   Q. *What is the second petition?*

        A. *Thy kingdom come.*
           That is:
           So rule us by Thy Word and Spirit
               that more and more we submit to Thee.[1]
           Preserve and increase Thy church.[2]
           Destroy the works of the devil,
               every power that raises itself against Thee,
               and every conspiracy
               against Thy holy Word.[3]
           Do all this
               until the fulness of Thy kingdom comes,
               wherein Thou shalt be all in all.[4]

[1] *Ps. 119:5, 105; 143:10; Matt. 6:33.*
[2] *Ps. 51:18; 122:6-9; Matt. 16:18; Acts 2:42-47.*
[3] *Rom. 16:20; I John 3:8.*
[4] *Rom. 8:22, 23; I Cor. 15:28; Rev. 22: 17, 20.*

A. NOTES

1. The kingdom of God is that state of affairs in which God is willingly and lovingly acknowledged as king. It existed in Paradise before the fall, but it was lost on earth because of sin. God did remain the king who reigned also on earth after the fall into sin, but he was no longer acknowledged and honoured as such thereafter. However, immediately after the fall Christ began to restore the kingdom of God on earth. It is often called the kingdom of heaven, because it is being restored on earth from heaven. Christ continues with this restoration until his return, when he will complete it. We pray for the continuation and completion of this restoration when we ask: Thy kingdom come.

2. As regards the form and the answer to this petition, the same comments as those made in connection with the first petition apply. (See LD 47, Q&A 122, Notes 1 and 2).

3. In this petition we ask first that the Lord will so rule us by his Word and Spirit that we will submit ourselves more and more to him. For that is how his kingdom comes, when we acknowledge him more and more in all things.

4. The church has a unique task in the acknowledgement of God as king over all things. The church is the army of God's kingdom. It proclaims the king's Word with authority. That is why the second petition also contains the plea: "Preserve and increase Thy church." Preserving means keeping to the Word. It is a very harmful error to suppose that the work for the coming of God's kingdom can continue powerfully, while one is unconcerned about the church and does not bother about the sins which destroy it.

5. We can be sure that there will be oppression by enemies, especially when God hears this petition and his kingdom is coming. The more God's kingdom becomes effective, the more the devil will become active. That is why the second petition also contains the plea: "Destroy the works of the devil, every power that raises itself against Thee, and every conspiracy against Thy holy Word." For nothing promotes the coming of God's kingdom as his Word, which announces and promises it and teaches us to seek it. That is why the devil roars more against the Bible than against anything else. He promotes all kinds of schemes to suppress the Bible in schools and army barracks, in the home and on ships, in newspapers and in the electronic media.

6. Thus, in the second petition we ask that God himself will teach us to serve him as king and promote all the means which contribute thereto, but also that he will destroy all opposition which raises itself against him. And we ask this in order that (for that is the purpose of this petition) the fullness of God's kingdom come, in which he shall be all in all.

7. We pray all this from the Lord. For only he can give it to us. And he has promised it!

B.   QUESTIONS

1.   What is the kingdom of God? When did it already exist? How was it lost? Who restores it? What do we ask for in the second petition with respect to this kingdom?

2.   What can you say about the form of this petition? Does the Lord answer this prayer. If so, how?

3.   What is the first thing we pray for in the second petition?

4.   What is the significance of the church for God's kingdom? What do we ask for the church?

5.   What other plea does the second petition contain?

6.   What is the ultimate purpose of the second petition?

7.   Why do we pray all this from the Lord?

124.   Q.   *What is the third petition?*

         A.   *Thy will be done,*
              on earth as it is in heaven.
          That is:
          Grant that we and all men
              may deny our own will,
              and without any murmuring
              obey Thy will,
              for it alone is good.[1]
          Grant also that everyone
              may carry out the duties
              of his office and calling[2]
              as willingly and faithfully
              as the angels in heaven.[3]

[1] Matt. 7:21; 16:24-26; Luke 22:42; Rom. 12:1, 2;
   Tit. 2:11, 12.
[2] I Cor. 7:17-24; Eph. 6:5-9.
[3] Ps. 103:20, 21.

A. NOTES

1. When we speak of God's will, we can think of his hidden will, or eternal counsel, by which the Lord determines what will happen to us, and of the Lord's revealed will, by which he tells us what we must do. This revealed will is made known to us (a) by the Word, and (b) by God's guidance in our lives. For by this guidance the Lord shows us our place and thereby also our task.

   This petition refers to God's revealed will, his commandment. For the addition, "on earth as it is in heaven," presupposes that God's will is done in heaven, but not yet on earth. That cannot be said of God's counsel. It is done just as punctually on earth as in heaven. However, his command is not opposed in heaven, but is opposed here on earth.

   Also this petition is not a wish: May what Thou wilt be done; but a plea: *Grant* that *we* and all men obey Thy commandment and fulfil and do Thy revealed will.

2. We ought not to think in this context about extraordinary things. The Catechism speaks beautifully about our office and calling. We must do God's will in them, in everyday life, as the Lord places it before us! And then we pray that we may do so as willingly and faithfully as the angels in heaven.

3. We are totally incapable of fulfilling God's will. We are inclined to contradict God's will. His will seems to us harmful and wrong. Our will, which seeks our own glory, resists God's will. That is why the third petition also contains the plea: Grant that we deny our own will, that we renounce it and refuse to follow it, and that we do THY will instead.

4. This is the last of the first three (the "Thy") petitions. Note how each successive petition flows from the one that precedes it. First: Hallowed be Thy Name. That is the main purpose which everyone who prays correctly has before him. If that purpose is to be achieved, then (second petition) God must be acknowledged as king. And to that end (third petition) it is necessary that his will be done.

B. QUESTIONS

1. What are the possible meanings of God's "will"? How is God's command made known to us? What must we think of when we pray the third petition? Why? What do we ask in this petition?

2. In what situations must God's will be done? How must this be done?

3. What else does the third petition contain? Why?

4. What is the relationship among the first three petitions?

125.   Q.   *What is the fourth petition?*

    A.   *Give us this day our daily bread.*
           That is:
           Provide us with all our bodily needs[1]
              so that we may acknowledge
              that Thou art the only fountain of all good,[2]
              and that our care and labour,
              and also Thy gifts,
              cannot do us any good
              without Thy blessing.[3]
           Grant therefore that we may
              withdraw our trust
              from all creatures,
              and place it only in Thee.[4]

[1] *Ps. 104:27-30; 145:15, 16; Matt. 6:25-34.*
[2] *Acts 14:17; 17:25; James 1:17.*
[3] *Deut. 8:3; Ps. 37:16; 127:1, 2; I Cor. 15:58.*
[4] *Ps. 55:22; 62; 146; Jer. 17:5-8; Heb. 13:5, 6.*

A. NOTES

1. The third petition already directed our attention to the earth when it spoke about office and calling. The fourth petition now asks that the Lord will maintain our earthly life. And this is also in order that his name be hallowed. For we may not separate the fourth petition from the first. We pray for bread, so that we may do God's will, in order that his kingdom come and his name be hallowed.

2. Christ teaches us to pray for BREAD. As the Catechism correctly states, this points to "all our bodily needs" (home and clothes, employees and employment, etc.). We employ the same concept when we say that a person "earns his bread," to indicate thereby that he has the necessaries of life. But by speaking of bread, the Master teaches us to be modest. And he curbs our desires even more by teaching us to pray for what we need today only.

   Give us THIS DAY; and our DAILY bread. The word "daily" also means "sufficient," or "adequate" in this context.

   The Lord promised us that he will give us what we need in our struggle and in our suffering in order to carry out his work. Christ teaches us to point to that promise when he teaches us to pray for OUR bread, that is, that which was promised to us for our livelihood.

3. The Lord does not teach us to pray for manna, but for bread. And bread does not fall from the sky, but comes about through much arduous work by people. If we are going to pray for our livelihood in the manner taught by the Lord, we must also be willing to work! But, however much we are required to work, we PRAY for our bread from the Lord. For we acknowledge "that Thou art the only fountain of all good, and that all our care and labour, and also Thy gifts, cannot do us any good without Thy blessing." For it is not the gifts, but only God's blessing which enriches and grants life. His blessing is more often over the lesser things than over the greater!

4. Of ourselves we place our trust in creatures. That is why this petition also contains the plea: Grant, therefore, that we may withdraw our trust (our trust is attached to, but must be withdrawn!) from all creatures and place it only in Thee.

5. Note that the Saviour teaches us to pray also for others. The petition does not say: Provide ME, but Provide US. The poor person may not forget the rich in his prayer and the rich may not forget the poor! Moreover, he who

receives much ought to bear in mind that he did not pray only for himself and that he did not receive only for himself. God places the bread of the servants in the hands of the masters and that of the poor in the hands of the rich.

B.   QUESTIONS

1.   Why do we pray for bread?
2.   What does the word "bread" point to? How does the Lord curb our desires in this petition? Why do we speak of OUR bread?
3.   Does this petition also point out that we must work? How does it do that? Why, then, must we still pray?
4.   Which plea does this petition also contain?
5.   Do we pray for bread only for ourselves? Does this have any significance for what we have? What?

126. Q. *What is the fifth petition?*

   A. *And forgive us our debts,*
          as we also have forgiven our debtors.
       That is:
       For the sake of Christ's blood,
          do not impute to us,
          wretched sinners;
          any of our transgressions,
          nor the evil which still clings to us,[1]
       as we also find this evidence of Thy grace in us
          that we are fully determined
          wholeheartedly to forgive our neighbour.[2]

   [1] *Ps. 51:1-7; 143:2; Rom. 8:1; I John 2:1, 2.*
   [2] *Matt. 6:14, 15; 18:21-35.*

A. NOTES

1. The last three petitions of the perfect prayer are all joined together by the conjunction, "and." They form a unit. If the Lord were to give us one thing, such as bread, but not the other, such as forgiveness, we would still have nothing. It is different with the first three petitions. Each of them encompasses everything.

   The Lord teaches us to speak of our debts. For our sins are not just deficiencies; by our sins we withhold from the Lord what we were obliged to give. Further, he teaches us to speak of our debts, in the plural, for our sins are many and great! The Catechism, in explaining the word "debts," correctly distinguishes between our "transgressions," *i.e.*, our wrongful conduct in thought, word and deed, and "the evil which still clings to us," *i.e.*, our wrong attitude and inclination, the depravity of our existence, which makes us guilty just as much as our transgressions.

2. We have nothing with which to pay our debts and to make things right again. For we increase our debt daily. We are "wretched sinners," *i.e.*, not pitiable sinners, but sinners who are powerless, who have no wherewithal to pay their debts. There is only one solution: forgiveness, remission of the debt. The Saviour teaches us to pray for that. And we may ask for it for the sake of Christ's blood, which is his sacrifice for reconciliation.

3. We are guilty not just because of what we do ourselves. We share each other's guilt, for we share in each other's sins. Did we warn the other person? Did we set a wrong example? We may not be unmoved by anyone else, even if we did not share in his sin directly. That is why the Saviour teaches us to pray for the forgiveness of *our* sins.

4. The addition, "as we also have forgiven our debtors," does not provide the basis for forgiveness. That is solely Christ's sacrifice. It also does not indicate the measure of forgiveness, as though we pray that God should forgive us as much and to the same extent as we do to our debtors. But the rule is, according to Mt 6:15:

   > But if you do not forgive men their trespasses, neither will your Father forgive your trespasses.

   For he who does not forgive another person has not recognized his own debts. And the Saviour wants us to keep this rule in mind when we pray for forgiveness. He structured the petition so that no one can ask it unless he is minded to forgive as well. He who wants to ask for forgiveness must find the evidence in himself of his complete determination wholeheartedly to forgive his neighbour. And the Catechism calls this "evidence of Thy grace," for no one forgives unless he learns to do so by grace. Thus, this evidence is also our guarantee of God's willingness to forgive. Would he, who taught us to forgive, not forgive?

B. QUESTIONS

1. What do you know about the last three petitions? What are our sins? Why are they called that? What distinction does the Catechism draw in its explanation of the word "debts"?

2. Can we set our debts to rights? What is the only solution? What is the basis for this solution?

3. Do we pray only because of our own debts? Do the debts of others concern us?

4. What is the rule of forgiveness? Do the words "as we also . . . " give the ground of forgiveness, or its measure? Why were they added to this petition?

127.   Q.   *What is the sixth petition?*

   A.   *And lead us not into temptation,*
             but deliver us from the evil one.
         That is:
         In ourselves we are so weak
             that we cannot stand even for a moment.[1]
         Moreover, our sworn enemies —
             the devil,[2] the world,[3] and our own flesh[4] —
             do not cease to attack us.
         Wilt Thou, therefore, uphold and strengthen us
             by the power of Thy Holy Spirit, so that in this
             spiritual war[5] we may not go down to defeat,
             but always firmly resist our enemies, until we finally
             obtain the complete victory.[6]
         [1] *Ps. 103:14-16; John 15:1-5.*
         [2] *II Cor. 11:14; Eph. 6:10-13; I Pet. 5:8.*
         [3] *John 15:18-21.*
         [4] *Rom. 7:23; Gal. 5:17.*
         [5] *Matt. 10:19, 20; 26:41; Mark 13:33; Rom. 5:3-5.*
         [6] *I Cor. 10:13; I Thess. 3:13; 5:23.*

128.   Q.   *How do you conclude your prayer?*

   A.   *For Thine is the kingdom,*
             and the power,
             and the glory, for ever.
         That is:
         All this we ask of Thee because, as our King,
             having power over all things,
             Thou art both willing and able
             to give us all that is good,[1]
         and because not we but Thy holy Name
             should so receive all glory for ever.[2]
         [1] *Rom. 10:11-13; II Pet 2:9.*
         [2] *Ps. 115:1; Jer. 33:8, 9; John 14:13.*

129.   Q.   *What does the word Amen mean?*

   A.   *Amen means:*
         It is true and certain.
         For God has much more certainly
         heard my prayer
         than I feel in my heart
         that I desire this of Him.[1]
         [1] *Is. 65:24; II Cor. 1:20; II Tim. 2:13.*

AND LEAD US NOT INTO TEMPTATION,
BUT DELIVER US FROM THE EVIL ONE

A. NOTES

1. There is a distinction between temptation and testing. Temptation is the deliberate attempt to persuade another person to do evil. The purpose of testing is to show the good by exertion. (The word "temptation" is used a few times in the KJV in the sense of "testing"). God does not tempt anyone (Jas 1:13). But that is all Satan does. However, God does sometimes *lead* into temptation. Sometimes he gives Satan the chance to use his power to tempt us (Mt 4:1). The Lord does this to reveal the power of his work in us, or to teach us to know our own weakness.

2. God always does it for a good reason. But it is hard for us. For we are so weak of ourselves that we cannot stand even for a moment. That is why the Master teaches us to pray that God will not lead us into temptation, but will spare us from temptation. He who asks this should not, of course, himself prevent the answer to his prayer by living rashly and imprudently, thereby placing himself in temptation!

3. We know, however, that God sometimes wants to lead us into temptation. That is why, in the second part of the petition, the petitioner asks that, in that event, God will deliver him from the evil one! Thus, we ask that God will uphold and strengthen us by the power of his holy Spirit, so that we do not succumb in this spiritual war, but always firmly resist our enemies, until we finally obtain the complete victory. For we shall do so. The victory is sure in Christ. Through him we are more than conquerors! (Rom 8:37).

4. The translation "evil," instead of "the evil one," is to be rejected. It is quite clear that the Saviour directed our attention to THE evil one, satan, in this petition. He did this constantly (see, *inter alia*, Mt 12:28, 29; 13:19; Mk 8:33; Lk 10:19). And the Catechism rightly notes that his two powerful allies, the world, full of temptation, and our own flesh, full of guile and craftiness, are also meant to be included with this Prince of Darkness. These three are our sworn enemies!

B. QUESTIONS

1. What is temptation? What is testing? Does God tempt? What does he do? Why does he do this?
2. What does the Saviour teach us to pray regarding temptation? How must we conduct ourselves regarding temptation? What else do we pray for in this petition? How does the Lord want to deliver us from the evil one?
3. Who is the evil one? Who are his allies?

Q. & A. 128
FOR THINE IS THE KINGDOM,
AND THE POWER, AND THE GLORY, FOR EVER

A. NOTES

1. Our prayer, in which we place ourselves before God's countenance and speak to him, may not consist solely of petitions. It must also include thanksgiving and adoration; thanksgiving for God's goodness and gifts; adoration in which to praise and extol his wonderful attributes and his greatness. The conclusion of the perfect prayer, in which we ask nothing more, but praise and extol God, teaches us to do this.

2. In this doxology we confess that God is king, the shepherd of his people. He is *willing* to hear our prayer (since he is king), and he has the ability to do so. For all power derives from him. He is *able* to hear us. And all glory comes from him. He only is exalted and wholly perfect. He will uphold his Word and, therefore, he *shall* hear us. Further, we confess in this doxology that God's glory is the purpose of our prayer. For we may not seek ourselves in our prayer. Rather, our goal must be God's honour. We pray, in the words of the Catechism, "because not we but Thy holy Name should so receive all glory for ever." This testimony is strengthened by the phrase, "for ever."

B. QUESTIONS

1. What must our prayer be in addition to petitions? For what ought we to give thanks? What do we do in adoration?
2. What do we confess when we say "Thine is the kingdom," "Thine is the power," and "Thine is the glory," respectively? What is the purpose of our prayer? Why does the doxology add the phrase, "for ever"?

Q. & A. 129
AMEN

A. NOTES

1. The word "amen" does not mean "it is finished," but "it is certain." The Lord Jesus often said: Amen, amen, I say to you; truly, truly, I say to you.

2. Thus, when we conclude our prayer with "amen," we say: "It is true and certain." Thereby we remove all doubt and confess, "God has much more certainly heard my prayer than I feel in my heart that I desire this of Him." We can be so certain about this because God promised to hear us! He hears our prayer!

Although he does not always remove distress, he does give strength to endure (2 Cor 12:7-9). He does not hear in accordance with our insight, but in accordance with his Fatherly wisdom. Nevertheless, he hears our prayer! And we must rise from our prayer in that confidence of faith, not doubting, but certain that "none that wait for thee [are] put to shame" (Ps 25:3). Therefore, in the words of Ps 103:1:

Bless the LORD, O my soul; and all that is within me, bless his holy name!

Amen.

B. QUESTIONS

1. What does "amen" mean? How did the Saviour often use it?

2. What do we testify when we conclude our prayer with "amen"? How can we say this with such certainty? Does the Father always hear our prayer in the way we would like?